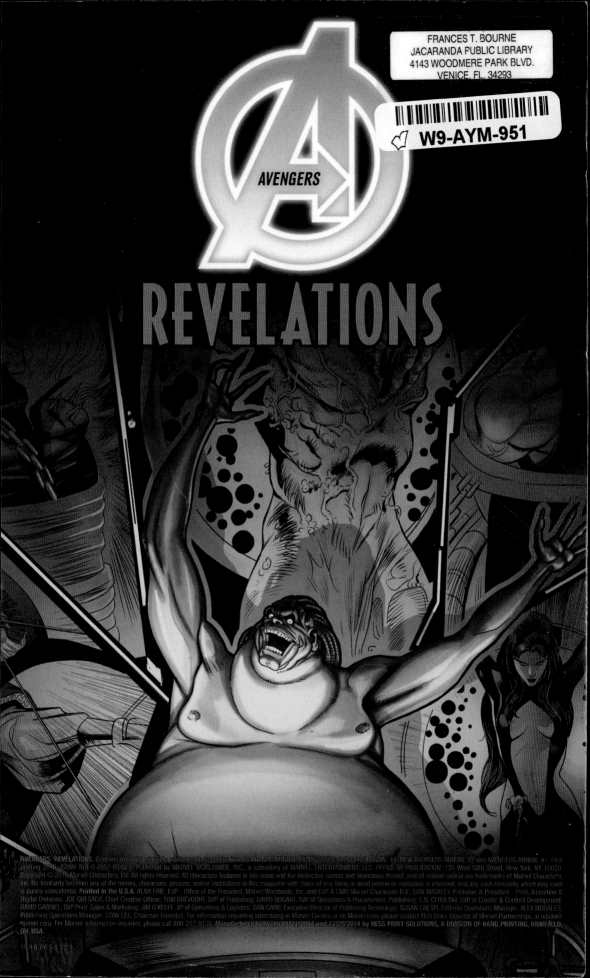

AVENGERS

REVELATIONS

AVENGERS: REVELATIONS. Contains material originally published in magazine form as THANOS ANNUAL #1, UNCANNY AVENGERS ANNUAL #1, NEW AVENGERS ANNUAL #1 and AVENGERS ANNUAL #1. First printing 2015. ISBN# 978-0-7851-9340-1. Published by MARVEL WORLDWIDE, INC., a subsidiary of MARVEL ENTERTAINMENT, LLC. OFFICE OF PUBLICATION: 135 West 50th Street, New York, NY 10020. Copyright © 2015 Marvel Characters, Inc. All rights reserved. All characters featured in this issue and the distinctive names and likenesses thereof, and all related indicia are trademarks of Marvel Characters, Inc. No similarity between any of the names, characters, persons, and/or institutions in this magazine with those of any living or dead person or institution is intended, and any such similarity which may exist is purely coincidental. Printed in the U.S.A. ALAN FINE, EVP - Office of the President, Marvel Worldwide, Inc. and EVP & CMO Marvel Characters B.V.; DAN BUCKLEY, Publisher & President - Print, Animation & Digital Divisions; JOE QUESADA, Chief Creative Officer; TOM BREVOORT, SVP of Publishing; DAVID BOGART, SVP of Operations & Procurement, Publishing; C.B. CEBULSKI, SVP of Creator & Content Development; DAVID GABRIEL, SVP Print, Sales & Marketing; JIM O'KEEFE, VP of Operations & Logistics; DAN CARR, Executive Director of Publishing Technology; SUSAN CRESPI, Editorial Operations Manager; ALEX MORALES, Publishing Operations Manager; STAN LEE, Chairman Emeritus. For information regarding advertising in Marvel Comics or on Marvel.com, please contact Niza Disla, Director of Marvel Partnerships, at ndisla@marvel.com. For Marvel subscription inquiries, please call 800-217-9158. Manufactured between 11/21/2014 and 12/29/2014 by HESS PRINT SOLUTIONS, A DIVISION OF BANG PRINTING, BRIMFIELD, OH, USA.

10 9 8 7 6 5 4 3 2 1

THANOS ANNUAL #1
WRITER: JIM STARLIN
PENCILER: RON LIM
INKER: ANDY SMITH
COLORIST: VAL STAPLES
LETTERER: VC'S JOE CARAMAGNA
COVER ART: DALE KEOWN & IVE SVORCINA
ASSISTANT EDITOR: JON MOISAN
EDITOR: WIL MOSS

UNCANNY AVENGERS ANNUAL #1
WRITER: RICK REMENDER
ARTIST: PAUL RENAUD
LETTERER: VC'S CLAYTON COWLES
COVER ART: ARTHUR ADAMS & JASON KEITH
EDITORS: TOM BREVOORT WITH DANIEL KETCHUM

NEW AVENGERS ANNUAL #1
WRITER: FRANK BARBIERE
ARTIST: MARCO RUDY
LETTERER: VC'S JOE CARAMAGNA
COVER ART: MARCO RUDY
EDITOR: JAKE THOMAS

AVENGERS ANNUAL #1
WRITER: KATHRYN IMMONEN
ARTIST: DAVID LAFUENTE
COLOR ARTISTS: RAIN BEREDO WITH LEE LOUGHRIDGE
LETTERER: VC'S CORY PETIT
COVER ART: DAVID LAFUENTE & LEE LOUGHRIDGE
EDITOR: JAKE THOMAS

EXECUTIVE EDITOR:
TOM BREVOORT

AVENGERS CREATED BY STAN LEE & JACK KIRBY

COLLECTION EDITOR: SARAH BRUNSTAD
ASSOCIATE MANAGING EDITOR: ALEX STARBUCK
EDITORS, SPECIAL PROJECTS:
JENNIFER GRÜNWALD & MARK D. BEAZLEY
SENIOR EDITOR, SPECIAL PROJECTS: JEFF YOUNGQUIST
SVP PRINT, SALES & MARKETING: DAVID GABRIEL
BOOK DESIGNER: NELSON RIBEIRO

EDITOR IN CHIEF: AXEL ALONSO
CHIEF CREATIVE OFFICER: JOE QUESADA
PUBLISHER: DAN BUCKLEY
EXECUTIVE PRODUCER: ALAN FINE

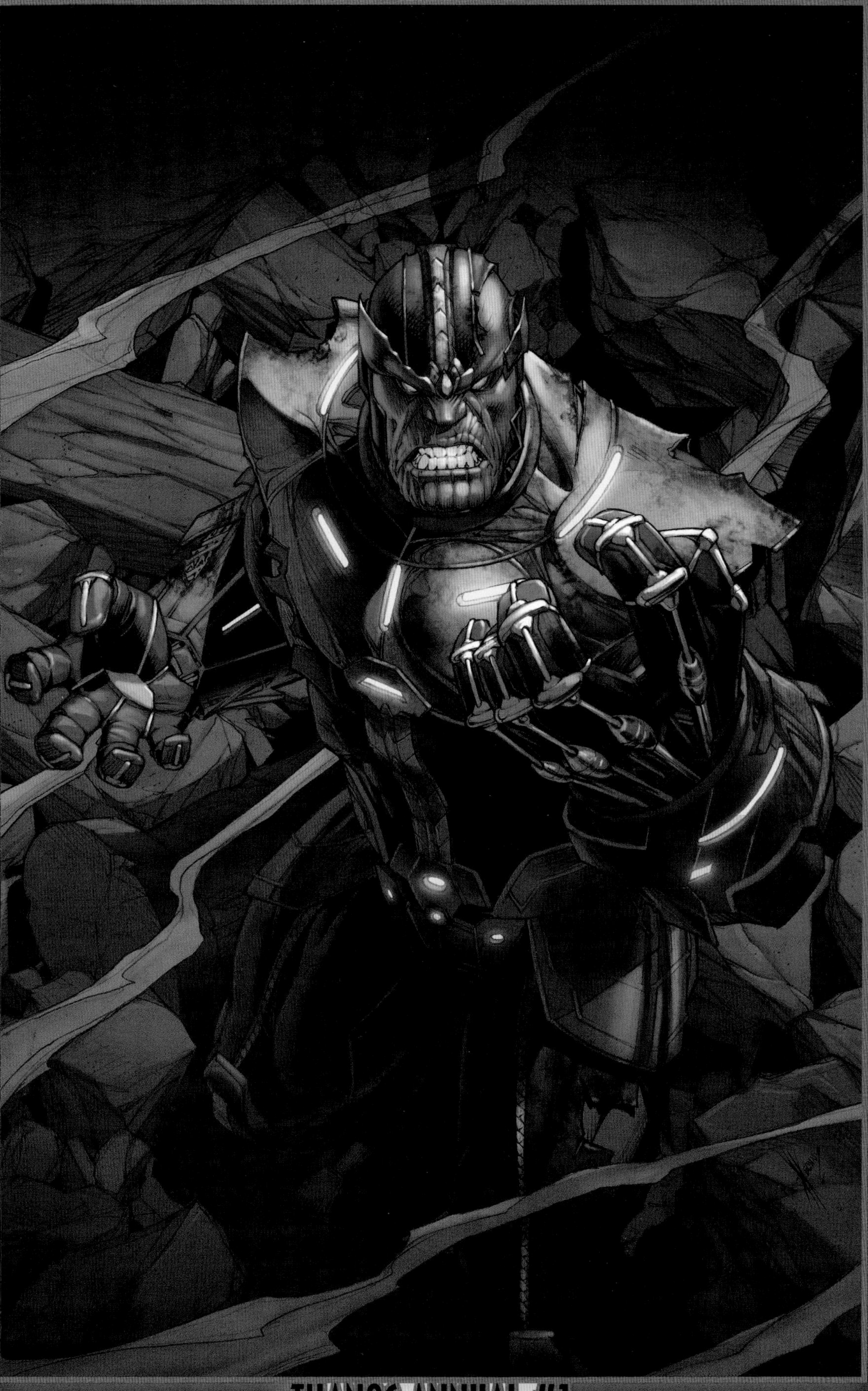

THANOS ANNUAL #1

The Mad Titan known as THANOS is obsessed with two things: power and death, the former of which he uses t bring about the latter.

In pursuit of these obsessions, Thanos gained control of the Infinity Gauntlet – a weapon of unimaginable powe – which briefly made him the equivalent of a god. Ever since, his life has often been intertwined with the Gauntle and its Gems in one way or another.

Currently Thanos is imprisoned on Earth, trapped in a "living death" by the very person he came there to kill: hi son Thane. But it is only a matter of time before the Mad Titan is free once more!

The following details a key moment in Thanos' life when he was faced with a future that may lead beyond deat itself...

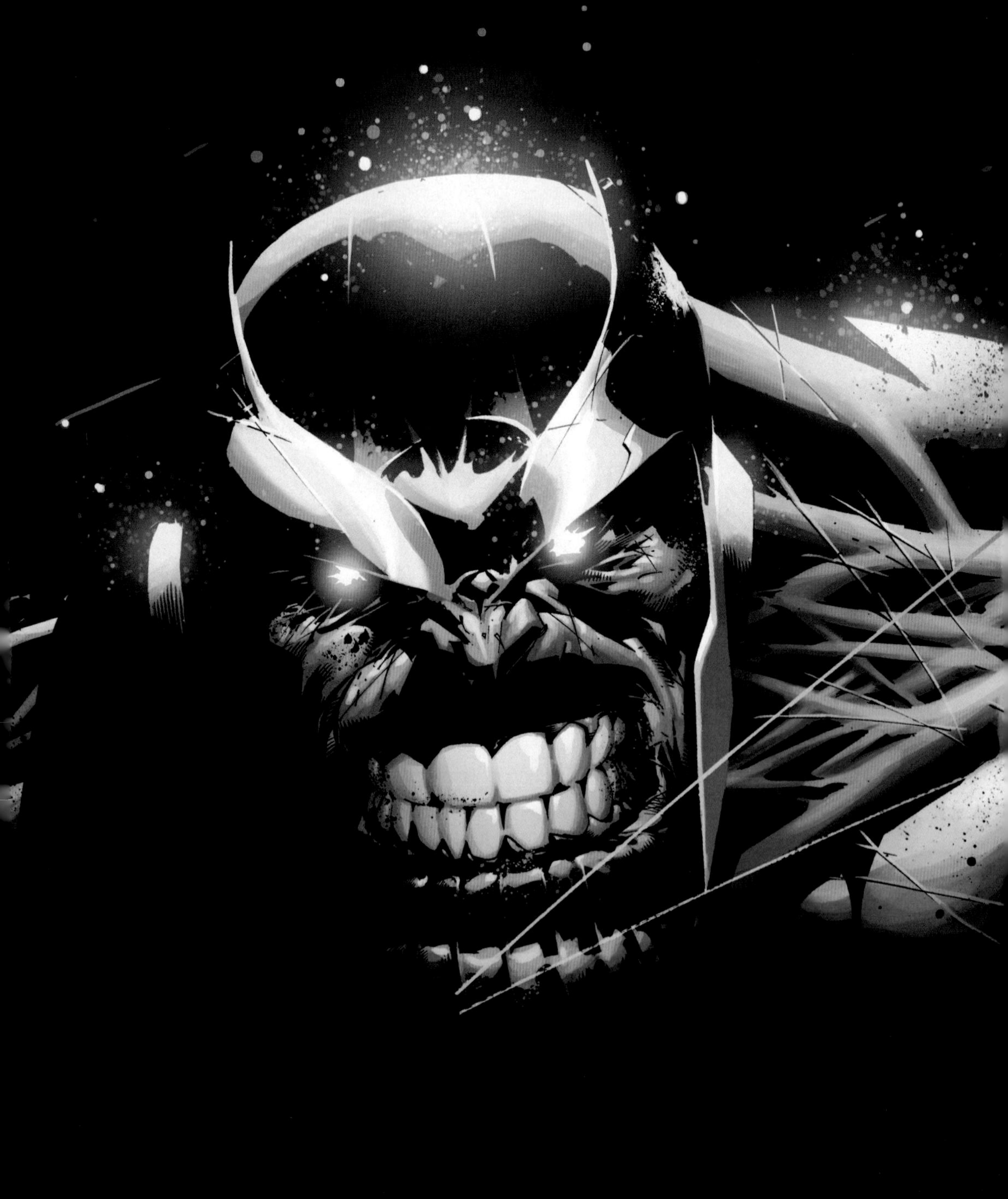

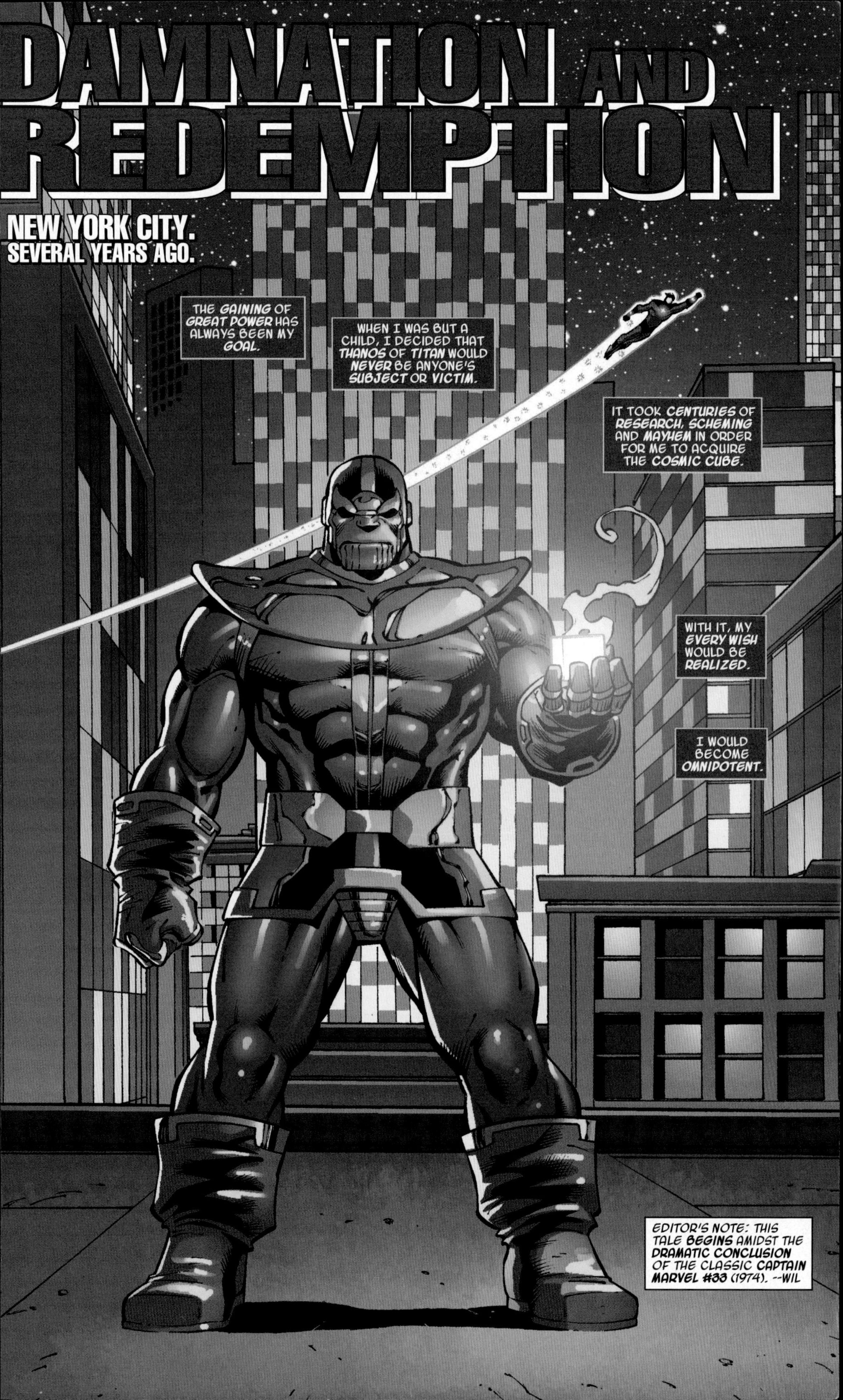
DAMNATION AND REDEMPTION
NEW YORK CITY. SEVERAL YEARS AGO.
THE GAINING OF GREAT POWER HAS ALWAYS BEEN MY GOAL.
WHEN I WAS BUT A CHILD, I DECIDED THAT THANOS OF TITAN WOULD NEVER BE ANYONE'S SUBJECT OR VICTIM.
IT TOOK CENTURIES OF RESEARCH, SCHEMING AND MAYHEM IN ORDER FOR ME TO ACQUIRE THE COSMIC CUBE.
WITH IT, MY EVERY WISH WOULD BE REALIZED.
I WOULD BECOME OMNIPOTENT.
EDITOR'S NOTE: THIS TALE BEGINS AMIDST THE DRAMATIC CONCLUSION OF THE CLASSIC CAPTAIN MARVEL #33 (1974). --WIL

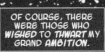

OF COURSE, THERE WERE THOSE WHO *WISHED* TO *THWART* MY *GRAND AMBITION.*

I HAD *ELIMINATED* MOST OF THE *OPPOSITION* BEFORE OR DIRECTLY AFTER GAINING *POSSESSION* OF THE *CUBE.*

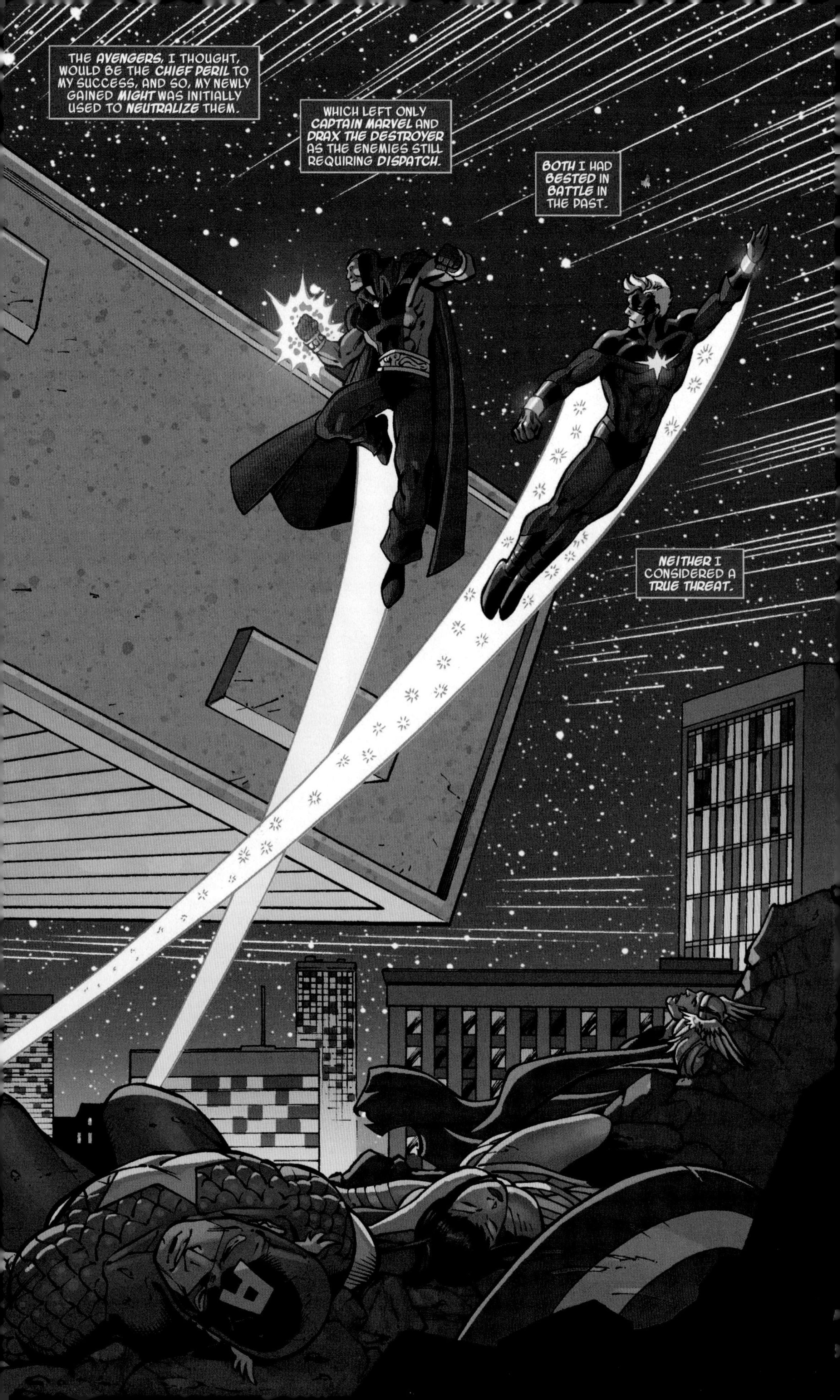
THE AVENGERS, I THOUGHT, WOULD BE THE CHIEF PERIL TO MY SUCCESS, AND SO, MY NEWLY GAINED MIGHT WAS INITIALLY USED TO NEUTRALIZE THEM.
WHICH LEFT ONLY CAPTAIN MARVEL AND DRAX THE DESTROYER AS THE ENEMIES STILL REQUIRING DISPATCH.
BOTH I HAD BESTED IN BATTLE IN THE PAST.
NEITHER I CONSIDERED A TRUE THREAT.

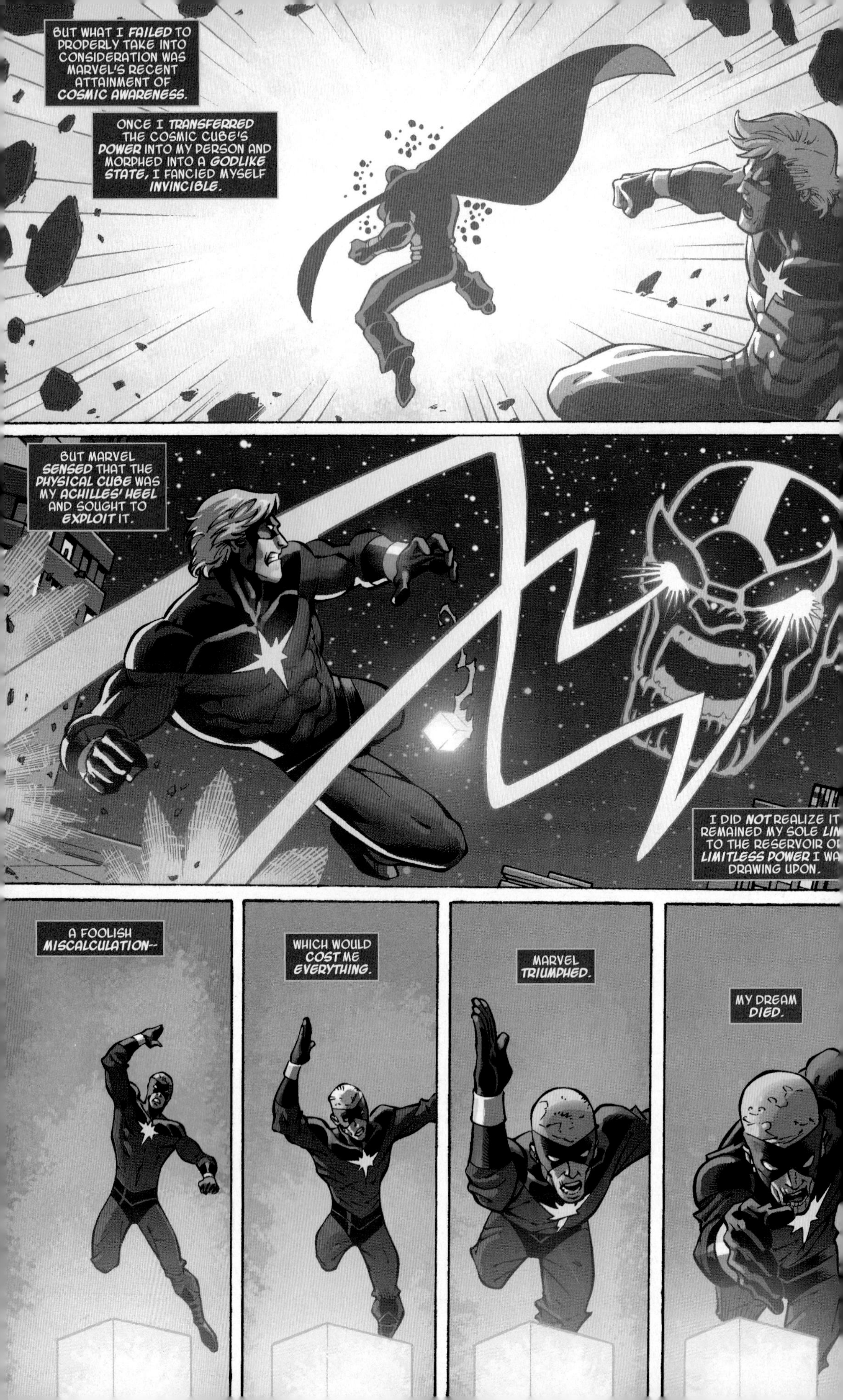
BUT WHAT I FAILED TO PROPERLY TAKE INTO CONSIDERATION WAS MARVEL'S RECENT ATTAINMENT OF COSMIC AWARENESS.
ONCE I TRANSFERRED THE COSMIC CUBE'S POWER INTO MY PERSON AND MORPHED INTO A GODLIKE STATE, I FANCIED MYSELF INVINCIBLE.
BUT MARVEL SENSED THAT THE PHYSICAL CUBE WAS MY ACHILLES' HEEL AND SOUGHT TO EXPLOIT IT.
I DID NOT REALIZE IT REMAINED MY SOLE LIN TO THE RESERVOIR O LIMITLESS POWER I WA DRAWING UPON.
A FOOLISH MISCALCULATION--
WHICH WOULD COST ME EVERYTHING.
MARVEL TRIUMPHED.
MY DREAM DIED.

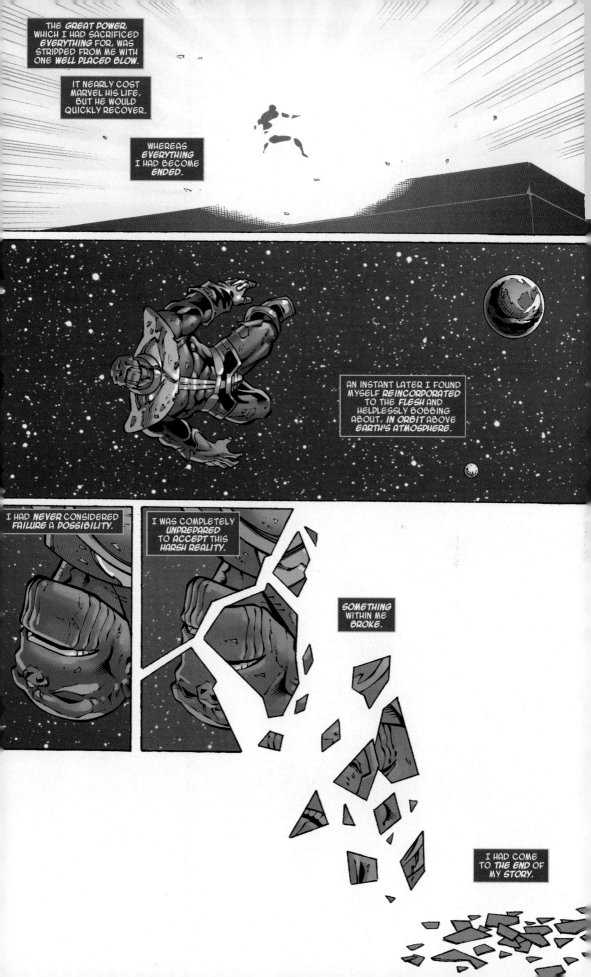

THE *GREAT POWER*, WHICH I HAD SACRIFICED *EVERYTHING* FOR, WAS STRIPPED FROM ME WITH ONE *WELL PLACED BLOW.*

IT NEARLY COST MARVEL HIS LIFE, BUT HE WOULD QUICKLY RECOVER.

WHEREAS *EVERYTHING* I HAD BECOME ENDED.

AN INSTANT LATER I FOUND MYSELF *REINCORPORATED* TO THE *FLESH* AND *HELPLESSLY BOBBING* ABOUT, *IN ORBIT* ABOVE *EARTH'S ATMOSPHERE.*

I HAD *NEVER* CONSIDERED FAILURE A *POSSIBILITY.*

I WAS COMPLETELY *UNPREPARED* TO ACCEPT THIS *HARSH REALITY.*

SOMETHING WITHIN ME *BROKE.*

I HAD COME TO *THE END* OF MY *STORY.*

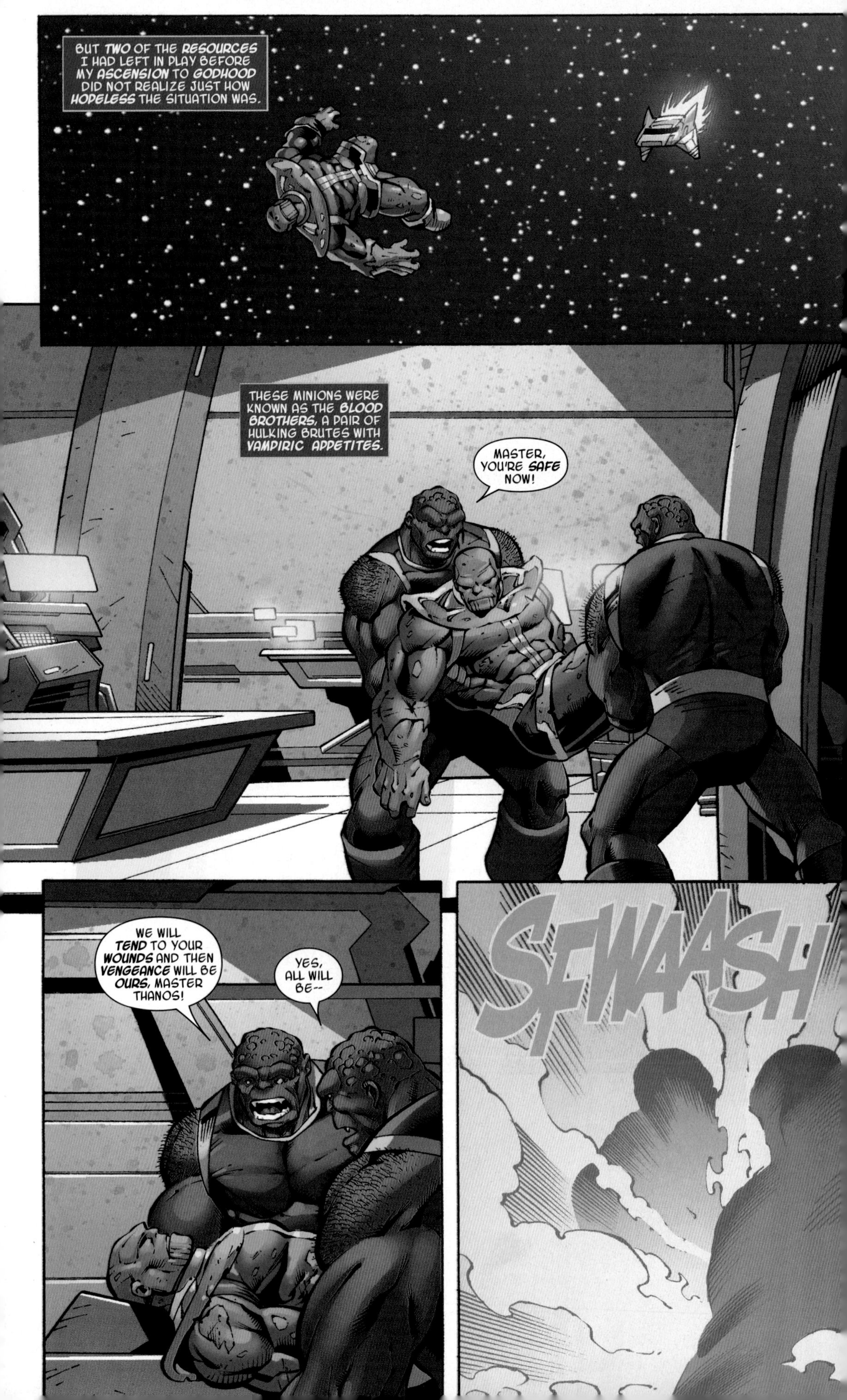
BUT TWO OF THE RESOURCES I HAD LEFT IN PLAY BEFORE MY ASCENSION TO GODHOOD DID NOT REALIZE JUST HOW HOPELESS THE SITUATION WAS.
THESE MINIONS WERE KNOWN AS THE BLOOD BROTHERS, A PAIR OF HULKING BRUTES WITH VAMPIRIC APPETITES.
MASTER, YOU'RE SAFE NOW!
WE WILL TEND TO YOUR WOUNDS AND THEN VENGEANCE WILL BE OURS, MASTER THANOS!
YES, ALL WILL BE--
SFWAASH

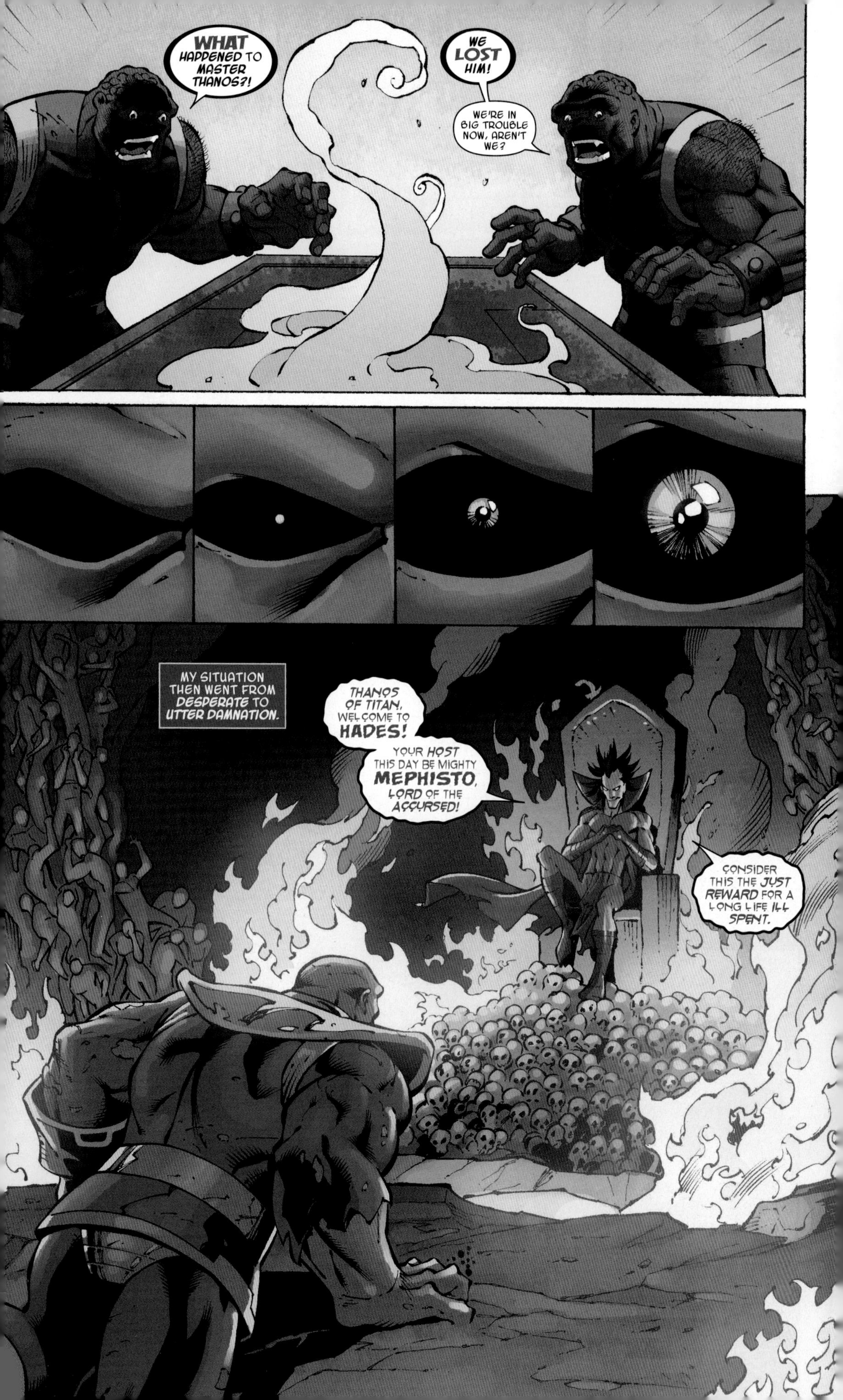
WHAT HAPPENED TO MASTER THANOS?!
WE LOST HIM!
WE'RE IN BIG TROUBLE NOW, AREN'T WE?
MY SITUATION THEN WENT FROM DESPERATE TO UTTER DAMNATION.
THANOS OF TITAN, WELCOME TO HADES!
YOUR HOST THIS DAY BE MIGHTY MEPHISTO, LORD OF THE ACCURSED!
CONSIDER THIS THE JUST REWARD FOR A LONG LIFE ILL SPENT.

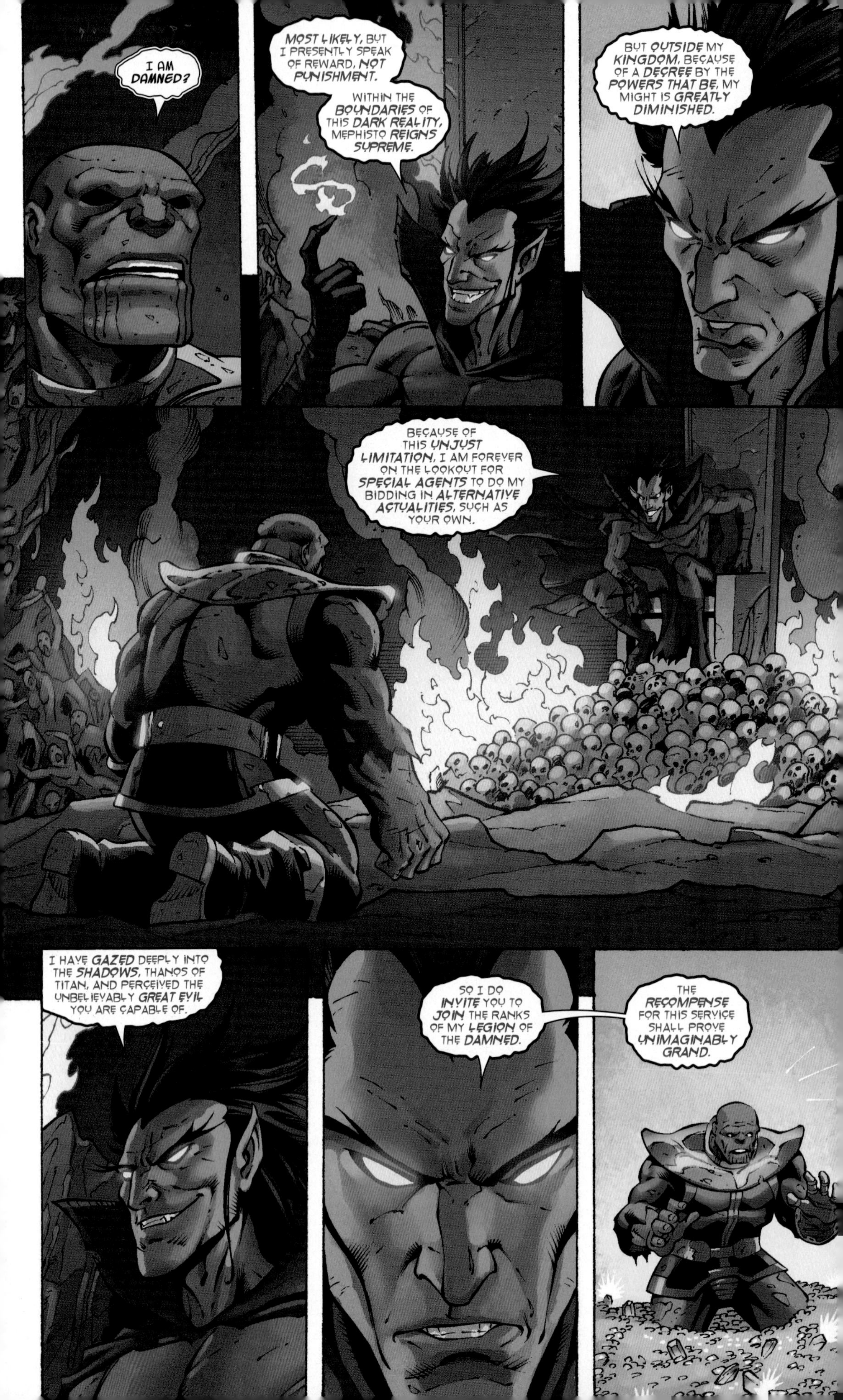
I AM DAMNED?
MOST LIKELY, BUT I PRESENTLY SPEAK OF REWARD, NOT PUNISHMENT.
WITHIN THE BOUNDARIES OF THIS DARK REALITY, MEPHISTO REIGNS SUPREME.
BUT OUTSIDE MY KINGDOM, BECAUSE OF A DECREE BY THE POWERS THAT BE, MY MIGHT IS GREATLY DIMINISHED.
BECAUSE OF THIS UNJUST LIMITATION, I AM FOREVER ON THE LOOKOUT FOR SPECIAL AGENTS TO DO MY BIDDING IN ALTERNATIVE ACTUALITIES, SUCH AS YOUR OWN.
I HAVE GAZED DEEPLY INTO THE SHADOWS, THANOS OF TITAN, AND PERCEIVED THE UNBELIEVABLY GREAT EVIL YOU ARE CAPABLE OF.
SO I DO INVITE YOU TO JOIN THE RANKS OF MY LEGION OF THE DAMNED.
THE RECOMPENSE FOR THIS SERVICE SHALL PROVE UNIMAGINABLY GRAND.

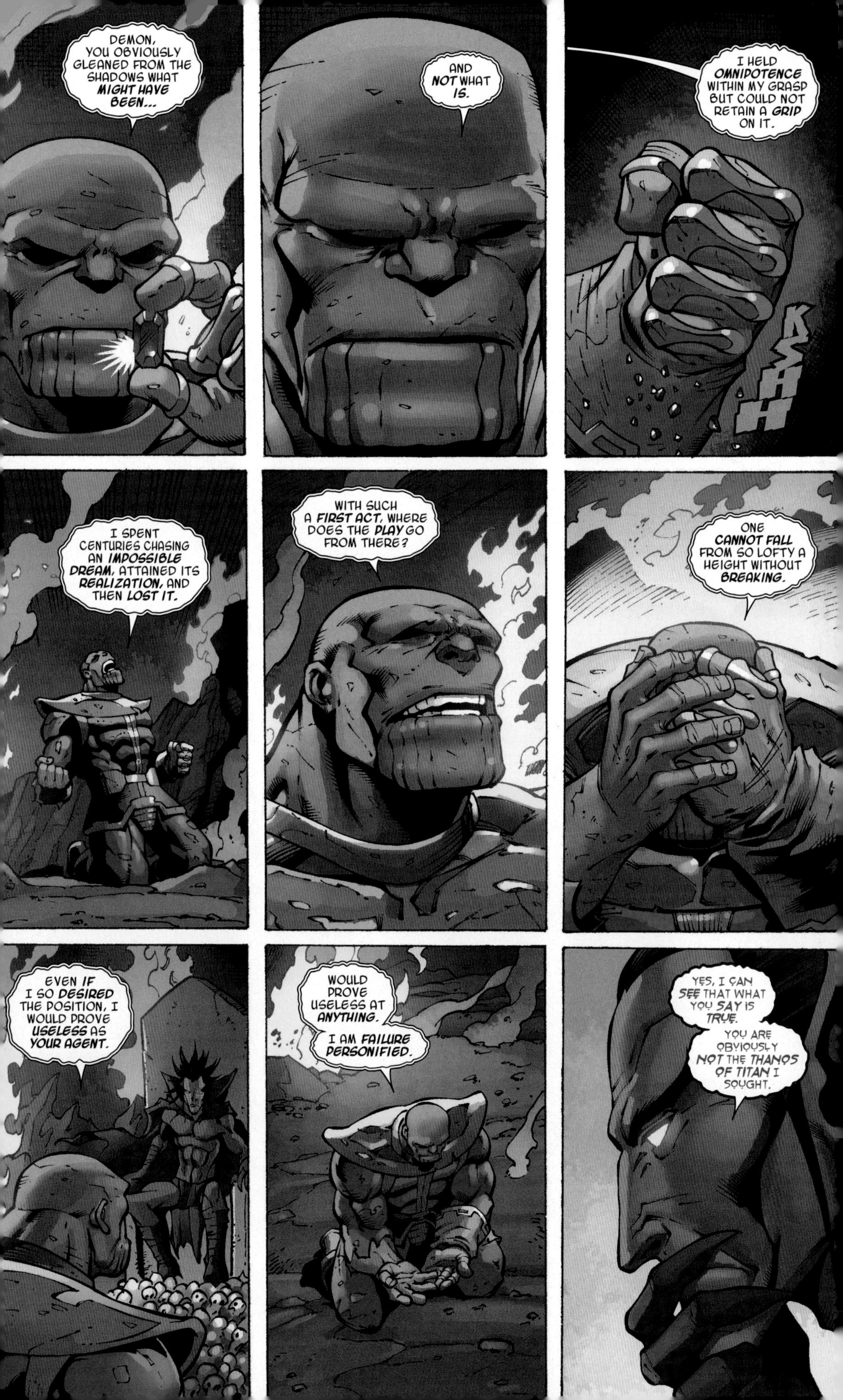
DEMON, YOU OBVIOUSLY GLEANED FROM THE SHADOWS WHAT MIGHT HAVE BEEN...
AND NOT WHAT IS.
I HELD OMNIPOTENCE WITHIN MY GRASP BUT COULD NOT RETAIN A GRIP ON IT.
KSHH
I SPENT CENTURIES CHASING AN IMPOSSIBLE DREAM, ATTAINED ITS REALIZATION, AND THEN LOST IT.
WITH SUCH A FIRST ACT, WHERE DOES THE PLAY GO FROM THERE?
ONE CANNOT FALL FROM SO LOFTY A HEIGHT WITHOUT BREAKING.
EVEN IF I SO DESIRED THE POSITION, I WOULD PROVE USELESS AS YOUR AGENT.
WOULD PROVE USELESS AT ANYTHING.
I AM FAILURE PERSONIFIED.
YES, I CAN SEE THAT WHAT YOU SAY IS TRUE.
YOU ARE OBVIOUSLY NOT THE THANOS OF TITAN I SOUGHT.

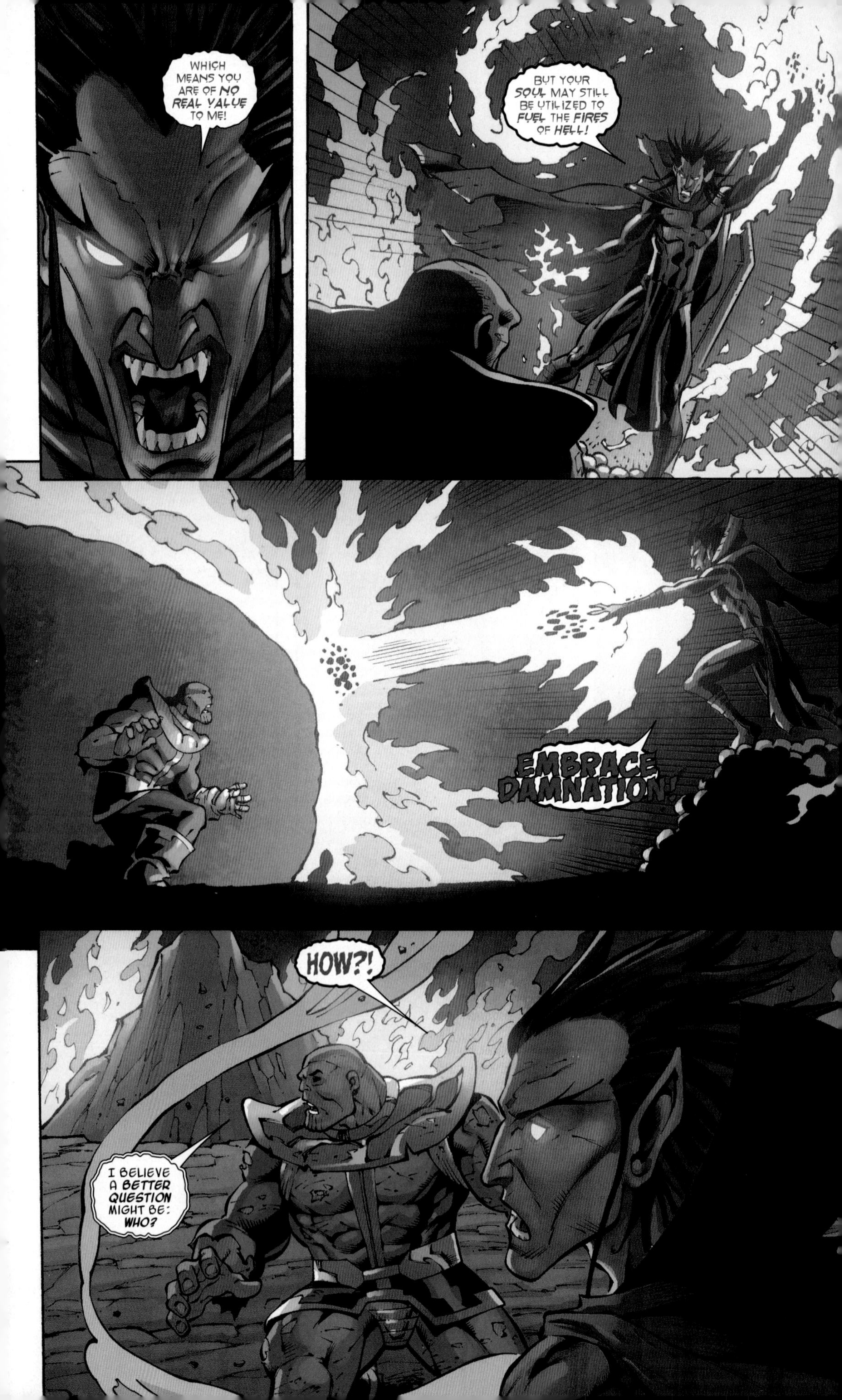
WHICH MEANS YOU ARE OF NO REAL VALUE TO ME!
BUT YOUR SOUL MAY STILL BE UTILIZED TO FUEL THE FIRES OF HELL!
EMBRACE DAMNATION!
HOW?!
I BELIEVE A BETTER QUESTION MIGHT BE: WHO?

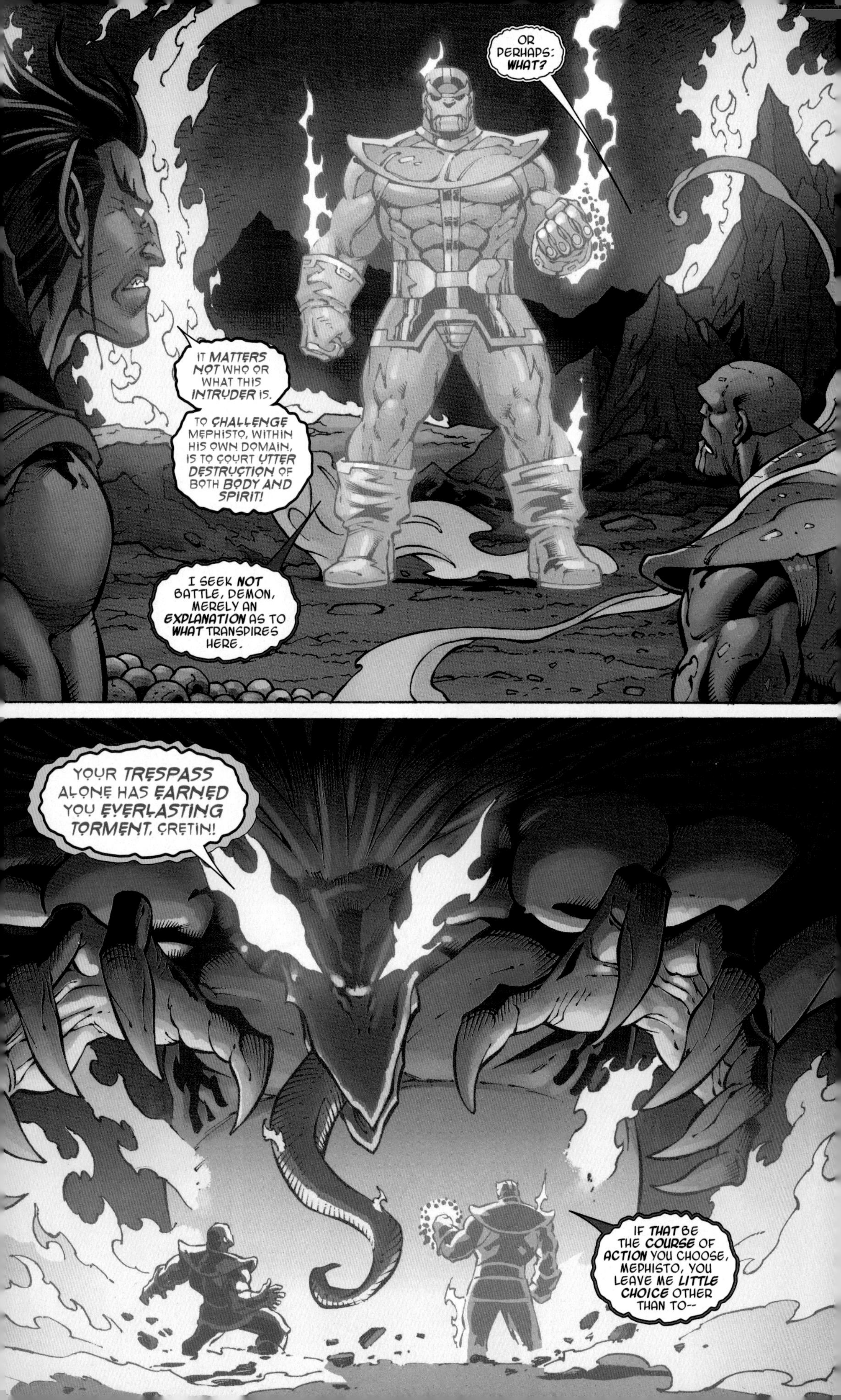
OR PERHAPS: WHAT?
IT MATTERS NOT WHO OR WHAT THIS INTRUDER IS.
TO CHALLENGE MEPHISTO, WITHIN HIS OWN DOMAIN, IS TO COURT UTTER DESTRUCTION OF BOTH BODY AND SPIRIT!
I SEEK NOT BATTLE, DEMON, MERELY AN EXPLANATION AS TO WHAT TRANSPIRES HERE.
YOUR TRESPASS ALONE HAS EARNED YOU EVERLASTING TORMENT, CRETIN!
IF THAT BE THE COURSE OF ACTION YOU CHOOSE, MEPHISTO, YOU LEAVE ME LITTLE CHOICE OTHER THAN TO--

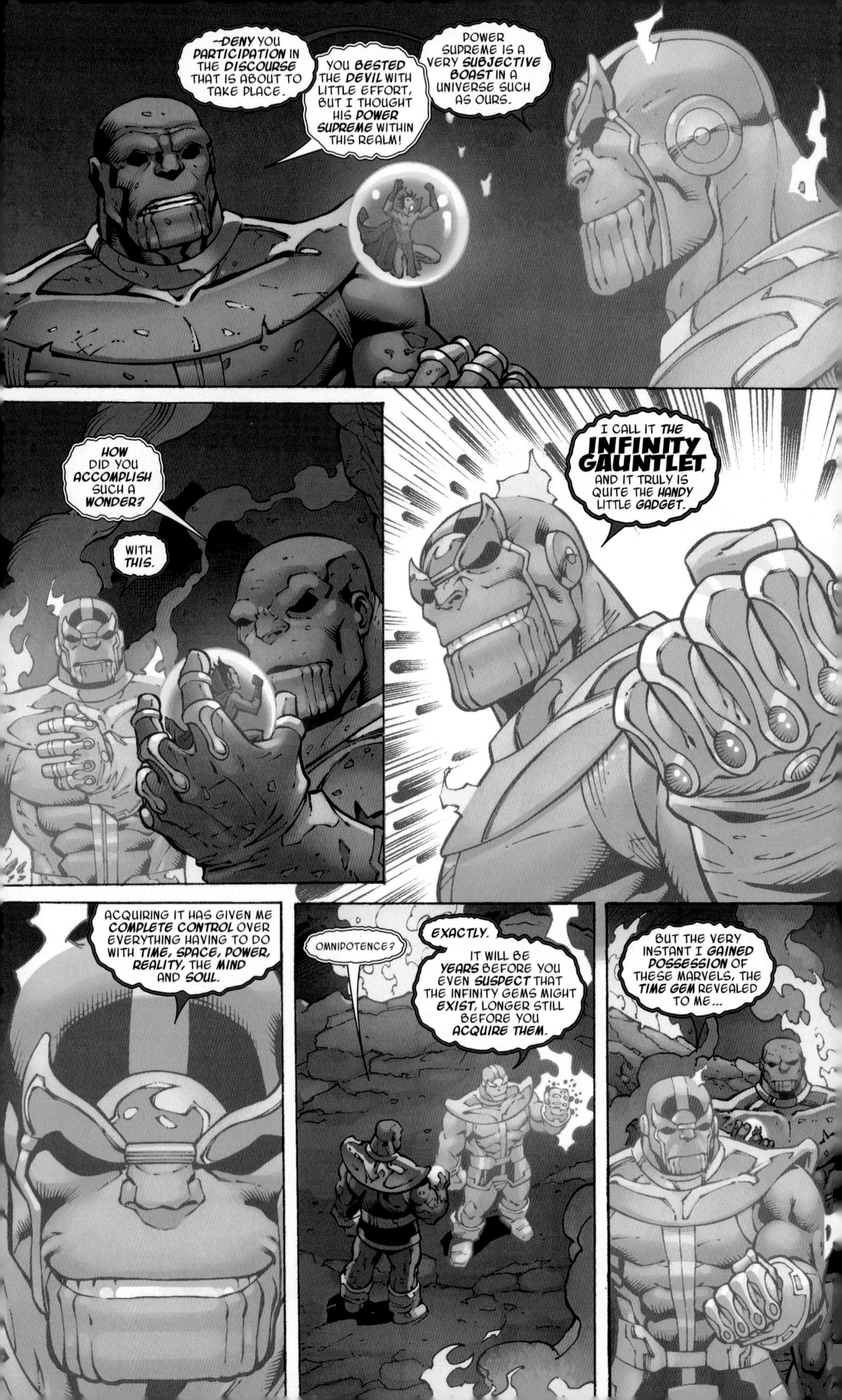
--DENY YOU PARTICIPATION IN THE DISCOURSE THAT IS ABOUT TO TAKE PLACE.
YOU BESTED THE DEVIL WITH LITTLE EFFORT, BUT I THOUGHT HIS POWER SUPREME WITHIN THIS REALM!
POWER SUPREME IS A VERY SUBJECTIVE BOAST IN A UNIVERSE SUCH AS OURS.
HOW DID YOU ACCOMPLISH SUCH A WONDER?
WITH THIS.
I CALL IT THE INFINITY GAUNTLET, AND IT TRULY IS QUITE THE HANDY LITTLE GADGET.
ACQUIRING IT HAS GIVEN ME COMPLETE CONTROL OVER EVERYTHING HAVING TO DO WITH TIME, SPACE, POWER, REALITY, THE MIND AND SOUL.
OMNIPOTENCE?
EXACTLY.
IT WILL BE YEARS BEFORE YOU EVEN SUSPECT THAT THE INFINITY GEMS MIGHT EXIST, LONGER STILL BEFORE YOU ACQUIRE THEM.
BUT THE VERY INSTANT I GAINED POSSESSION OF THESE MARVELS, THE TIME GEM REVEALED TO ME...

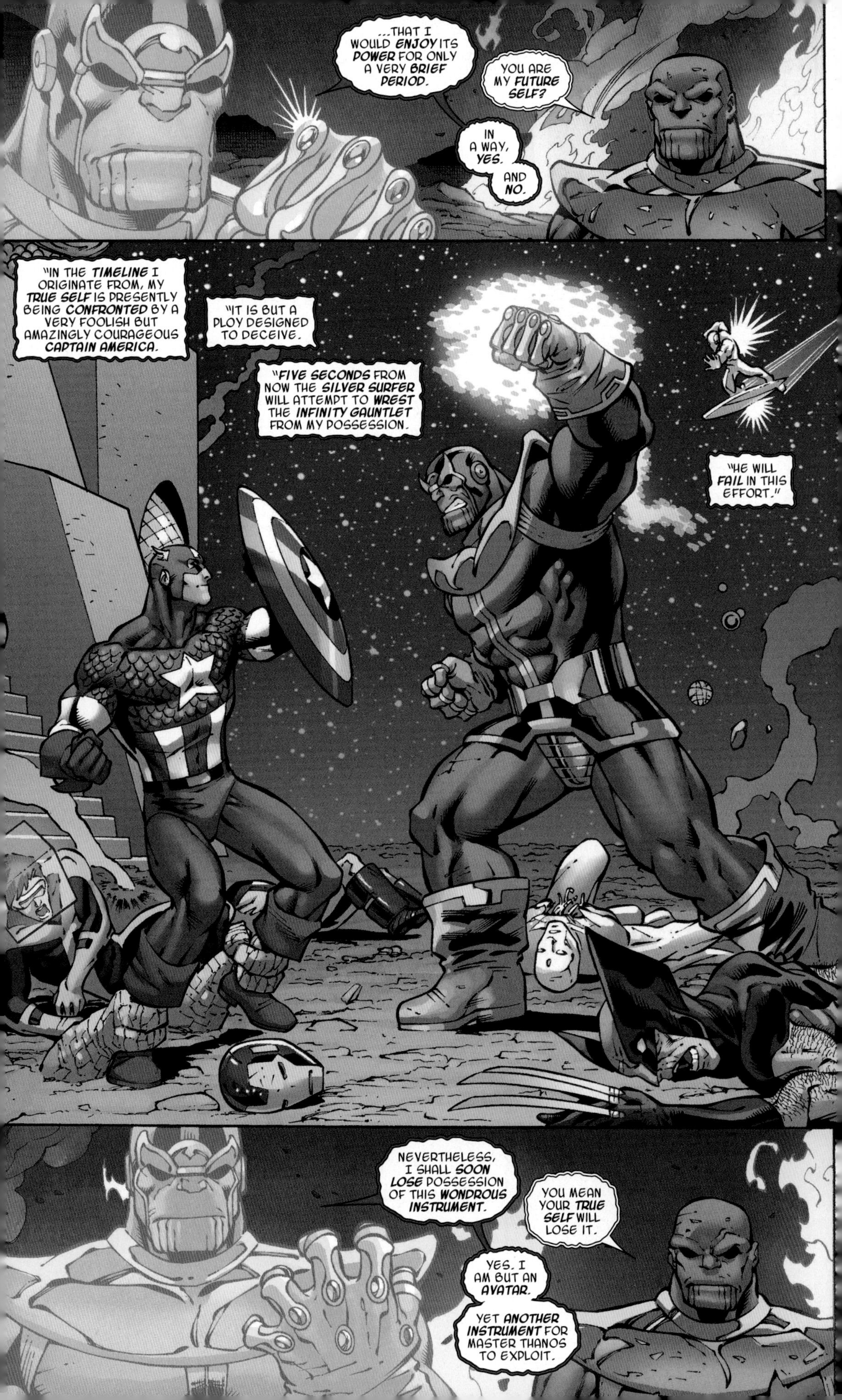

...THAT I WOULD ENJOY ITS POWER FOR ONLY A VERY BRIEF PERIOD.
YOU ARE MY FUTURE SELF?
IN A WAY, YES.
AND NO.
"IN THE TIMELINE I ORIGINATE FROM, MY TRUE SELF IS PRESENTLY BEING CONFRONTED BY A VERY FOOLISH BUT AMAZINGLY COURAGEOUS CAPTAIN AMERICA.
"IT IS BUT A PLOY DESIGNED TO DECEIVE.
"FIVE SECONDS FROM NOW THE SILVER SURFER WILL ATTEMPT TO WREST THE INFINITY GAUNTLET FROM MY POSSESSION.
"HE WILL FAIL IN THIS EFFORT."
NEVERTHELESS, I SHALL SOON LOSE POSSESSION OF THIS WONDROUS INSTRUMENT.
YOU MEAN YOUR TRUE SELF WILL LOSE IT.
YES. I AM BUT AN AVATAR.
YET ANOTHER INSTRUMENT FOR MASTER THANOS TO EXPLOIT.

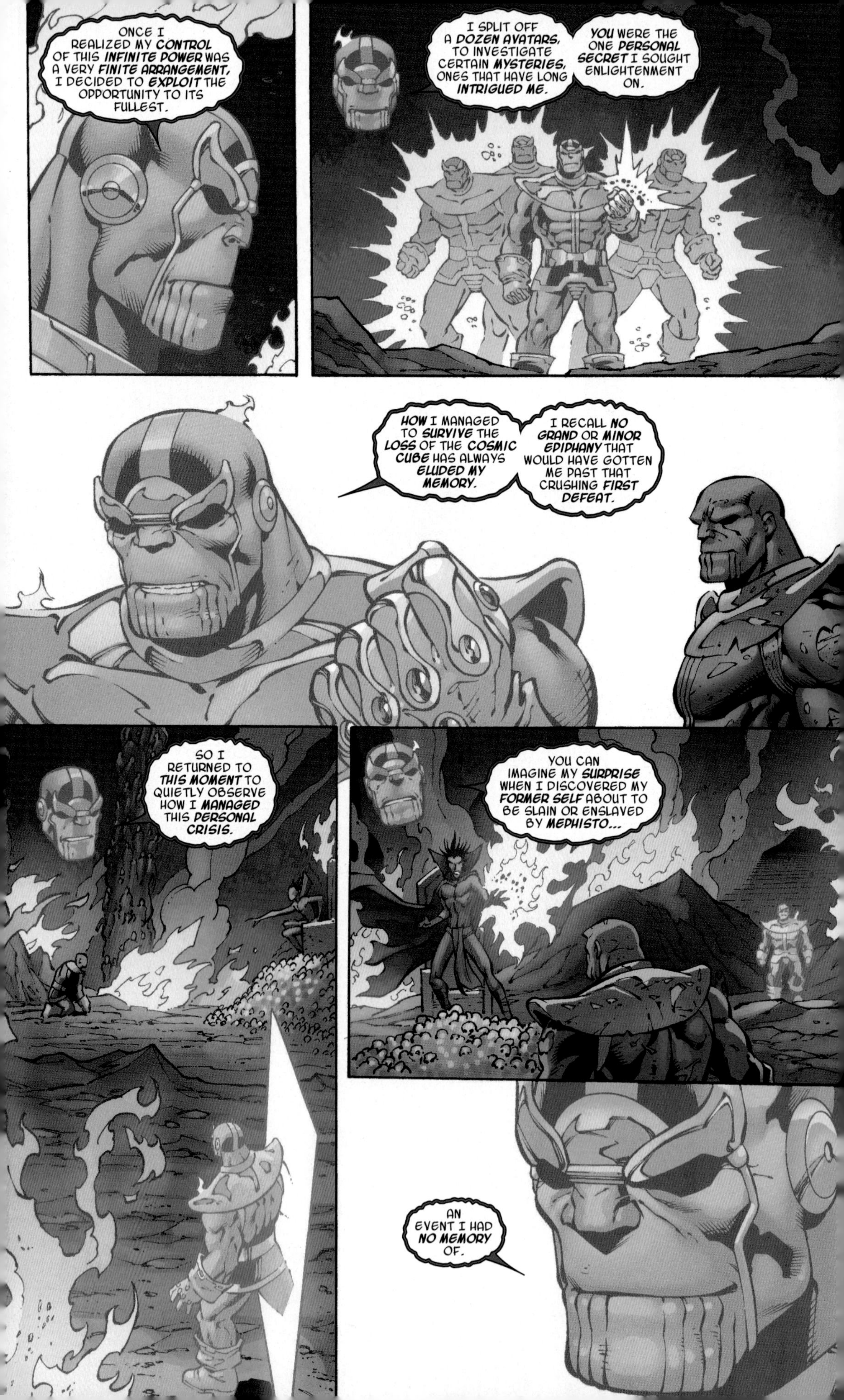

ONCE I REALIZED MY CONTROL OF THIS INFINITE POWER WAS A VERY FINITE ARRANGEMENT, I DECIDED TO EXPLOIT THE OPPORTUNITY TO ITS FULLEST.
I SPLIT OFF A DOZEN AVATARS, TO INVESTIGATE CERTAIN MYSTERIES, ONES THAT HAVE LONG INTRIGUED ME.
YOU WERE THE ONE PERSONAL SECRET I SOUGHT ENLIGHTENMENT ON.
HOW I MANAGED TO SURVIVE THE LOSS OF THE COSMIC CUBE HAS ALWAYS ELUDED MY MEMORY.
I RECALL NO GRAND OR MINOR EPIPHANY THAT WOULD HAVE GOTTEN ME PAST THAT CRUSHING FIRST DEFEAT.
SO I RETURNED TO THIS MOMENT TO QUIETLY OBSERVE HOW I MANAGED THIS PERSONAL CRISIS.
YOU CAN IMAGINE MY SURPRISE WHEN I DISCOVERED MY FORMER SELF ABOUT TO BE SLAIN OR ENSLAVED BY MEPHISTO...
AN EVENT I HAD NO MEMORY OF.

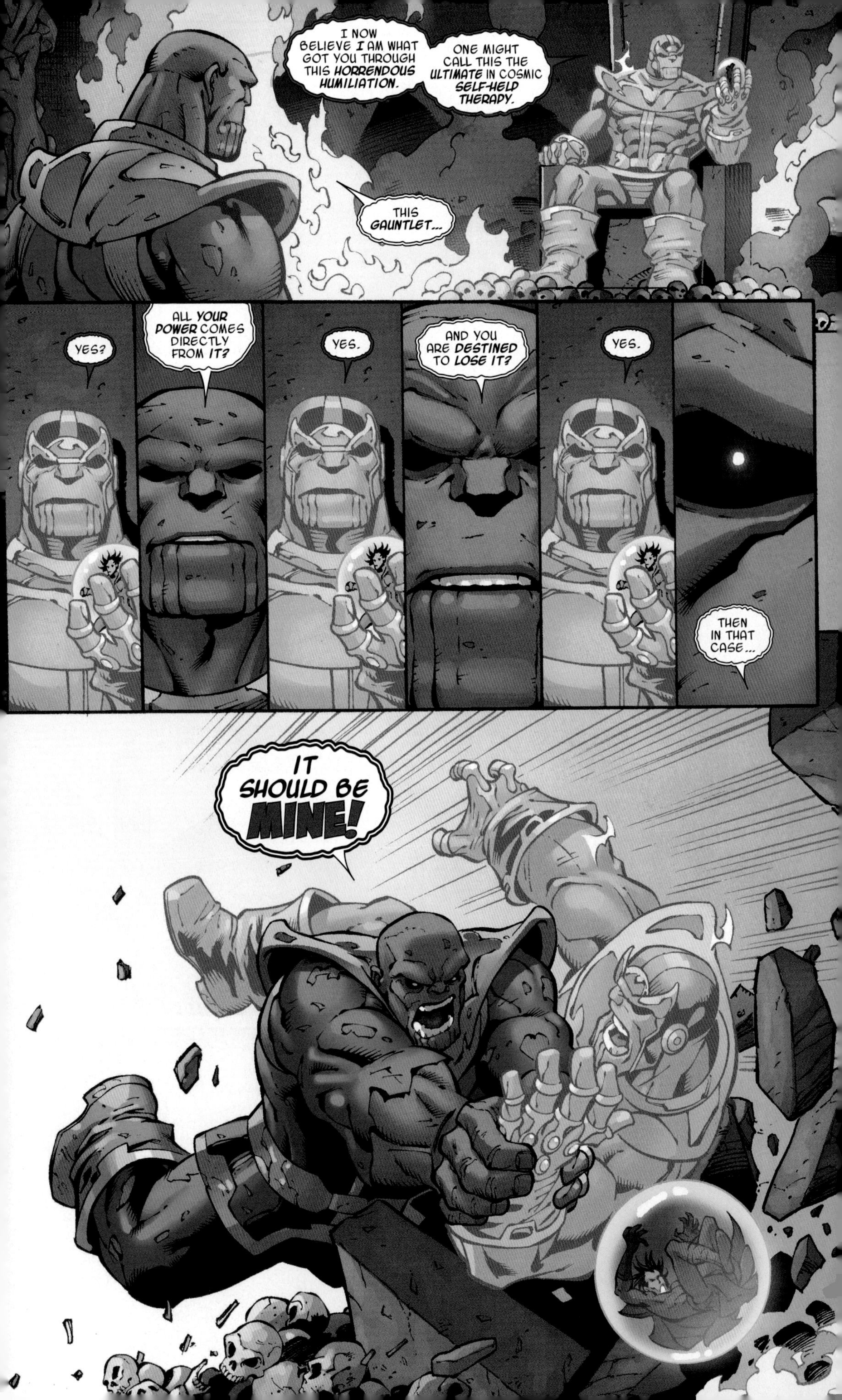
I NOW BELIEVE I AM WHAT GOT YOU THROUGH THIS HORRENDOUS HUMILIATION.
ONE MIGHT CALL THIS THE ULTIMATE IN COSMIC SELF-HELP THERAPY.
THIS GAUNTLET...
YES?
ALL YOUR POWER COMES DIRECTLY FROM IT?
YES.
AND YOU ARE DESTINED TO LOSE IT?
YES.
THEN IN THAT CASE...
IT SHOULD BE MINE!

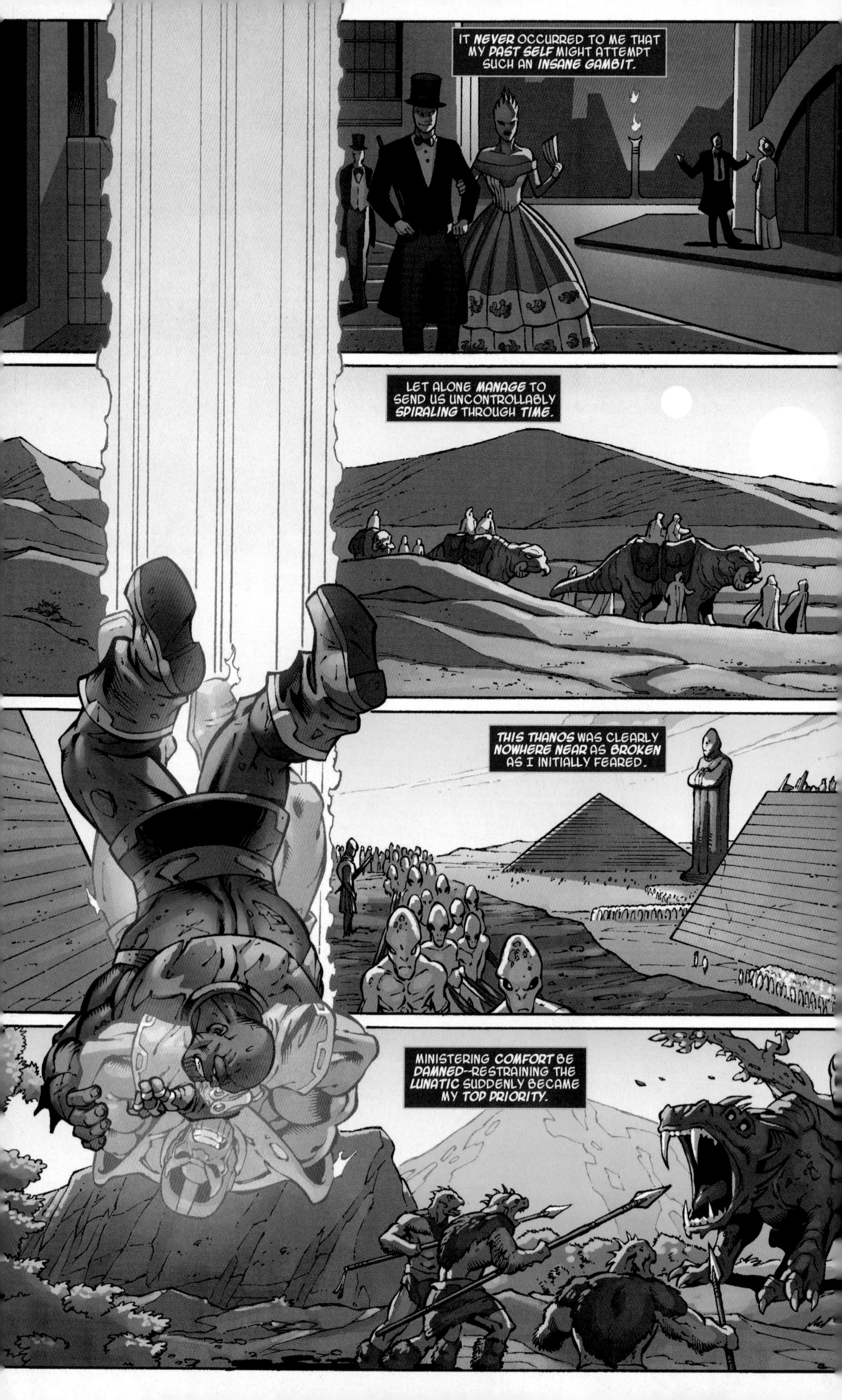
IT NEVER OCCURRED TO ME THAT MY PAST SELF MIGHT ATTEMPT SUCH AN INSANE GAMBIT.
LET ALONE MANAGE TO SEND US UNCONTROLLABLY SPIRALING THROUGH TIME.
THIS THANOS WAS CLEARLY NOWHERE NEAR AS BROKEN AS I INITIALLY FEARED.
MINISTERING COMFORT BE DAMNED--RESTRAINING THE LUNATIC SUDDENLY BECAME MY TOP PRIORITY.

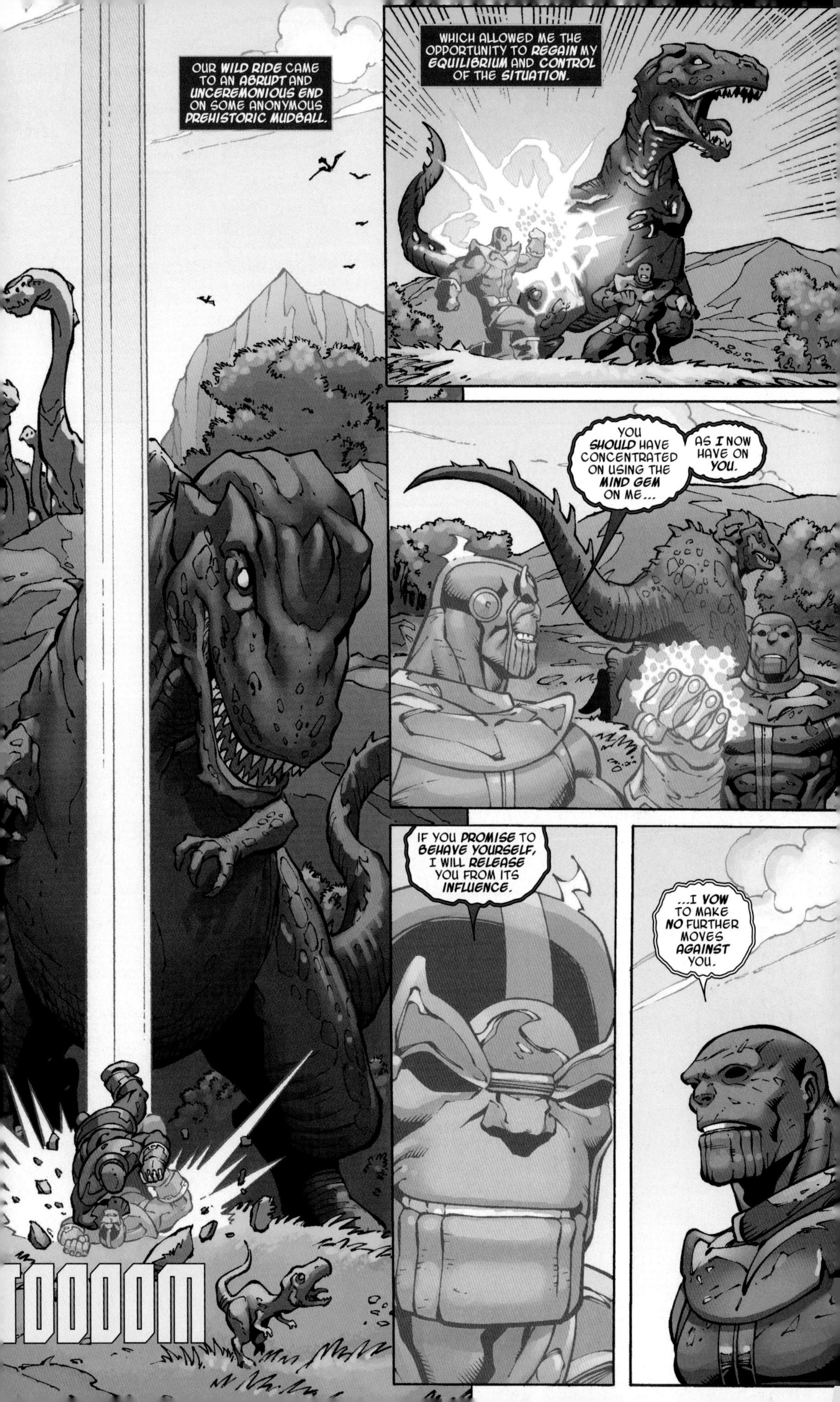
OUR WILD RIDE CAME TO AN ABRUPT AND UNCEREMONIOUS END ON SOME ANONYMOUS PREHISTORIC MUDBALL.
TOOOOM
WHICH ALLOWED ME THE OPPORTUNITY TO REGAIN MY EQUILIBRIUM AND CONTROL OF THE SITUATION.
YOU SHOULD HAVE CONCENTRATED ON USING THE MIND GEM ON ME...
AS I NOW HAVE ON YOU.
IF YOU PROMISE TO BEHAVE YOURSELF, I WILL RELEASE YOU FROM ITS INFLUENCE.
...I VOW TO MAKE NO FURTHER MOVES AGAINST YOU.

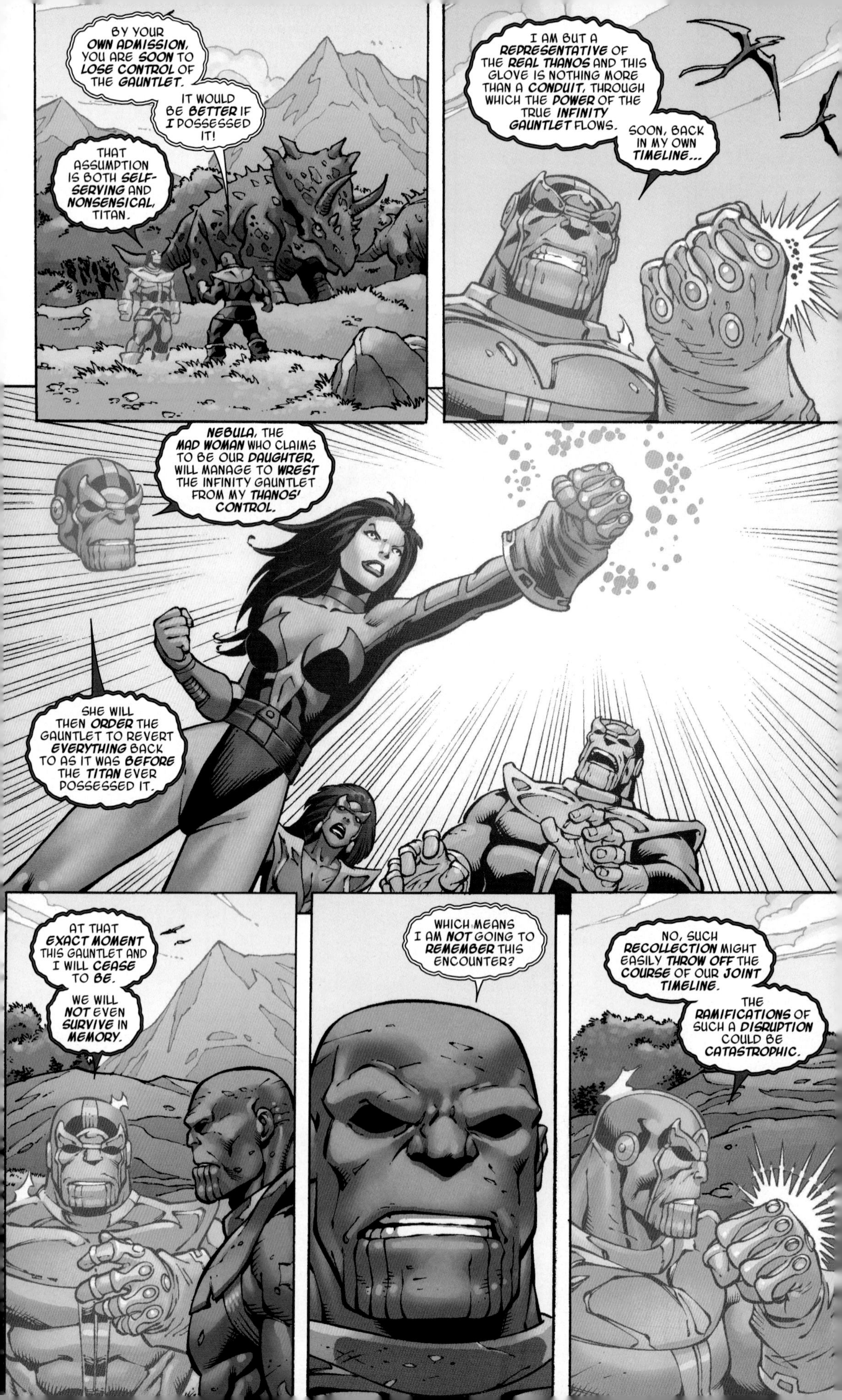
BY YOUR OWN ADMISSION, YOU ARE SOON TO LOSE CONTROL OF THE GAUNTLET.
IT WOULD BE BETTER IF I POSSESSED IT!
THAT ASSUMPTION IS BOTH SELF-SERVING AND NONSENSICAL, TITAN.
I AM BUT A REPRESENTATIVE OF THE REAL THANOS AND THIS GLOVE IS NOTHING MORE THAN A CONDUIT, THROUGH WHICH THE POWER OF THE TRUE INFINITY GAUNTLET FLOWS.
SOON, BACK IN MY OWN TIMELINE...
NEBULA, THE MAD WOMAN WHO CLAIMS TO BE OUR DAUGHTER, WILL MANAGE TO WREST THE INFINITY GAUNTLET FROM MY THANOS' CONTROL.
SHE WILL THEN ORDER THE GAUNTLET TO REVERT EVERYTHING BACK TO AS IT WAS BEFORE THE TITAN EVER POSSESSED IT.
AT THAT EXACT MOMENT THIS GAUNTLET AND I WILL CEASE TO BE.
WE WILL NOT EVEN SURVIVE IN MEMORY.
WHICH MEANS I AM NOT GOING TO REMEMBER THIS ENCOUNTER?
NO, SUCH RECOLLECTION MIGHT EASILY THROW OFF THE COURSE OF OUR JOINT TIMELINE.
THE RAMIFICATIONS OF SUCH A DISRUPTION COULD BE CATASTROPHIC.

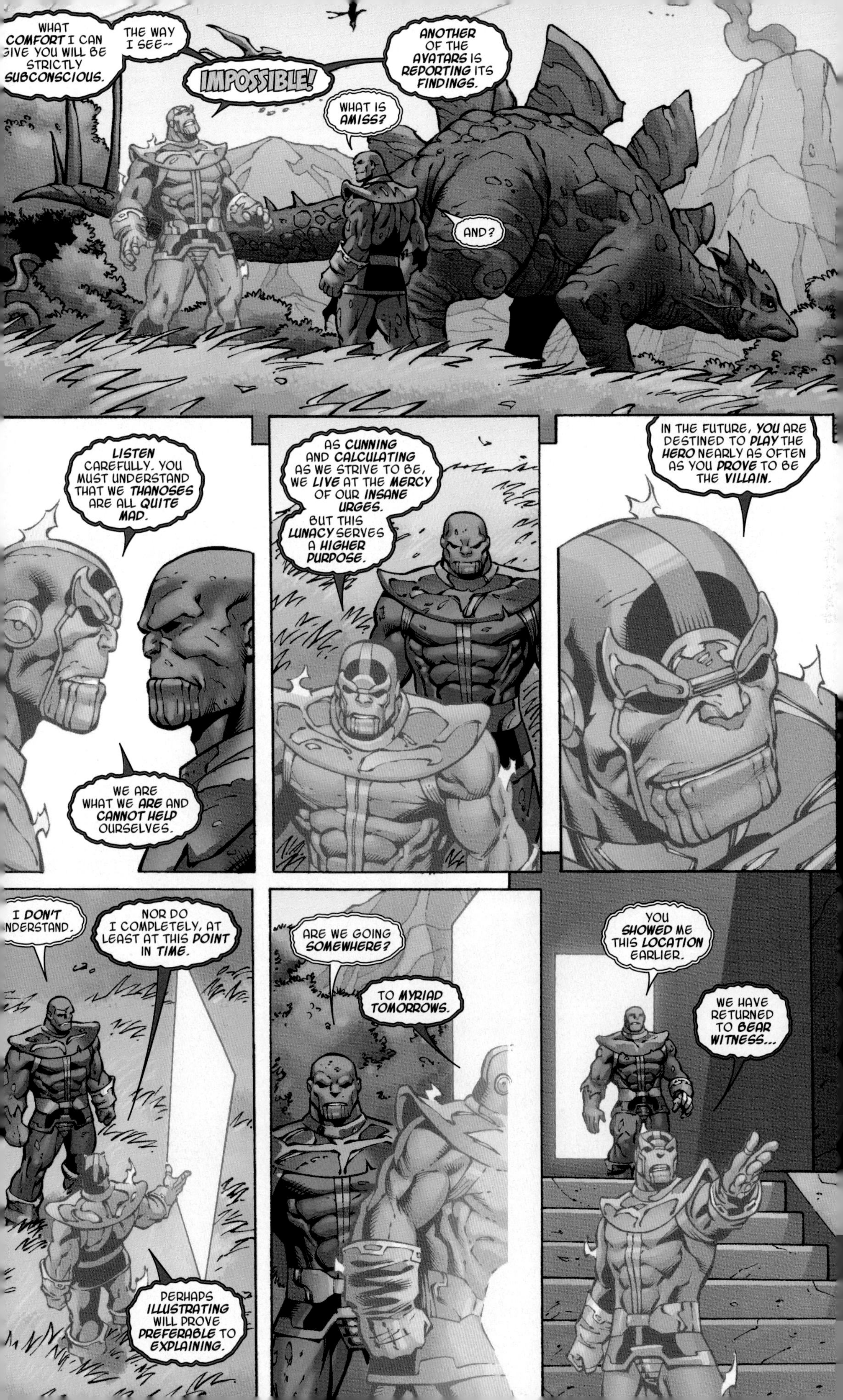

WHAT COMFORT I CAN GIVE YOU WILL BE STRICTLY SUBCONSCIOUS.
THE WAY I SEE--
IMPOSSIBLE!
ANOTHER OF THE AVATARS IS REPORTING ITS FINDINGS.
WHAT IS AMISS?
AND?
LISTEN CAREFULLY. YOU MUST UNDERSTAND THAT WE THANOSES ARE ALL QUITE MAD.
WE ARE WHAT WE ARE AND CANNOT HELP OURSELVES.
AS CUNNING AND CALCULATING AS WE STRIVE TO BE, WE LIVE AT THE MERCY OF OUR INSANE URGES.
BUT THIS LUNACY SERVES A HIGHER PURPOSE.
IN THE FUTURE, YOU ARE DESTINED TO PLAY THE HERO NEARLY AS OFTEN AS YOU PROVE TO BE THE VILLAIN.
I DON'T UNDERSTAND.
NOR DO I COMPLETELY, AT LEAST AT THIS POINT IN TIME.
PERHAPS ILLUSTRATING WILL PROVE PREFERABLE TO EXPLAINING.
ARE WE GOING SOMEWHERE?
TO MYRIAD TOMORROWS.
YOU SHOWED ME THIS LOCATION EARLIER.
WE HAVE RETURNED TO BEAR WITNESS...

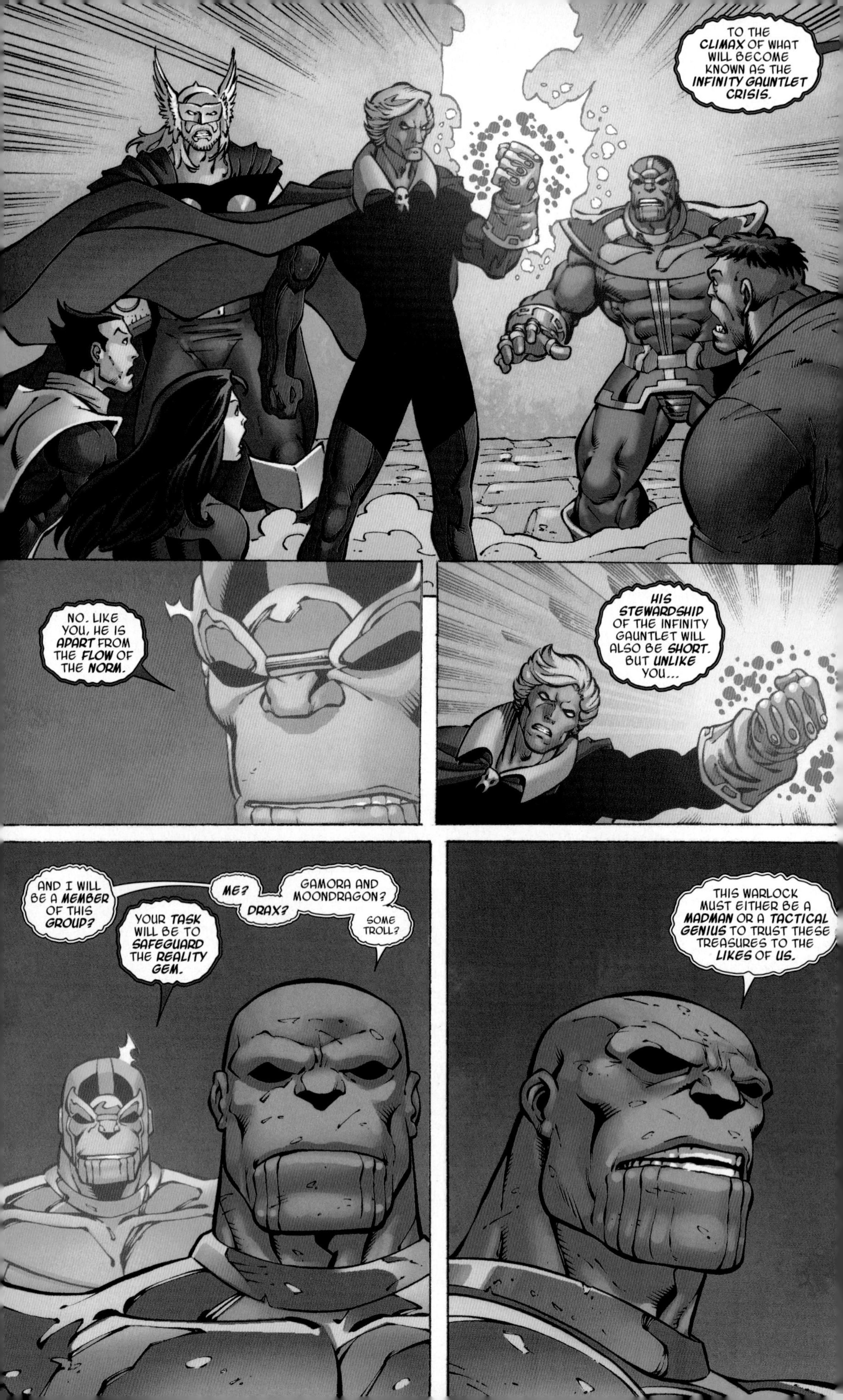
TO THE CLIMAX OF WHAT WILL BECOME KNOWN AS THE INFINITY GAUNTLET CRISIS.
NO. LIKE YOU, HE IS APART FROM THE FLOW OF THE NORM.
HIS STEWARDSHIP OF THE INFINITY GAUNTLET WILL ALSO BE SHORT. BUT UNLIKE YOU...
AND I WILL BE A MEMBER OF THIS GROUP?
ME?
DRAX?
GAMORA AND MOONDRAGON?
SOME TROLL?
YOUR TASK WILL BE TO SAFEGUARD THE REALITY GEM.
THIS WARLOCK MUST EITHER BE A MADMAN OR A TACTICAL GENIUS TO TRUST THESE TREASURES TO THE LIKES OF US.

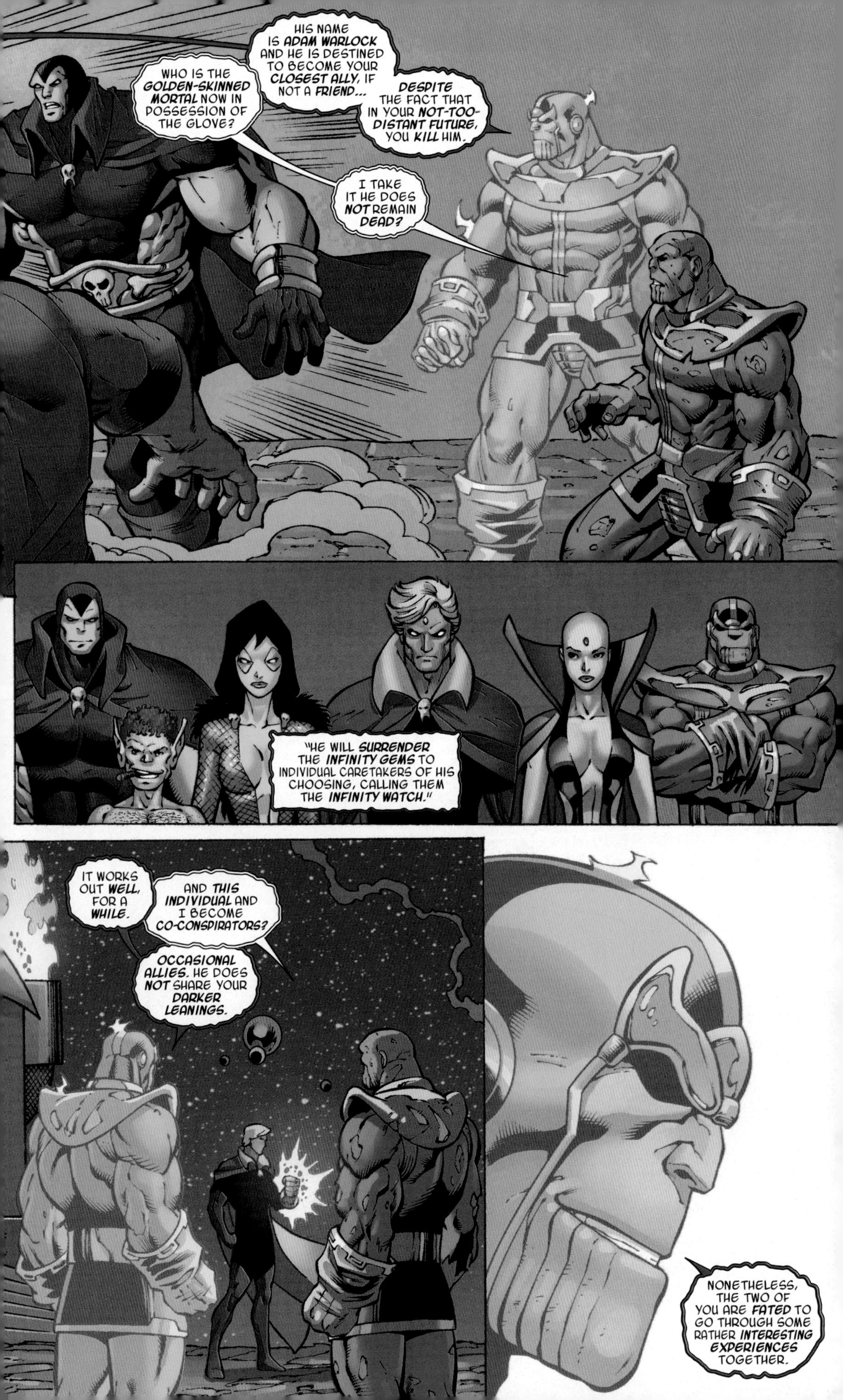
WHO IS THE GOLDEN-SKINNED MORTAL NOW IN POSSESSION OF THE GLOVE?
HIS NAME IS ADAM WARLOCK AND HE IS DESTINED TO BECOME YOUR CLOSEST ALLY, IF NOT A FRIEND...
DESPITE THE FACT THAT IN YOUR NOT-TOO-DISTANT FUTURE, YOU KILL HIM.
I TAKE IT HE DOES NOT REMAIN DEAD?
"HE WILL SURRENDER THE INFINITY GEMS TO INDIVIDUAL CARETAKERS OF HIS CHOOSING, CALLING THEM THE INFINITY WATCH."
IT WORKS OUT WELL, FOR A WHILE.
AND THIS INDIVIDUAL AND I BECOME CO-CONSPIRATORS?
OCCASIONAL ALLIES. HE DOES NOT SHARE YOUR DARKER LEANINGS.
NONETHELESS, THE TWO OF YOU ARE FATED TO GO THROUGH SOME RATHER INTERESTING EXPERIENCES TOGETHER.

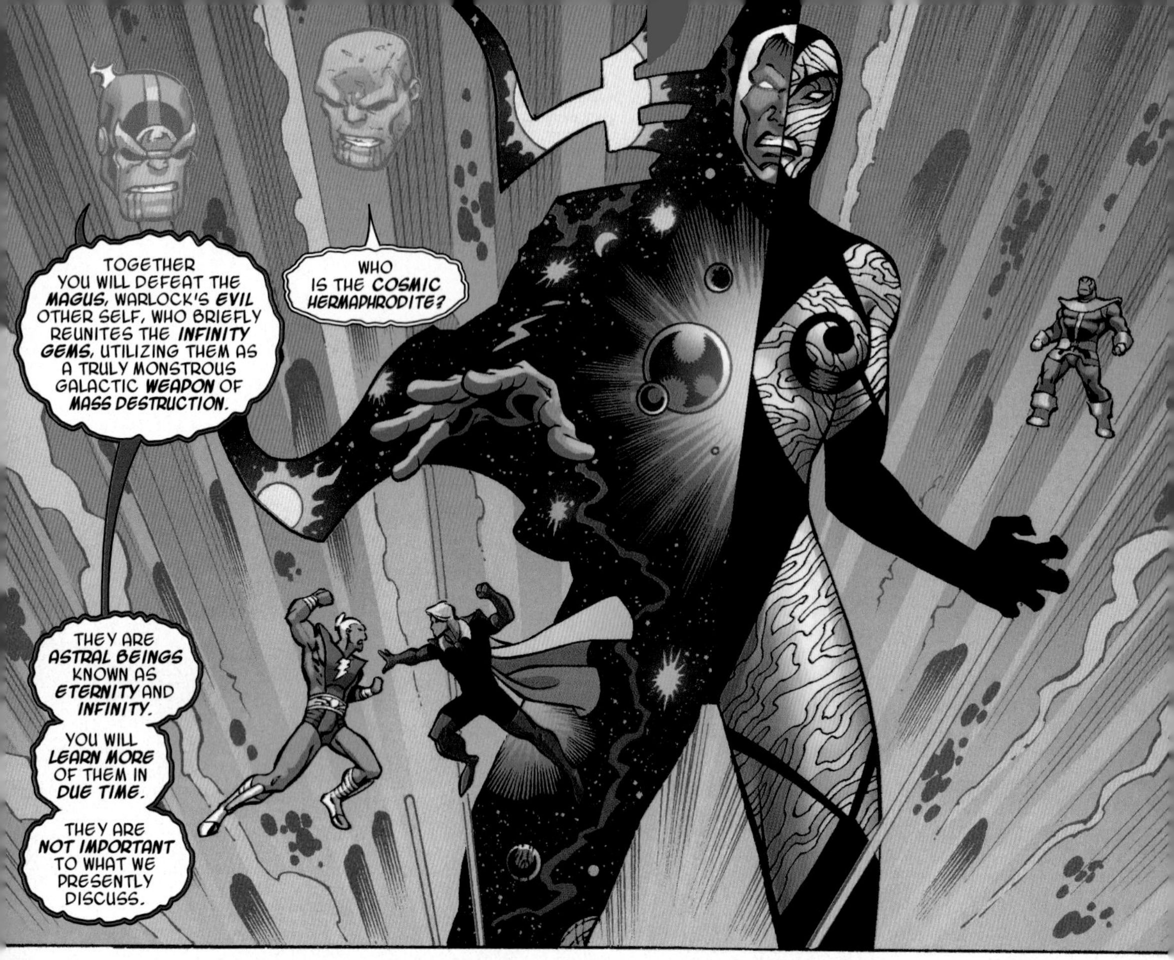
TOGETHER YOU WILL DEFEAT THE MAGUS, WARLOCK'S EVIL OTHER SELF, WHO BRIEFLY REUNITES THE INFINITY GEMS, UTILIZING THEM AS A TRULY MONSTROUS GALACTIC WEAPON OF MASS DESTRUCTION.
WHO IS THE COSMIC HERMAPHRODITE?
THEY ARE ASTRAL BEINGS KNOWN AS ETERNITY AND INFINITY.
YOU WILL LEARN MORE OF THEM IN DUE TIME.
THEY ARE NOT IMPORTANT TO WHAT WE PRESENTLY DISCUSS.

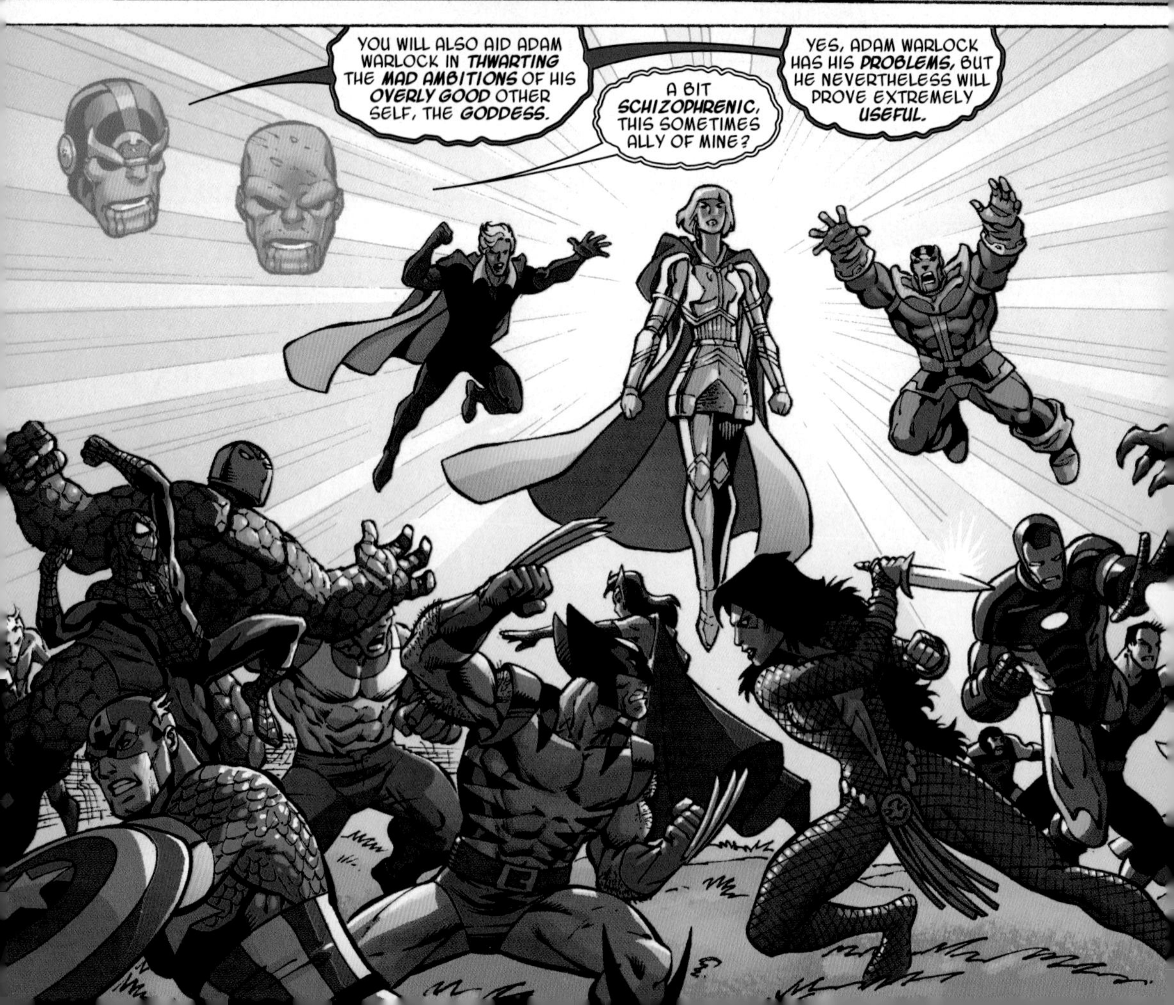
YOU WILL ALSO AID ADAM WARLOCK IN THWARTING THE MAD AMBITIONS OF HIS OVERLY GOOD OTHER SELF, THE GODDESS.
A BIT SCHIZOPHRENIC, THIS SOMETIMES ALLY OF MINE?
YES, ADAM WARLOCK HAS HIS PROBLEMS, BUT HE NEVERTHELESS WILL PROVE EXTREMELY USEFUL.

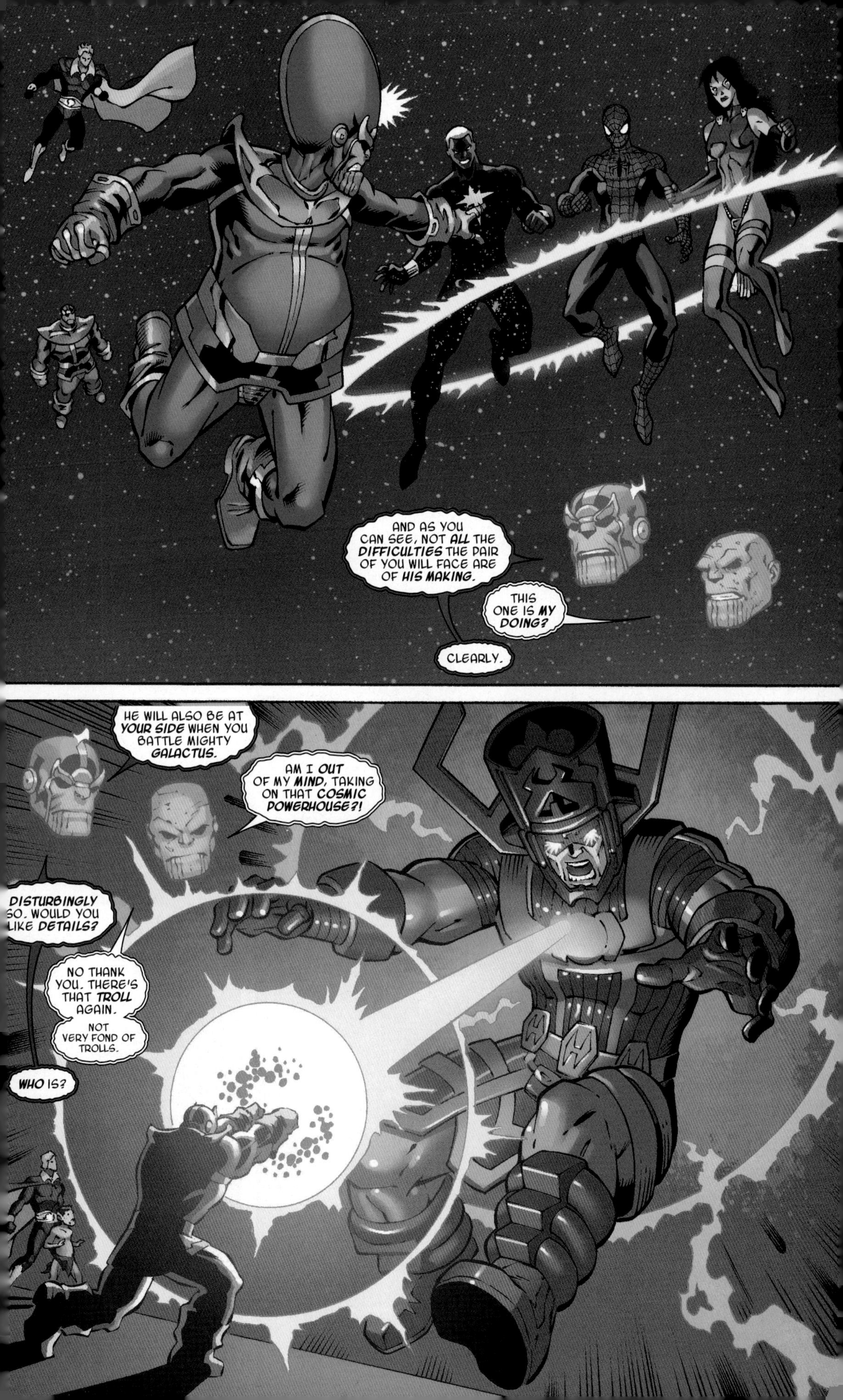
AND AS YOU CAN SEE, NOT ALL THE DIFFICULTIES THE PAIR OF YOU WILL FACE ARE OF HIS MAKING.
THIS ONE IS MY DOING?
CLEARLY.
HE WILL ALSO BE AT YOUR SIDE WHEN YOU BATTLE MIGHTY GALACTUS.
AM I OUT OF MY MIND, TAKING ON THAT COSMIC POWERHOUSE?!
DISTURBINGLY SO. WOULD YOU LIKE DETAILS?
NO THANK YOU. THERE'S THAT TROLL AGAIN.
NOT VERY FOND OF TROLLS.
WHO IS?

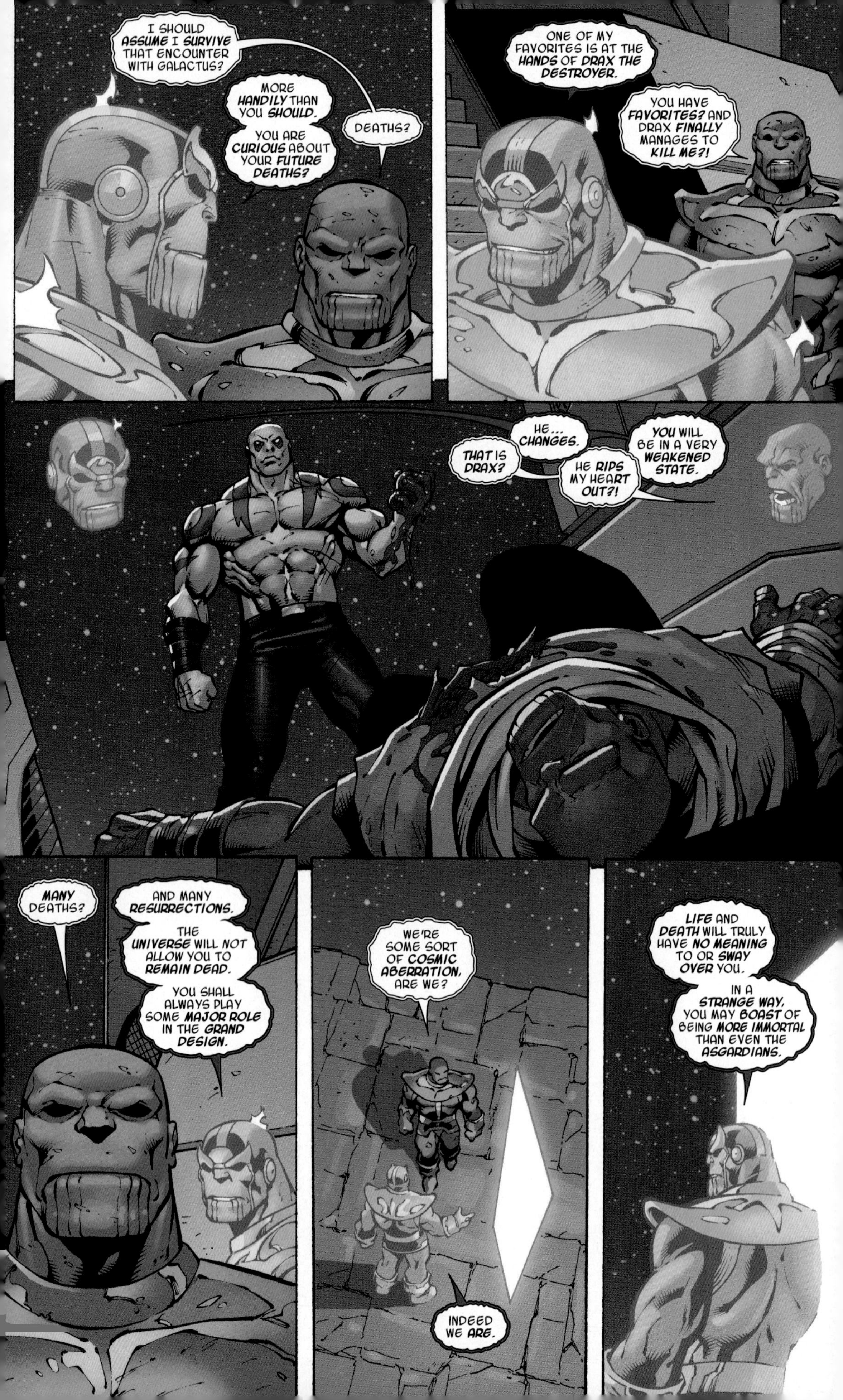
I SHOULD ASSUME I SURVIVE THAT ENCOUNTER WITH GALACTUS?
MORE HANDILY THAN YOU SHOULD.
YOU ARE CURIOUS ABOUT YOUR FUTURE DEATHS?
DEATHS?
ONE OF MY FAVORITES IS AT THE HANDS OF DRAX THE DESTROYER.
YOU HAVE FAVORITES? AND DRAX FINALLY MANAGES TO KILL ME?!
THAT IS DRAX?
HE... CHANGES.
HE RIPS MY HEART OUT?!
YOU WILL BE IN A VERY WEAKENED STATE.
MANY DEATHS?
AND MANY RESURRECTIONS.
THE UNIVERSE WILL NOT ALLOW YOU TO REMAIN DEAD.
YOU SHALL ALWAYS PLAY SOME MAJOR ROLE IN THE GRAND DESIGN.
WE'RE SOME SORT OF COSMIC ABERRATION, ARE WE?
INDEED WE ARE.
LIFE AND DEATH WILL TRULY HAVE NO MEANING TO OR SWAY OVER YOU.
IN A STRANGE WAY, YOU MAY BOAST OF BEING MORE IMMORTAL THAN EVEN THE ASGARDIANS.

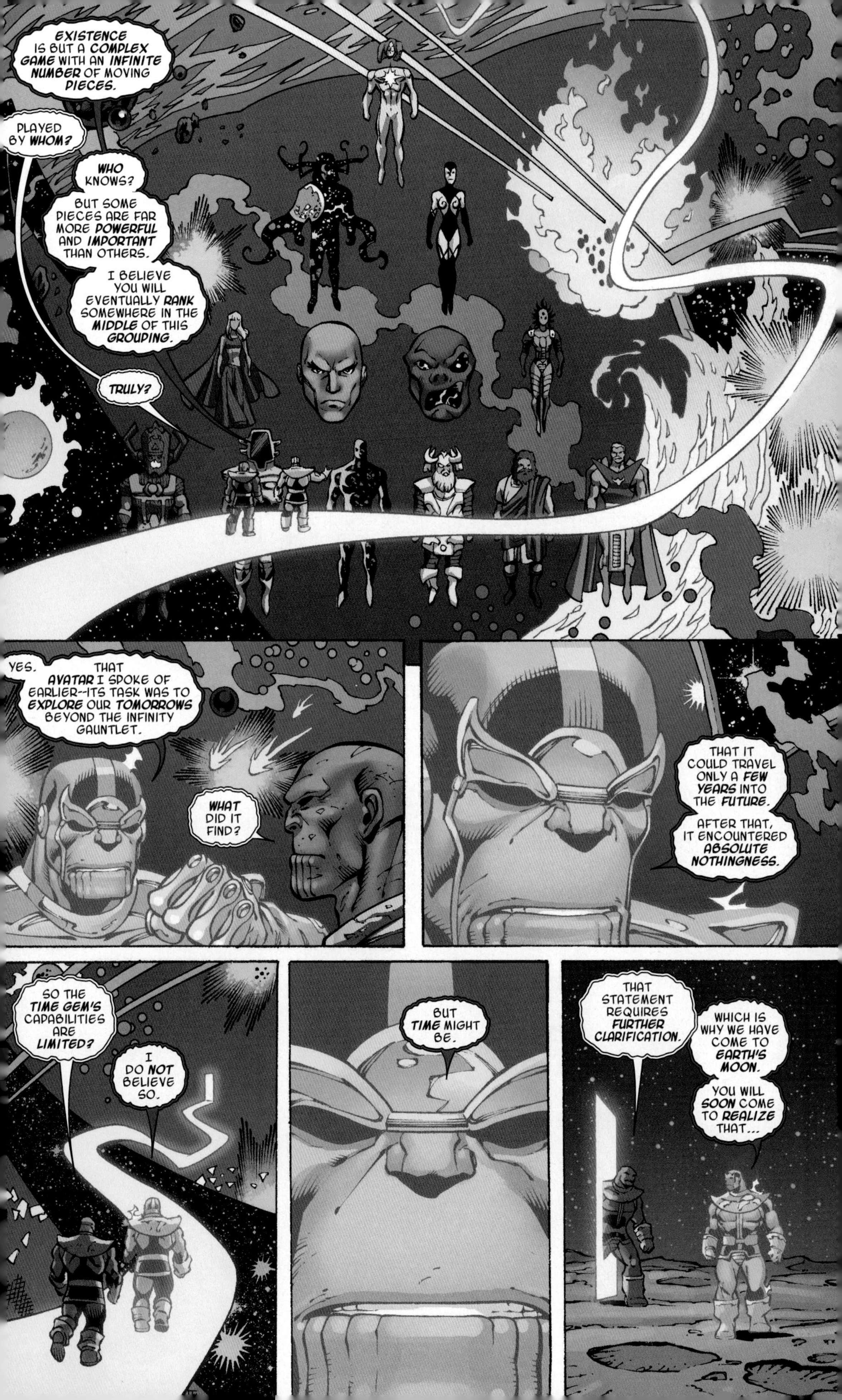
EXISTENCE IS BUT A COMPLEX GAME WITH AN INFINITE NUMBER OF MOVING PIECES.
PLAYED BY WHOM?
WHO KNOWS?
BUT SOME PIECES ARE FAR MORE POWERFUL AND IMPORTANT THAN OTHERS.
I BELIEVE YOU WILL EVENTUALLY RANK SOMEWHERE IN THE MIDDLE OF THIS GROUPING.
TRULY?
YES. THAT AVATAR I SPOKE OF EARLIER--ITS TASK WAS TO EXPLORE OUR TOMORROWS BEYOND THE INFINITY GAUNTLET.
WHAT DID IT FIND?
THAT IT COULD TRAVEL ONLY A FEW YEARS INTO THE FUTURE.
AFTER THAT, IT ENCOUNTERED ABSOLUTE NOTHINGNESS.
SO THE TIME GEM'S CAPABILITIES ARE LIMITED?
I DO NOT BELIEVE SO.
BUT TIME MIGHT BE.
THAT STATEMENT REQUIRES FURTHER CLARIFICATION.
WHICH IS WHY WE HAVE COME TO EARTH'S MOON.
YOU WILL SOON COME TO REALIZE THAT...

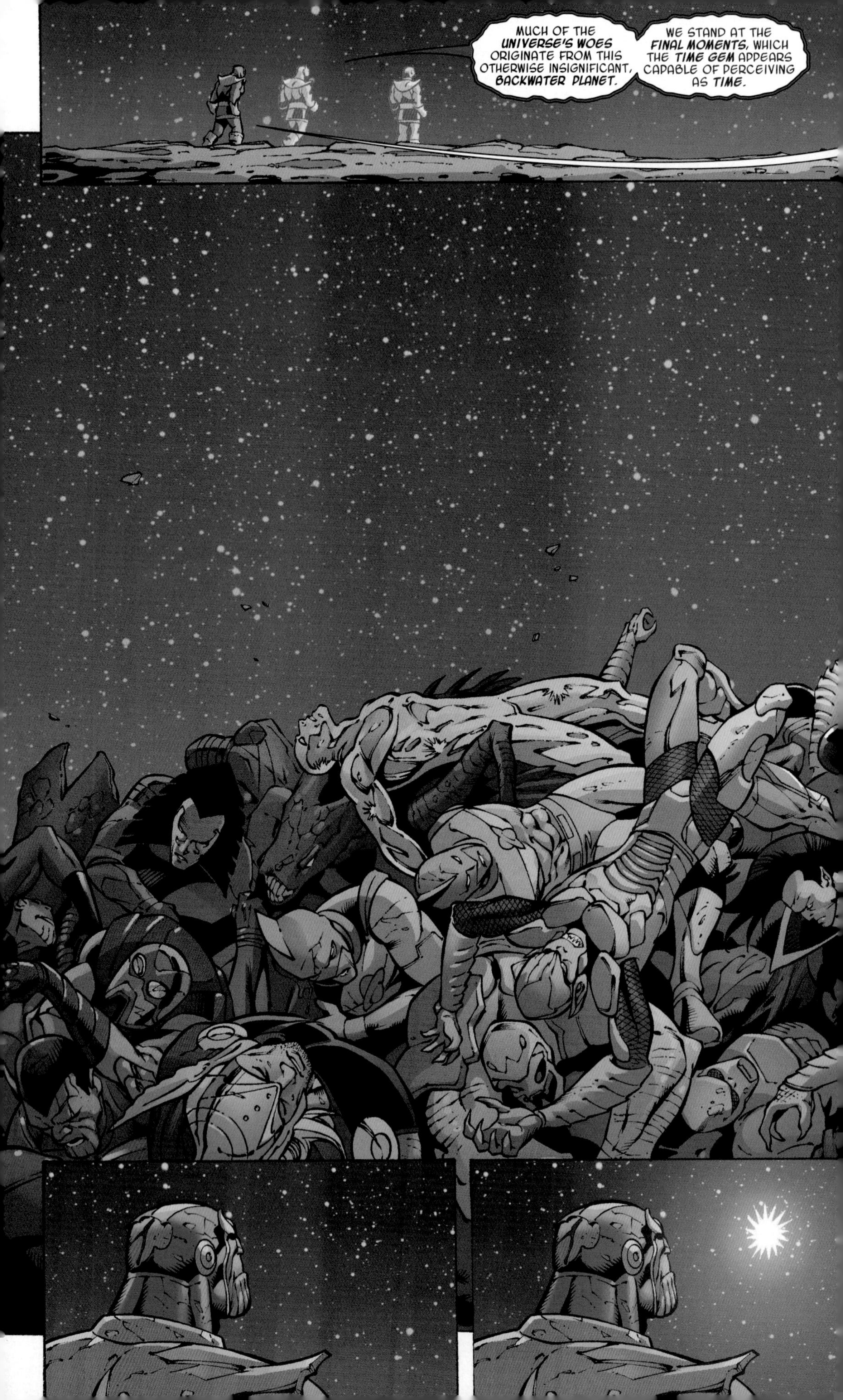
MUCH OF THE UNIVERSE'S WOES ORIGINATE FROM THIS OTHERWISE INSIGNIFICANT, BACKWATER PLANET.
WE STAND AT THE FINAL MOMENTS, WHICH THE TIME GEM APPEARS CAPABLE OF PERCEIVING AS TIME.

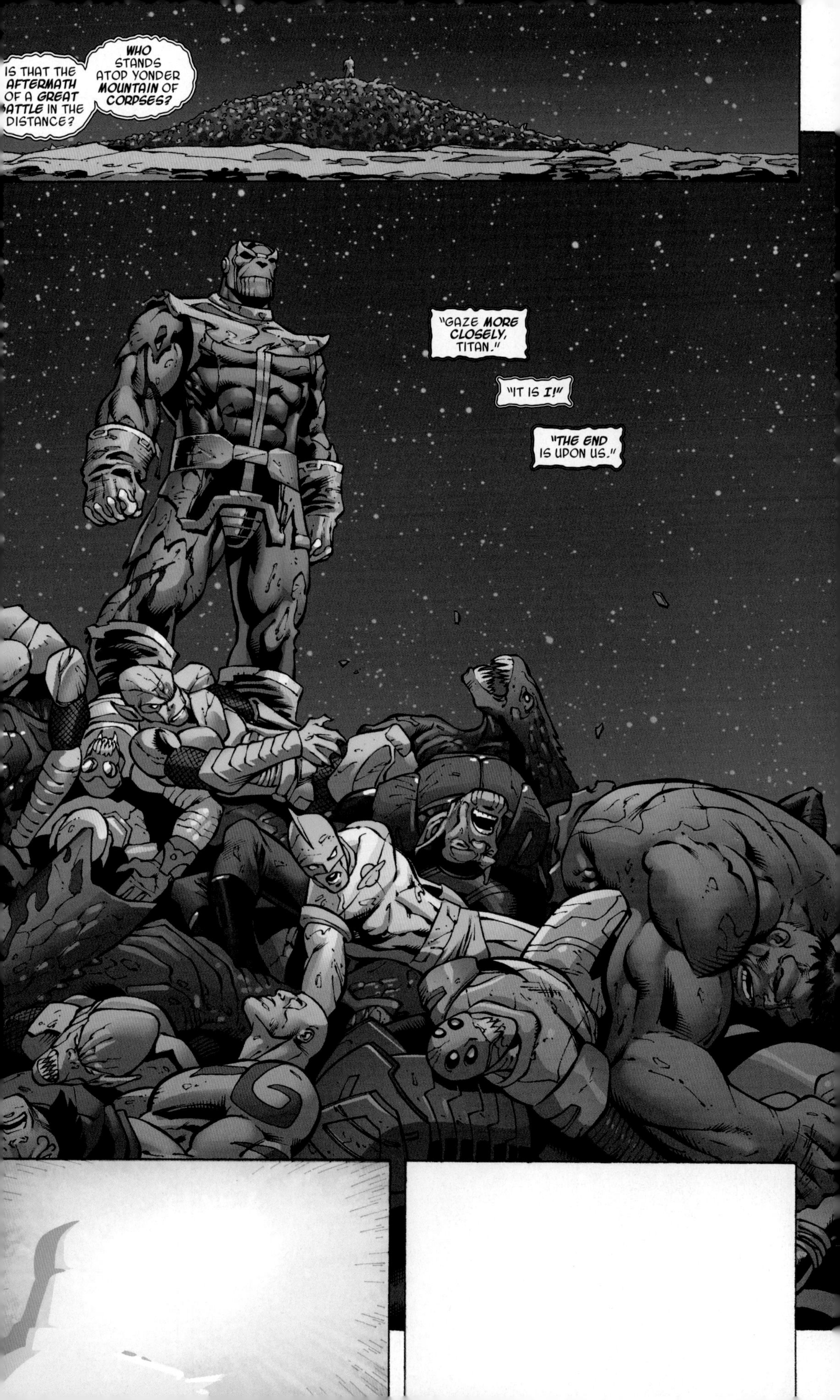

IS THAT THE AFTERMATH OF A GREAT BATTLE IN THE DISTANCE?
WHO STANDS ATOP YONDER MOUNTAIN OF CORPSES?
"GAZE MORE CLOSELY, TITAN."
"IT IS I!"
"THE END IS UPON US."

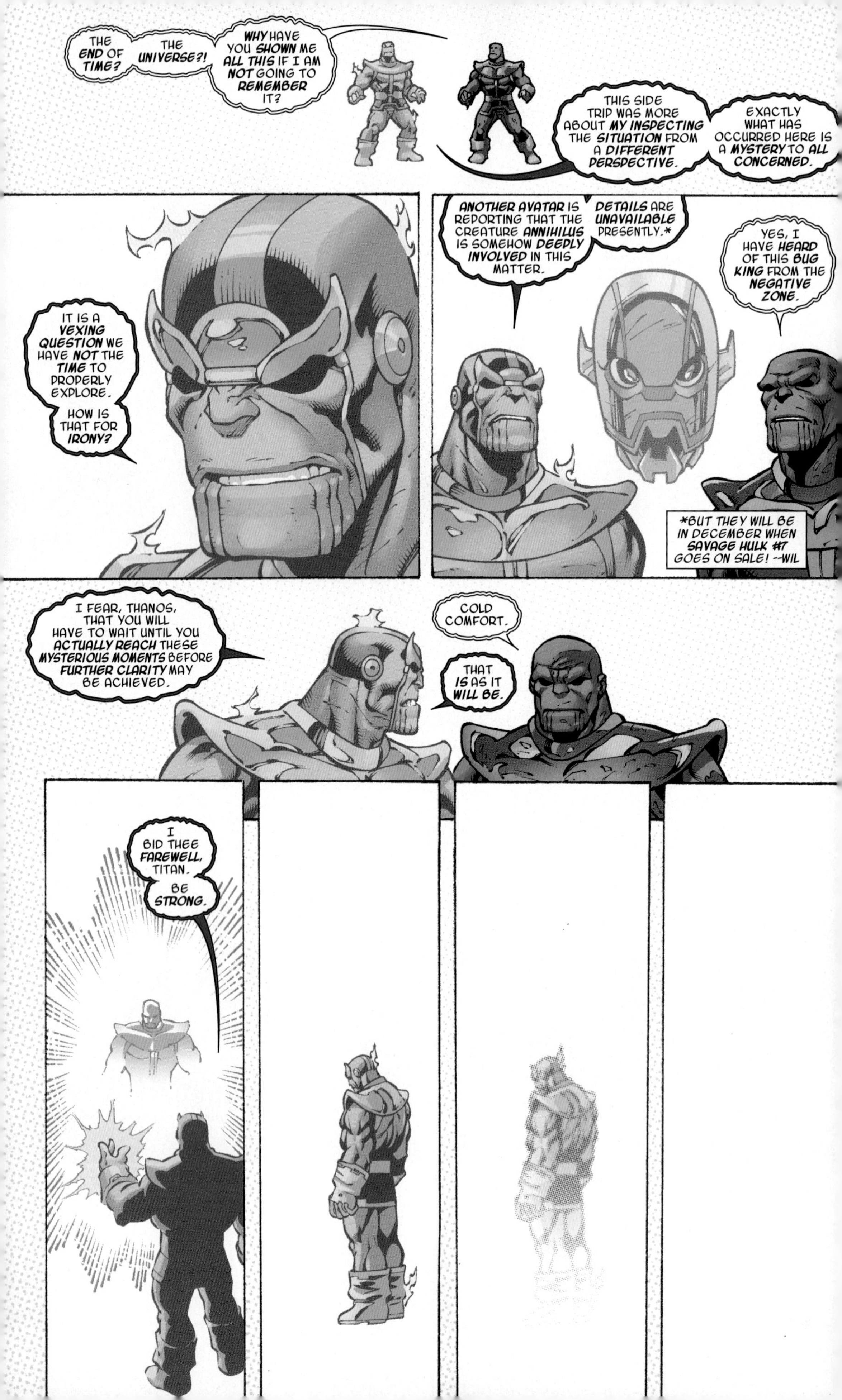
THE END OF TIME?
THE UNIVERSE?!
WHY HAVE YOU SHOWN ME ALL THIS IF I AM NOT GOING TO REMEMBER IT?
THIS SIDE TRIP WAS MORE ABOUT MY INSPECTING THE SITUATION FROM A DIFFERENT PERSPECTIVE.
EXACTLY WHAT HAS OCCURRED HERE IS A MYSTERY TO ALL CONCERNED.
IT IS A VEXING QUESTION WE HAVE NOT THE TIME TO PROPERLY EXPLORE.
HOW IS THAT FOR IRONY?
ANOTHER AVATAR IS REPORTING THAT THE CREATURE ANNIHILUS IS SOMEHOW DEEPLY INVOLVED IN THIS MATTER.
DETAILS ARE UNAVAILABLE PRESENTLY.*
YES, I HAVE HEARD OF THIS BUG KING FROM THE NEGATIVE ZONE.
*BUT THEY WILL BE IN DECEMBER WHEN SAVAGE HULK #7 GOES ON SALE! --WIL
I FEAR, THANOS, THAT YOU WILL HAVE TO WAIT UNTIL YOU ACTUALLY REACH THESE MYSTERIOUS MOMENTS BEFORE FURTHER CLARITY MAY BE ACHIEVED.
COLD COMFORT.
THAT IS AS IT WILL BE.
I BID THEE FAREWELL, TITAN.
BE STRONG.

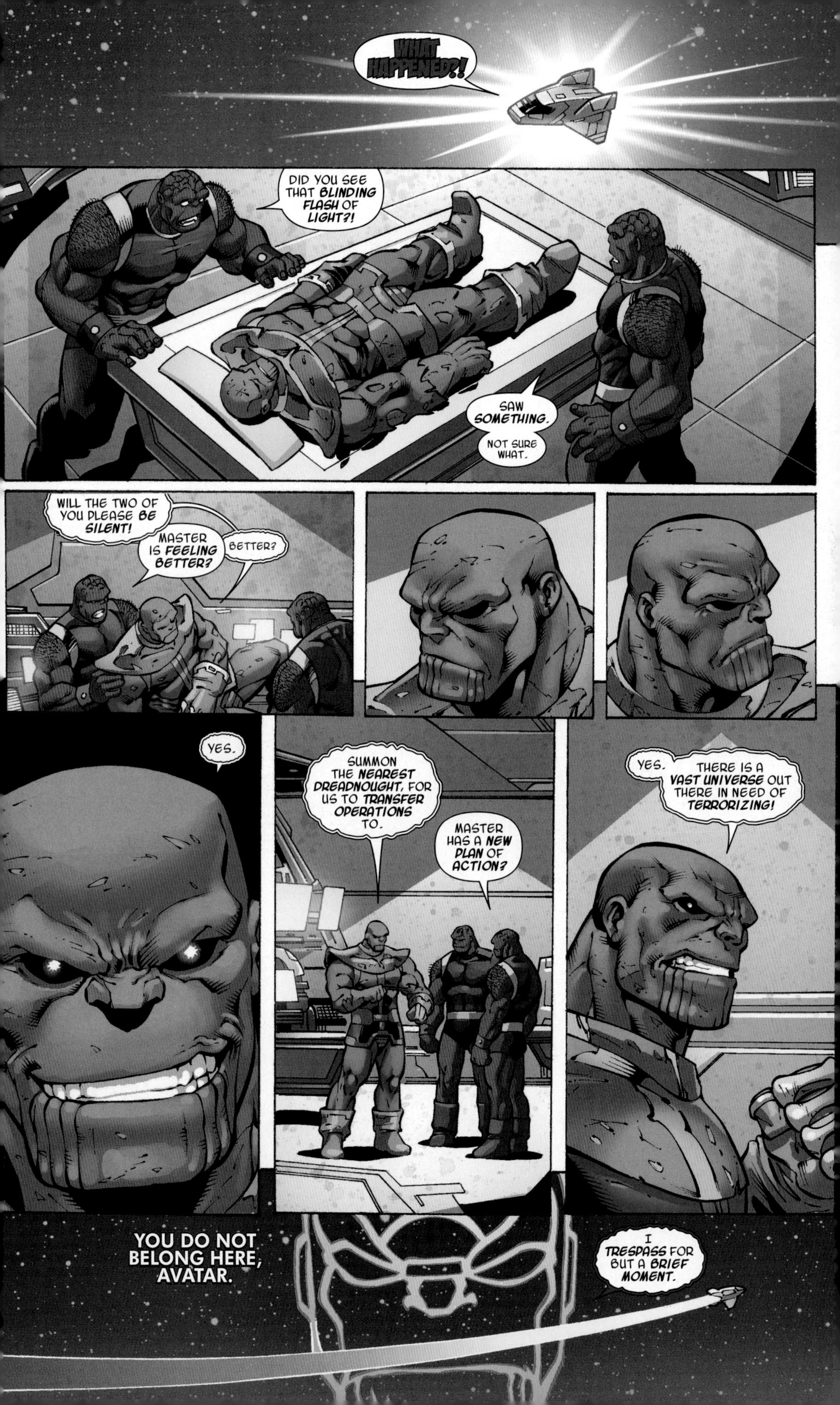
WHAT HAPPENED?!
DID YOU SEE THAT BLINDING FLASH OF LIGHT?!
SAW SOMETHING.
NOT SURE WHAT.
WILL THE TWO OF YOU PLEASE BE SILENT!
MASTER IS FEELING BETTER?
BETTER?
YES.
SUMMON THE NEAREST DREADNOUGHT, FOR US TO TRANSFER OPERATIONS TO.
MASTER HAS A NEW PLAN OF ACTION?
YES.
THERE IS A VAST UNIVERSE OUT THERE IN NEED OF TERRORIZING!
YOU DO NOT BELONG HERE, AVATAR.
I TRESPASS FOR BUT A BRIEF MOMENT.

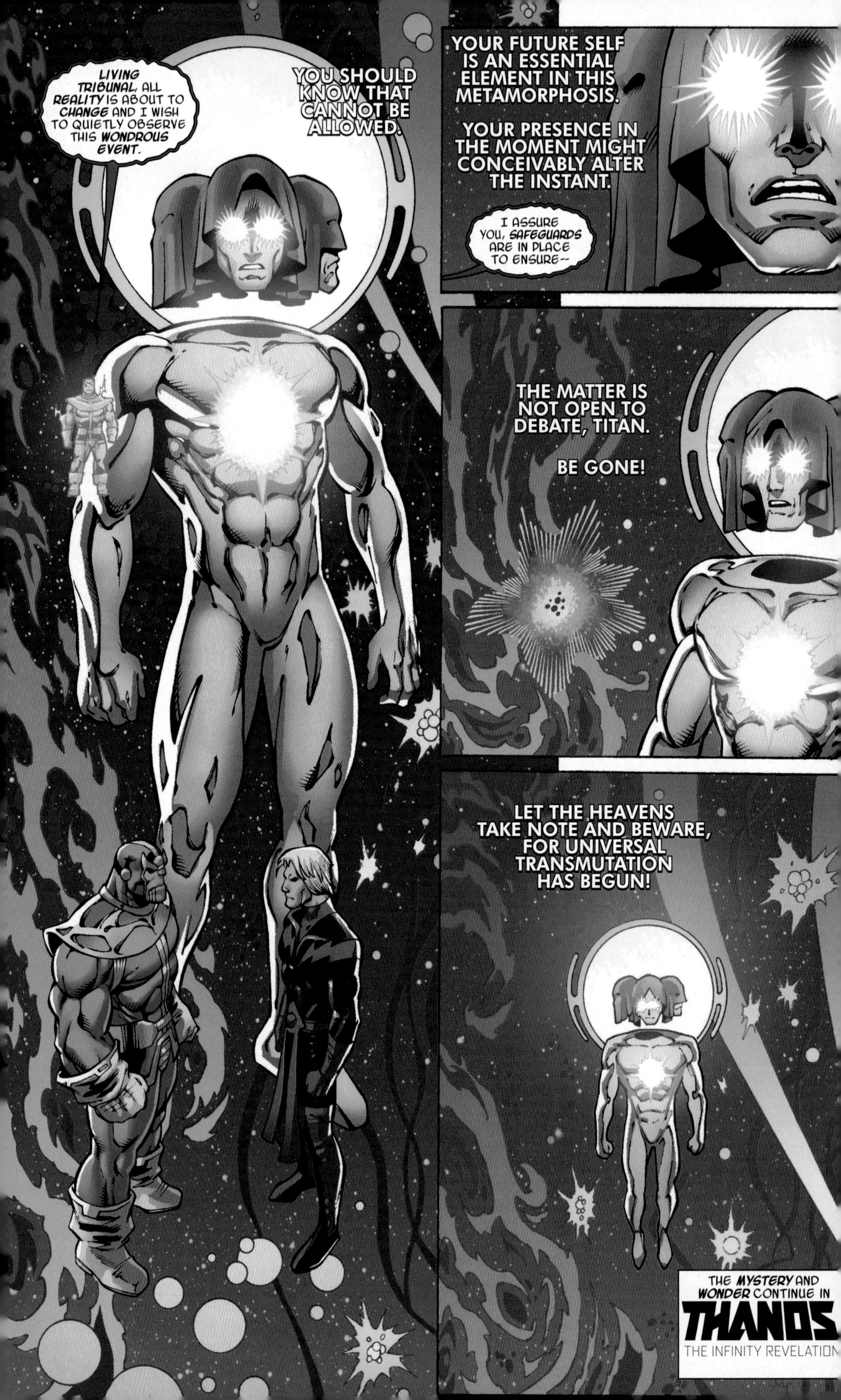
LIVING TRIBUNAL, ALL REALITY IS ABOUT TO CHANGE AND I WISH TO QUIETLY OBSERVE THIS WONDROUS EVENT.
YOU SHOULD KNOW THAT CANNOT BE ALLOWED.
YOUR FUTURE SELF IS AN ESSENTIAL ELEMENT IN THIS METAMORPHOSIS.
YOUR PRESENCE IN THE MOMENT MIGHT CONCEIVABLY ALTER THE INSTANT.
I ASSURE YOU, SAFEGUARDS ARE IN PLACE TO ENSURE--
THE MATTER IS NOT OPEN TO DEBATE, TITAN.
BE GONE!
LET THE HEAVENS TAKE NOTE AND BEWARE, FOR UNIVERSAL TRANSMUTATION HAS BEGUN!
THE MYSTERY AND WONDER CONTINUE IN
THANOS
THE INFINITY REVELATION

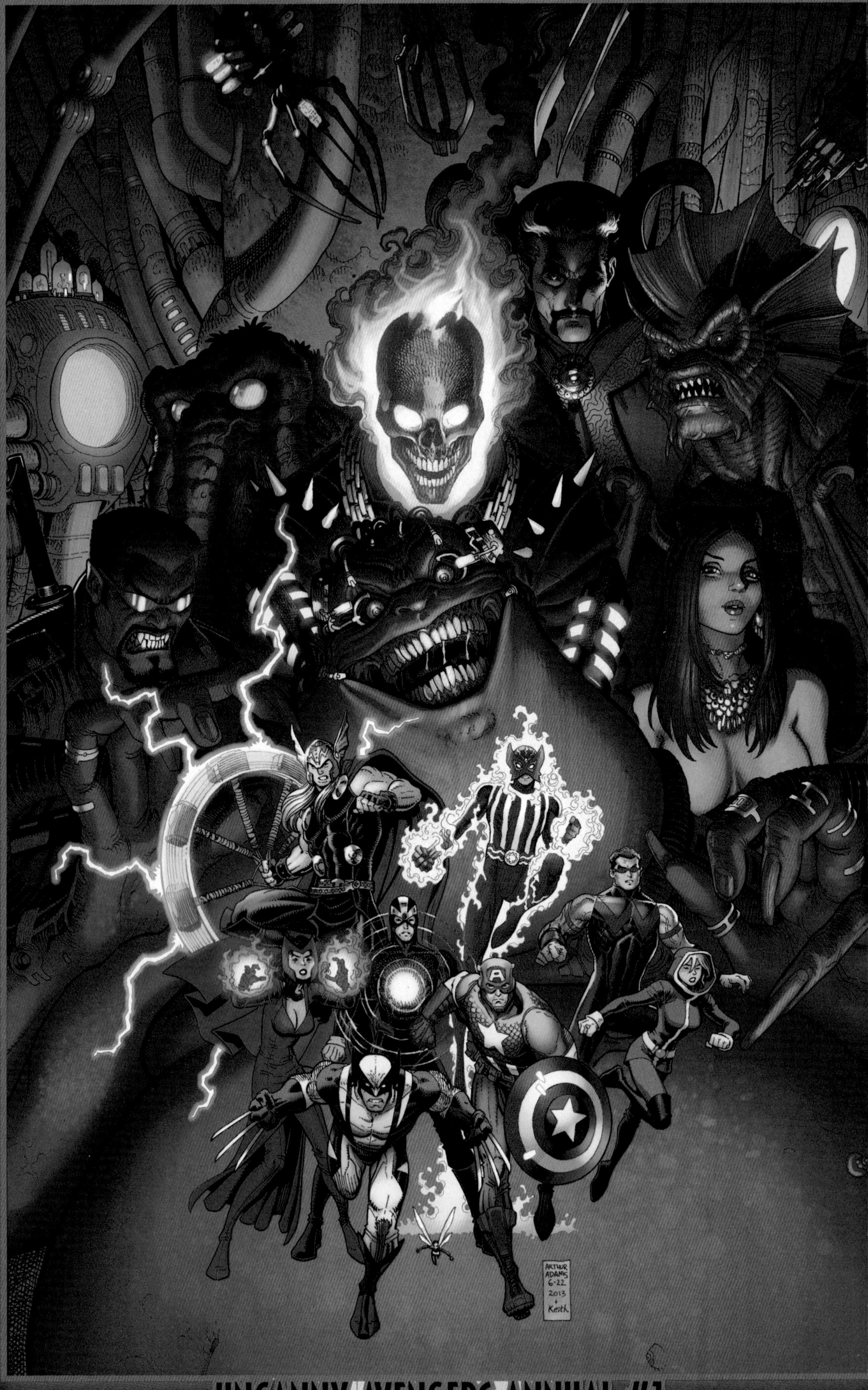
ARTHUR ADAMS 6-22 2013 + Keith

UNCANNY AVENGERS ANNUAL #1

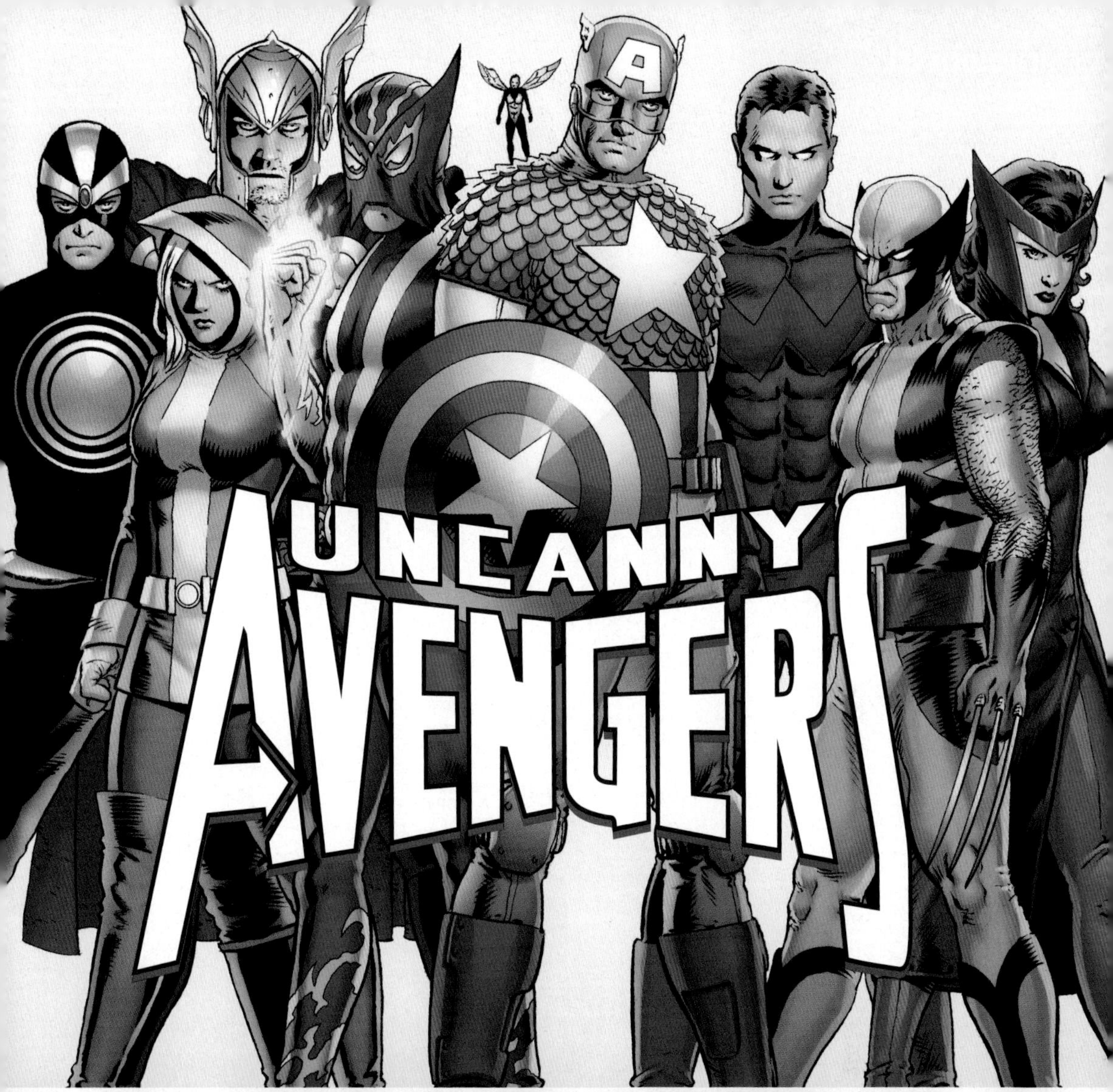
UNCANNY
AVENGERS

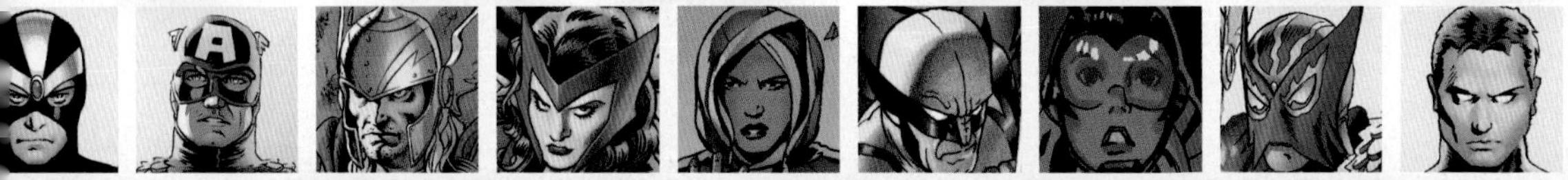

HAVOK | CAPTAIN AMERICA | THOR | SCARLET WITCH | ROGUE | WOLVERINE | WASP | SUNFIRE | WONDER MAN

FOLLOWING THE DEATH OF PROFESSOR CHARLES XAVIER, FOUNDER AND LEADER OF THE X-MEN, THE MUTANT RACE FOUND THEMSELVES IN A WORLD THAT HAD NEVER HATED NOR FEARED THEM MORE. HOPING TO SET AN EXAMPLE FOR THE REST OF THE WORLD TO FOLLOW, CAPTAIN AMERICA APPROACHED LONGTIME X-MAN HAVOK TO LEAD A TEAM OF AVENGERS THAT WOULD DEMONSTRATE MUTANTS AND HUMANS CAN WORK SIDE BY SIDE.

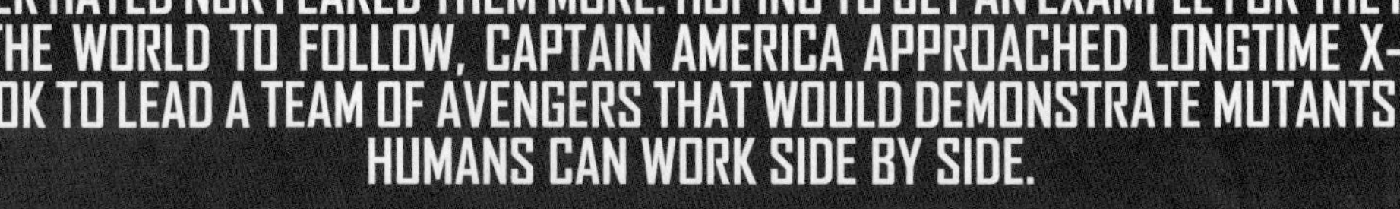

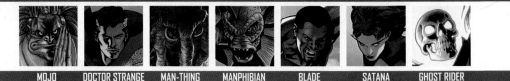

MOJO | DOCTOR STRANGE | MAN-THING | MANPHIBIAN | BLADE | SATANA | GHOST RIDER

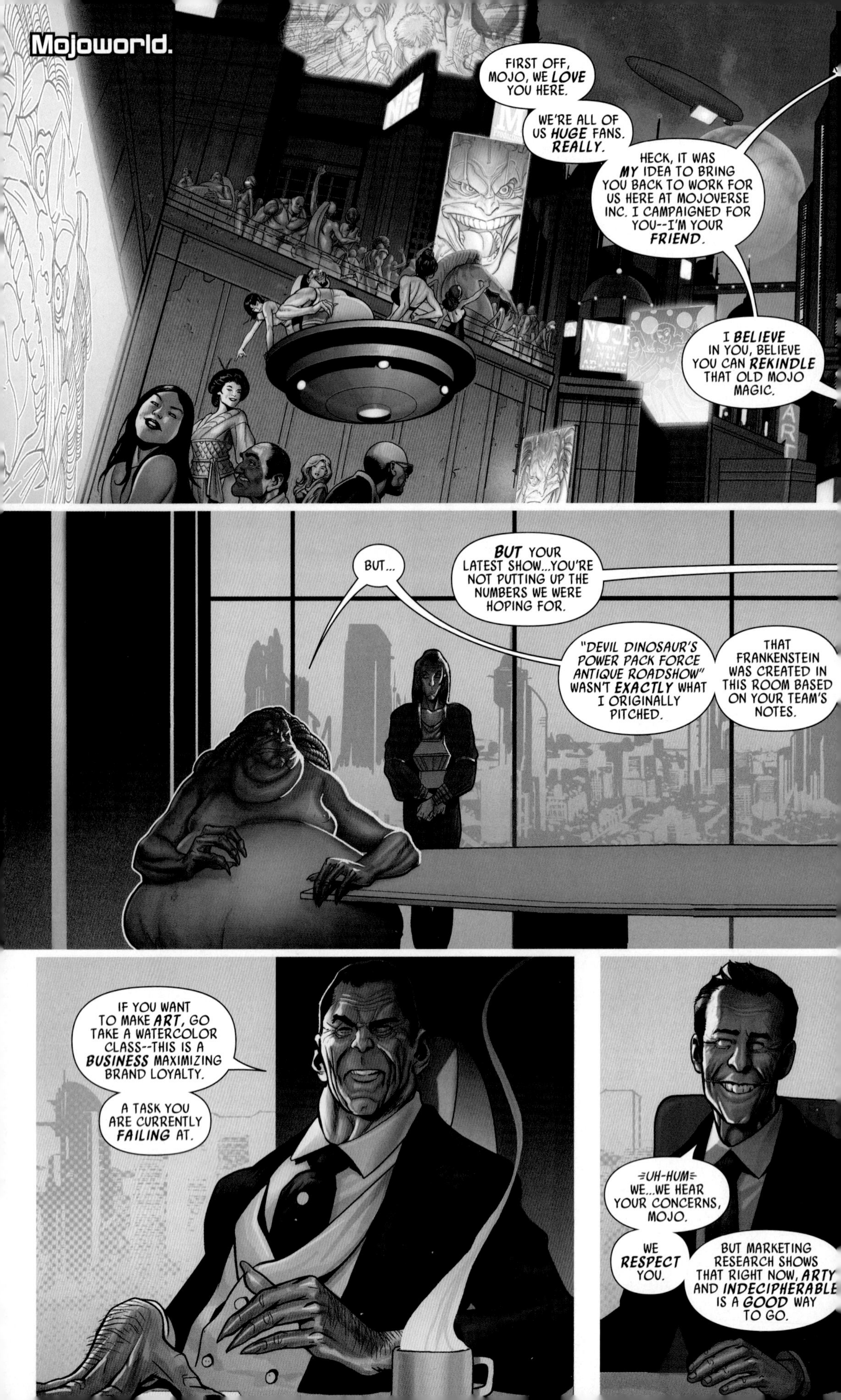

Mojoworld.
FIRST OFF, MOJO, WE LOVE YOU HERE.
WE'RE ALL OF US HUGE FANS. REALLY.
HECK, IT WAS MY IDEA TO BRING YOU BACK TO WORK FOR US HERE AT MOJOVERSE INC. I CAMPAIGNED FOR YOU--I'M YOUR FRIEND.
I BELIEVE IN YOU, BELIEVE YOU CAN REKINDLE THAT OLD MOJO MAGIC.
BUT YOUR LATEST SHOW...YOU'RE NOT PUTTING UP THE NUMBERS WE WERE HOPING FOR.
BUT...
"DEVIL DINOSAUR'S POWER PACK FORCE ANTIQUE ROADSHOW" WASN'T EXACTLY WHAT I ORIGINALLY PITCHED.
THAT FRANKENSTEIN WAS CREATED IN THIS ROOM BASED ON YOUR TEAM'S NOTES.
IF YOU WANT TO MAKE ART, GO TAKE A WATERCOLOR CLASS--THIS IS A BUSINESS MAXIMIZING BRAND LOYALTY.
A TASK YOU ARE CURRENTLY FAILING AT.
=UH-HUM= WE...WE HEAR YOUR CONCERNS, MOJO.
WE RESPECT YOU.
BUT MARKETING RESEARCH SHOWS THAT RIGHT NOW, ARTY AND INDECIPHERABLE IS A GOOD WAY TO GO.

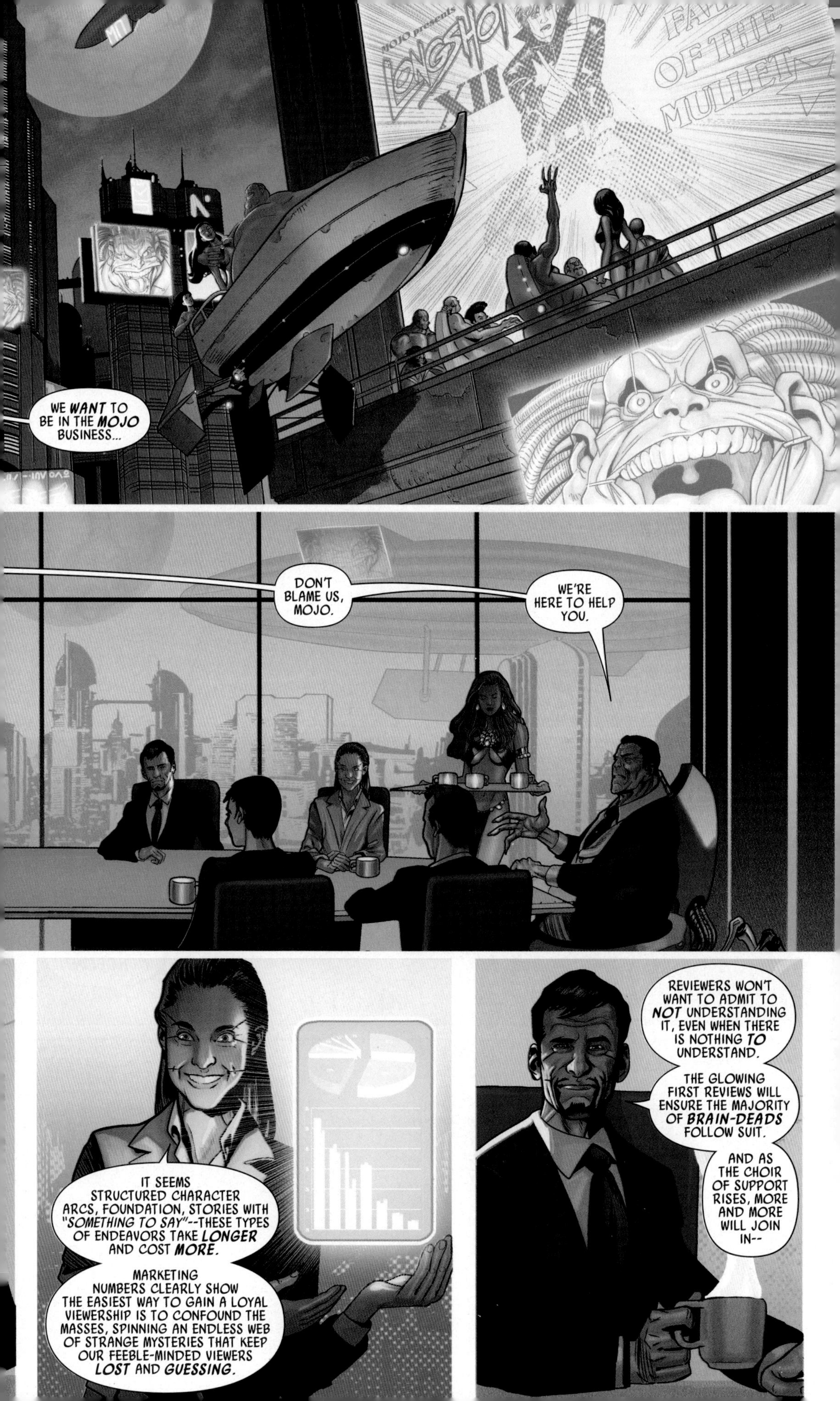
MOJO presents
LONGSHOT XII
FALL OF THE MULLET
WE WANT TO BE IN THE MOJO BUSINESS...
DON'T BLAME US, MOJO.
WE'RE HERE TO HELP YOU.
IT SEEMS STRUCTURED CHARACTER ARCS, FOUNDATION, STORIES WITH "SOMETHING TO SAY"--THESE TYPES OF ENDEAVORS TAKE LONGER AND COST MORE.
MARKETING NUMBERS CLEARLY SHOW THE EASIEST WAY TO GAIN A LOYAL VIEWERSHIP IS TO CONFOUND THE MASSES, SPINNING AN ENDLESS WEB OF STRANGE MYSTERIES THAT KEEP OUR FEEBLE-MINDED VIEWERS LOST AND GUESSING.
REVIEWERS WON'T WANT TO ADMIT TO NOT UNDERSTANDING IT, EVEN WHEN THERE IS NOTHING TO UNDERSTAND.
THE GLOWING FIRST REVIEWS WILL ENSURE THE MAJORITY OF BRAIN-DEADS FOLLOW SUIT.
AND AS THE CHOIR OF SUPPORT RISES, MORE AND MORE WILL JOIN IN--

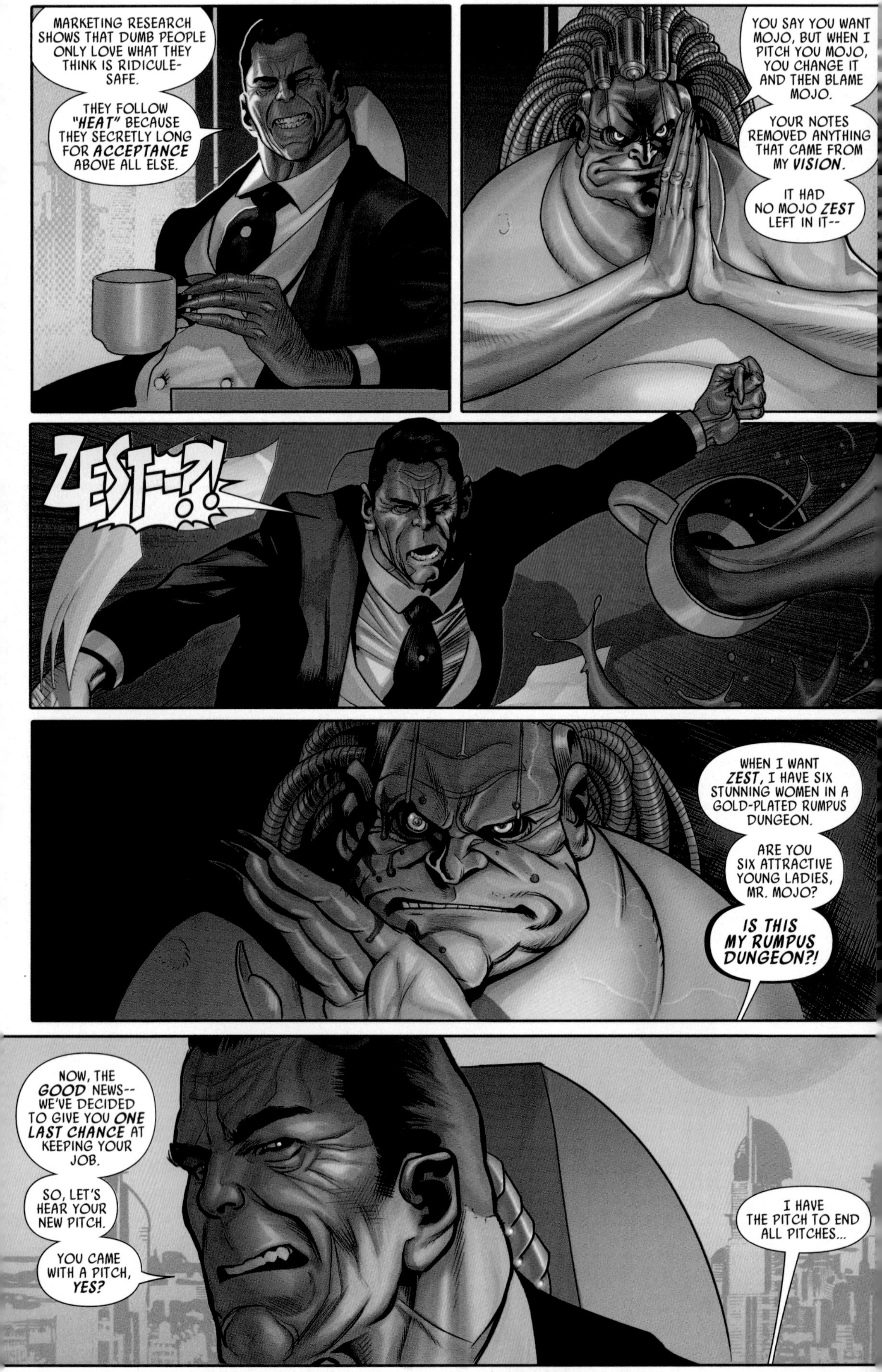
MARKETING RESEARCH SHOWS THAT DUMB PEOPLE ONLY LOVE WHAT THEY THINK IS RIDICULE-SAFE.
THEY FOLLOW "HEAT" BECAUSE THEY SECRETLY LONG FOR ACCEPTANCE ABOVE ALL ELSE.
YOU SAY YOU WANT MOJO, BUT WHEN I PITCH YOU MOJO, YOU CHANGE IT AND THEN BLAME MOJO.
YOUR NOTES REMOVED ANYTHING THAT CAME FROM MY VISION.
IT HAD NO MOJO ZEST LEFT IN IT--
ZEST--?!
WHEN I WANT ZEST, I HAVE SIX STUNNING WOMEN IN A GOLD-PLATED RUMPUS DUNGEON.
ARE YOU SIX ATTRACTIVE YOUNG LADIES, MR. MOJO?
IS THIS MY RUMPUS DUNGEON?!
NOW, THE GOOD NEWS-- WE'VE DECIDED TO GIVE YOU ONE LAST CHANCE AT KEEPING YOUR JOB.
SO, LET'S HEAR YOUR NEW PITCH.
YOU CAME WITH A PITCH, YES?
I HAVE THE PITCH TO END ALL PITCHES...

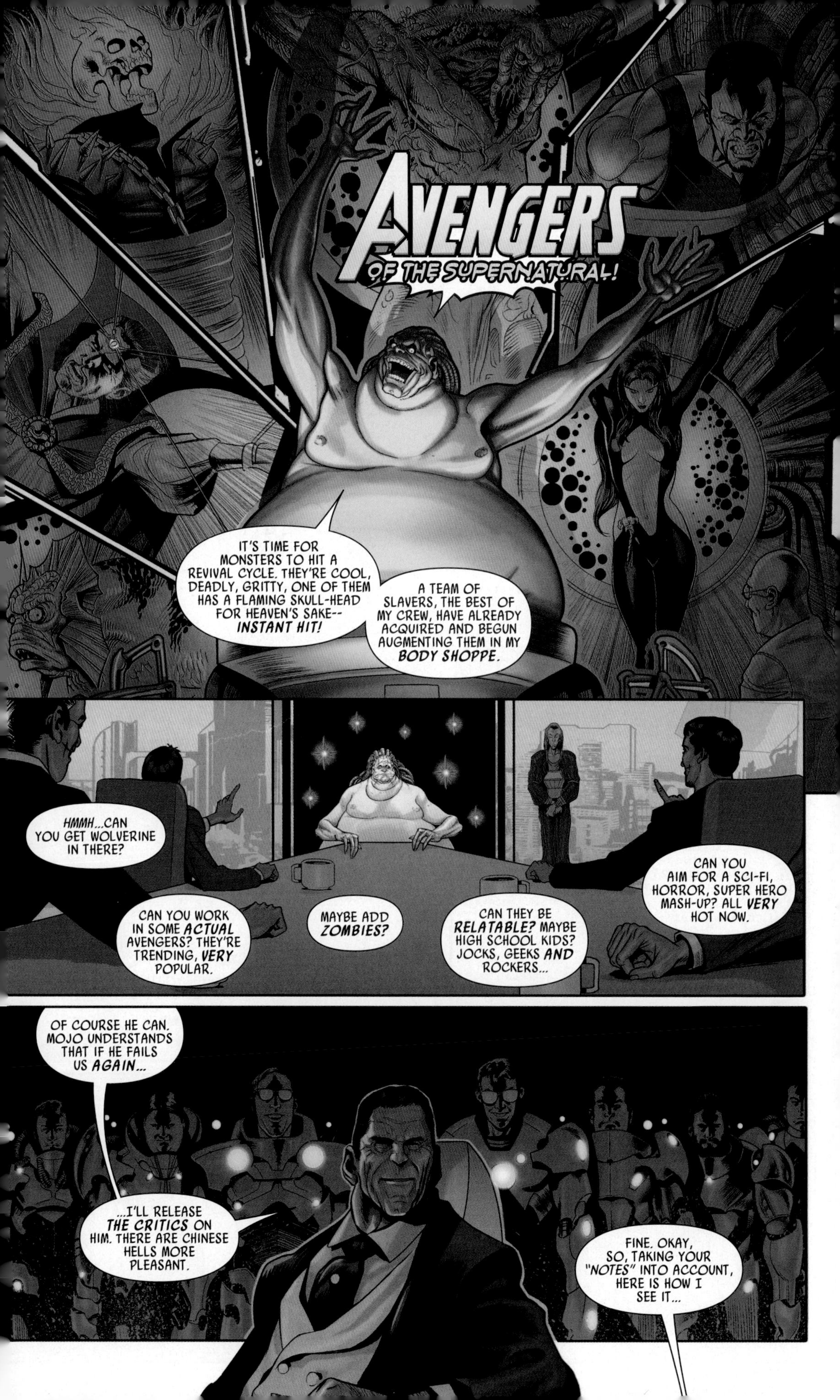
AVENGERS
OF THE SUPERNATURAL!
IT'S TIME FOR MONSTERS TO HIT A REVIVAL CYCLE. THEY'RE COOL, DEADLY, GRITTY, ONE OF THEM HAS A FLAMING SKULL-HEAD FOR HEAVEN'S SAKE-- INSTANT HIT!
A TEAM OF SLAVERS, THE BEST OF MY CREW, HAVE ALREADY ACQUIRED AND BEGUN AUGMENTING THEM IN MY BODY SHOPPE.
HMMH...CAN YOU GET WOLVERINE IN THERE?
CAN YOU WORK IN SOME ACTUAL AVENGERS? THEY'RE TRENDING, VERY POPULAR.
MAYBE ADD ZOMBIES?
CAN THEY BE RELATABLE? MAYBE HIGH SCHOOL KIDS? JOCKS, GEEKS AND ROCKERS...
CAN YOU AIM FOR A SCI-FI, HORROR, SUPER HERO MASH-UP? ALL VERY HOT NOW.
OF COURSE HE CAN. MOJO UNDERSTANDS THAT IF HE FAILS US AGAIN...
...I'LL RELEASE THE CRITICS ON HIM. THERE ARE CHINESE HELLS MORE PLEASANT.
FINE. OKAY, SO, TAKING YOUR "NOTES" INTO ACCOUNT, HERE IS HOW I SEE IT...

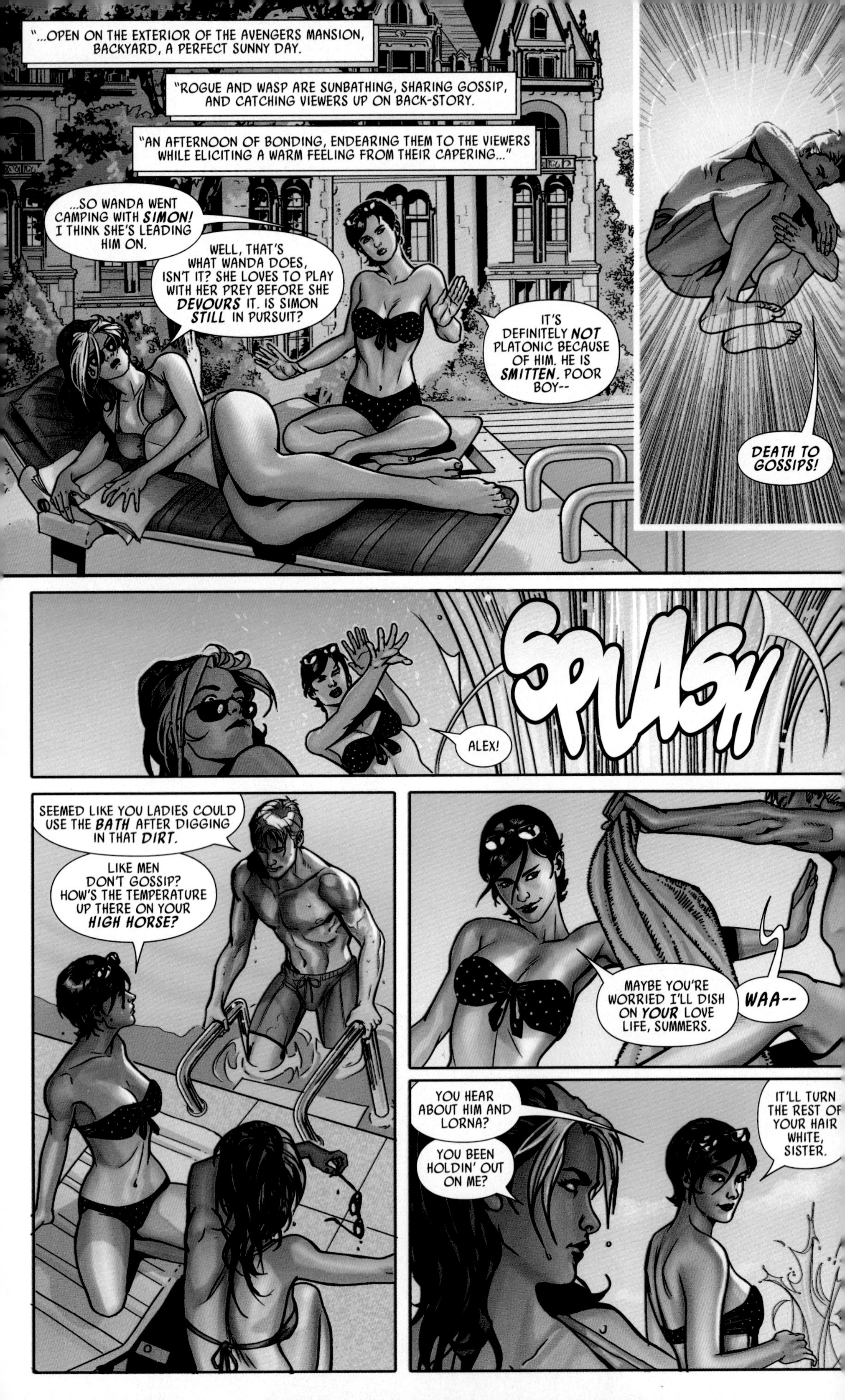
"...OPEN ON THE EXTERIOR OF THE AVENGERS MANSION, BACKYARD, A PERFECT SUNNY DAY.
"ROGUE AND WASP ARE SUNBATHING, SHARING GOSSIP, AND CATCHING VIEWERS UP ON BACK-STORY.
"AN AFTERNOON OF BONDING, ENDEARING THEM TO THE VIEWERS WHILE ELICITING A WARM FEELING FROM THEIR CAPERING..."
...SO WANDA WENT CAMPING WITH SIMON! I THINK SHE'S LEADING HIM ON.
WELL, THAT'S WHAT WANDA DOES, ISN'T IT? SHE LOVES TO PLAY WITH HER PREY BEFORE SHE DEVOURS IT. IS SIMON STILL IN PURSUIT?
IT'S DEFINITELY NOT PLATONIC BECAUSE OF HIM. HE IS SMITTEN. POOR BOY--
DEATH TO GOSSIPS!
SPLASH
ALEX!
SEEMED LIKE YOU LADIES COULD USE THE BATH AFTER DIGGING IN THAT DIRT.
LIKE MEN DON'T GOSSIP? HOW'S THE TEMPERATURE UP THERE ON YOUR HIGH HORSE?
MAYBE YOU'RE WORRIED I'LL DISH ON YOUR LOVE LIFE, SUMMERS.
WAA--
YOU HEAR ABOUT HIM AND LORNA?
YOU BEEN HOLDIN' OUT ON ME?
IT'LL TURN THE REST OF YOUR HAIR WHITE, SISTER.

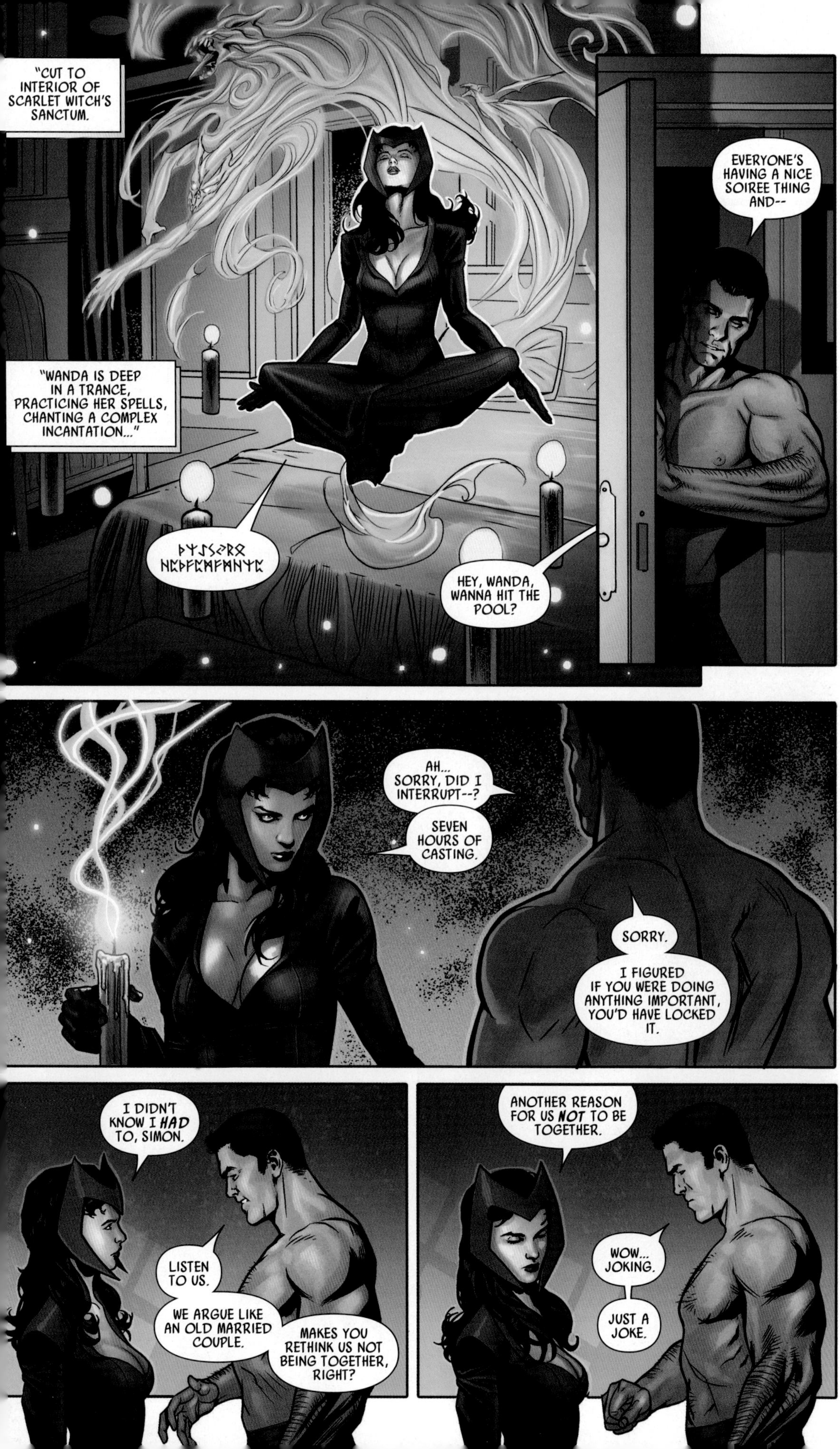

"CUT TO INTERIOR OF SCARLET WITCH'S SANCTUM.
"WANDA IS DEEP IN A TRANCE, PRACTICING HER SPELLS, CHANTING A COMPLEX INCANTATION..."
EVERYONE'S HAVING A NICE SOIREE THING AND--
HEY, WANDA, WANNA HIT THE POOL?
AH... SORRY, DID I INTERRUPT--?
SEVEN HOURS OF CASTING.
SORRY.
I FIGURED IF YOU WERE DOING ANYTHING IMPORTANT, YOU'D HAVE LOCKED IT.
I DIDN'T KNOW I HAD TO, SIMON.
LISTEN TO US.
WE ARGUE LIKE AN OLD MARRIED COUPLE.
MAKES YOU RETHINK US NOT BEING TOGETHER, RIGHT?
ANOTHER REASON FOR US NOT TO BE TOGETHER.
WOW... JOKING.
JUST A JOKE.

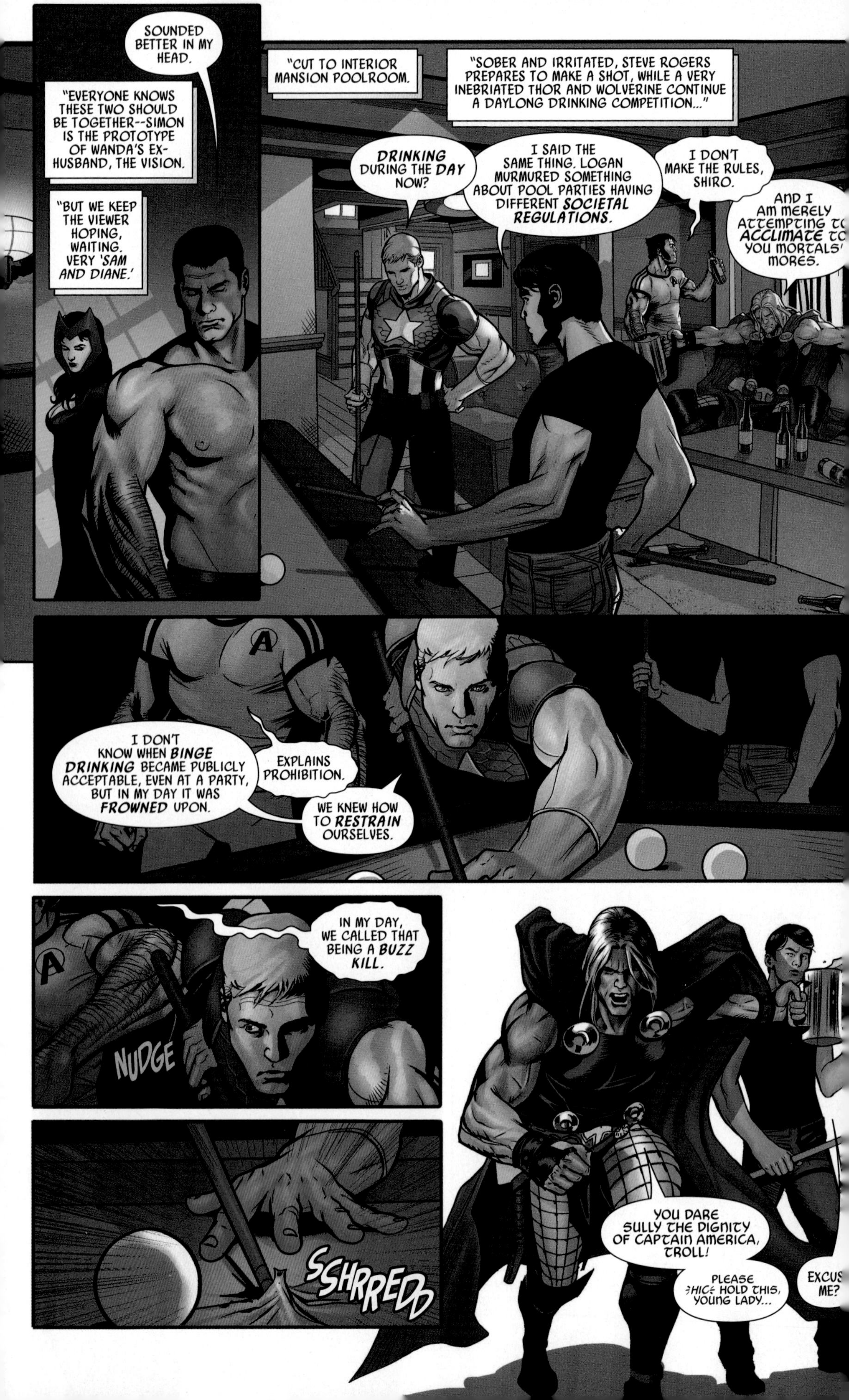

SOUNDED BETTER IN MY HEAD.
"EVERYONE KNOWS THESE TWO SHOULD BE TOGETHER--SIMON IS THE PROTOTYPE OF WANDA'S EX-HUSBAND, THE VISION.
"BUT WE KEEP THE VIEWER HOPING, WAITING. VERY 'SAM AND DIANE.'
"CUT TO INTERIOR MANSION POOLROOM.
"SOBER AND IRRITATED, STEVE ROGERS PREPARES TO MAKE A SHOT, WHILE A VERY INEBRIATED THOR AND WOLVERINE CONTINUE A DAYLONG DRINKING COMPETITION..."
DRINKING DURING THE DAY NOW?
I SAID THE SAME THING. LOGAN MURMURED SOMETHING ABOUT POOL PARTIES HAVING DIFFERENT SOCIETAL REGULATIONS.
I DON'T MAKE THE RULES, SHIRO.
AND I AM MERELY ATTEMPTING TO ACCLIMATE TO YOU MORTALS' MORES.
I DON'T KNOW WHEN BINGE DRINKING BECAME PUBLICLY ACCEPTABLE, EVEN AT A PARTY, BUT IN MY DAY IT WAS FROWNED UPON.
EXPLAINS PROHIBITION.
WE KNEW HOW TO RESTRAIN OURSELVES.
IN MY DAY, WE CALLED THAT BEING A BUZZ KILL.
NUDGE
SSHRREDD
YOU DARE SULLY THE DIGNITY OF CAPTAIN AMERICA, TROLL!
PLEASE *HIC* HOLD THIS, YOUNG LADY...
EXCUS ME?

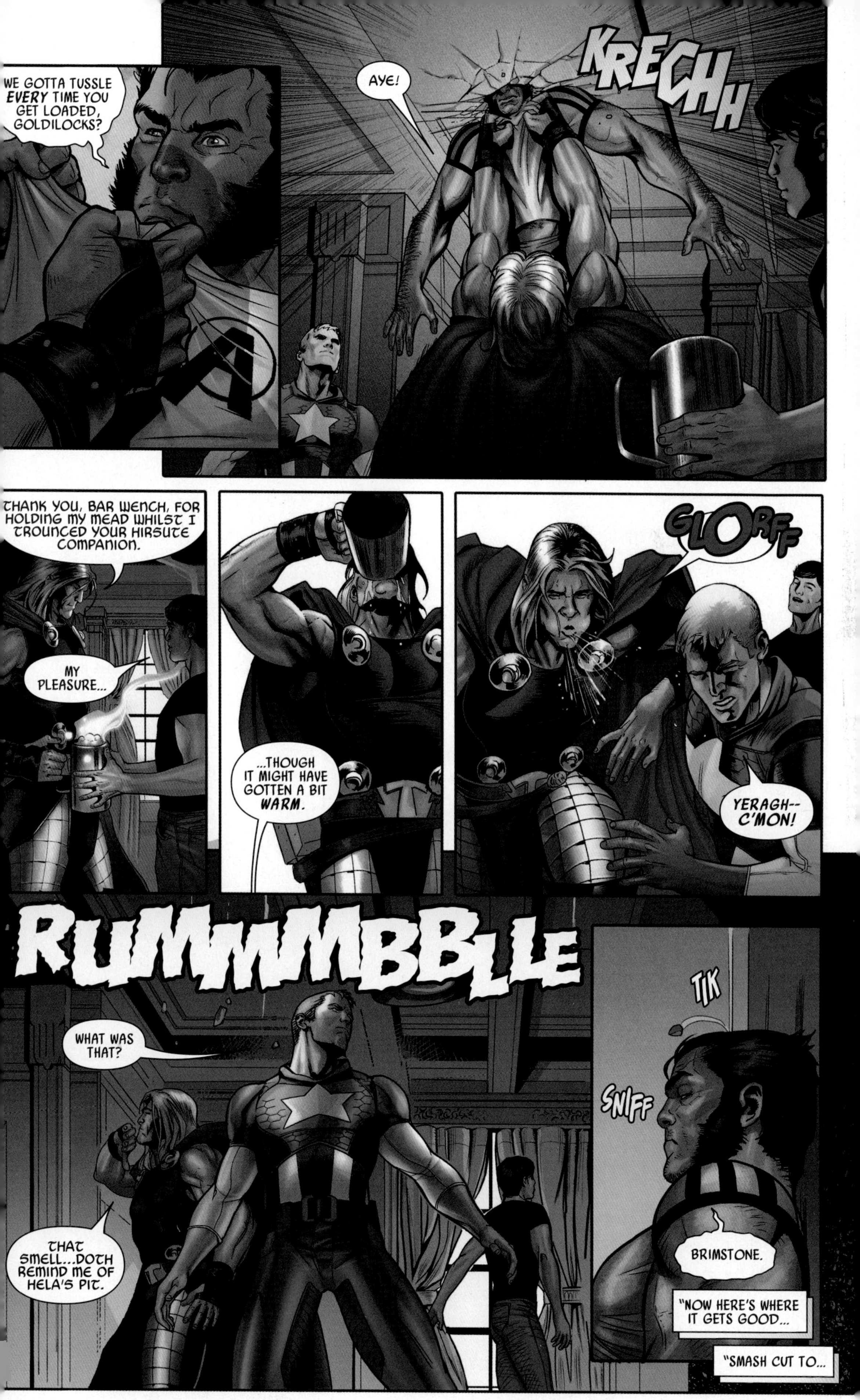

WE GOTTA TUSSLE EVERY TIME YOU GET LOADED, GOLDILOCKS?
AYE!
KRECHH
THANK YOU, BAR WENCH, FOR HOLDING MY MEAD WHILST I TROUNCED YOUR HIRSUTE COMPANION.
MY PLEASURE...
...THOUGH IT MIGHT HAVE GOTTEN A BIT WARM.
GLORFF
YERAGH-- C'MON!
RUMMMBBLLE
WHAT WAS THAT?
THAT SMELL...DOTH REMIND ME OF HELA'S PIT.
TIK
SNIFF
BRIMSTONE.
"NOW HERE'S WHERE IT GETS GOOD...
"SMASH CUT TO...

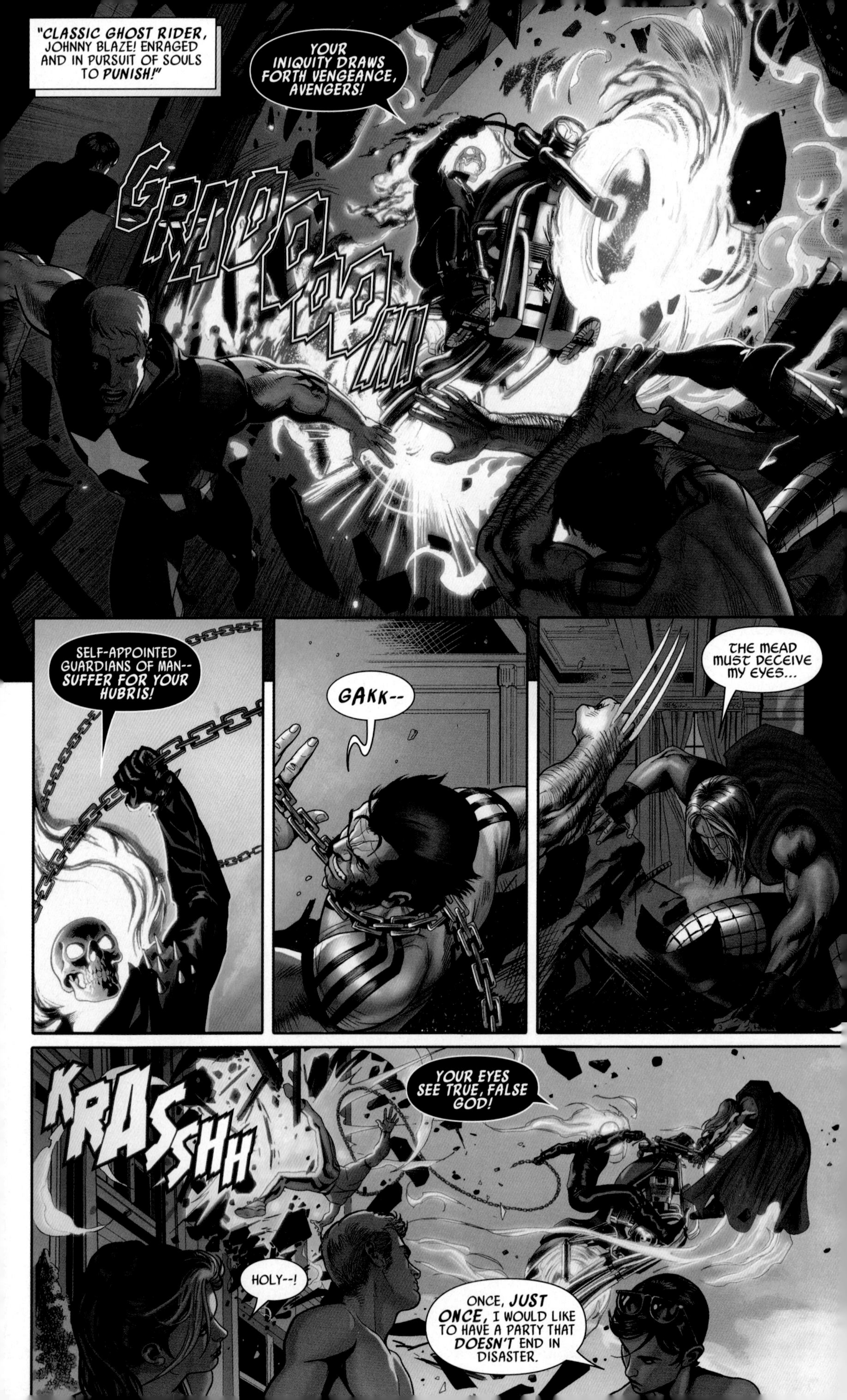
"CLASSIC GHOST RIDER, JOHNNY BLAZE! ENRAGED AND IN PURSUIT OF SOULS TO PUNISH!"
YOUR INIQUITY DRAWS FORTH VENGEANCE, AVENGERS!
GRAAOOOM
SELF-APPOINTED GUARDIANS OF MAN-- SUFFER FOR YOUR HUBRIS!
GAKK--
THE MEAD MUST DECEIVE MY EYES...
KRASSHH
YOUR EYES SEE TRUE, FALSE GOD!
HOLY--!
ONCE, JUST ONCE, I WOULD LIKE TO HAVE A PARTY THAT DOESN'T END IN DISASTER.

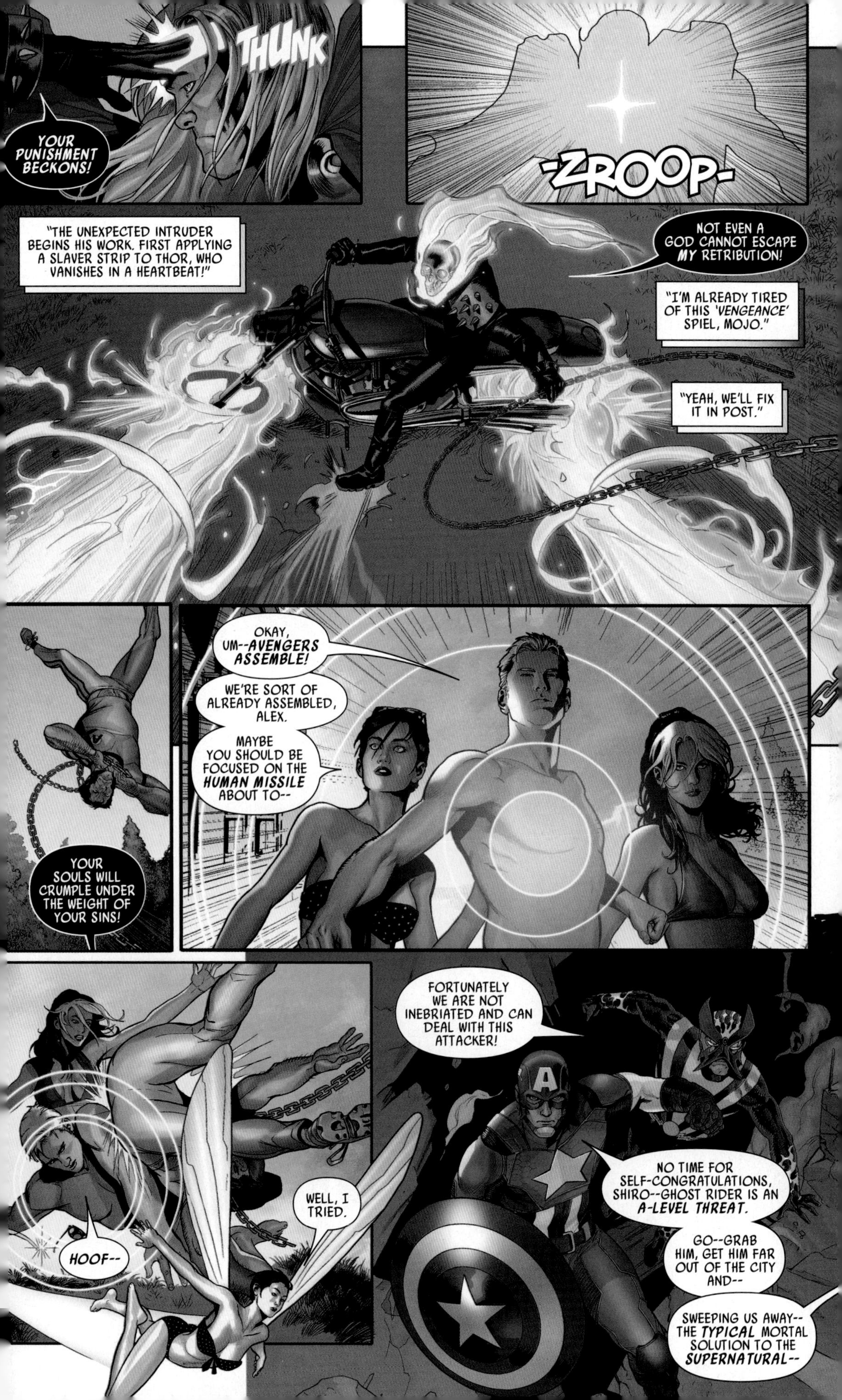

THUNK
YOUR PUNISHMENT BECKONS!
-ZROOP-
"THE UNEXPECTED INTRUDER BEGINS HIS WORK. FIRST APPLYING A SLAVER STRIP TO THOR, WHO VANISHES IN A HEARTBEAT!"
NOT EVEN A GOD CANNOT ESCAPE *MY* RETRIBUTION!
"I'M ALREADY TIRED OF THIS *'VENGEANCE'* SPIEL, MOJO."
"YEAH, WE'LL FIX IT IN POST."
YOUR SOULS WILL CRUMPLE UNDER THE WEIGHT OF YOUR SINS!
OKAY, UM--*AVENGERS ASSEMBLE!*
WE'RE SORT OF ALREADY ASSEMBLED, ALEX.
MAYBE YOU SHOULD BE FOCUSED ON THE *HUMAN MISSILE* ABOUT TO--
HOOF--
WELL, I TRIED.
FORTUNATELY WE ARE NOT INEBRIATED AND CAN DEAL WITH THIS ATTACKER!
NO TIME FOR SELF-CONGRATULATIONS, SHIRO--GHOST RIDER IS AN *A-LEVEL THREAT*.
GO--GRAB HIM, GET HIM FAR OUT OF THE CITY AND--
SWEEPING US AWAY--THE *TYPICAL* MORTAL SOLUTION TO THE *SUPERNATURAL*--

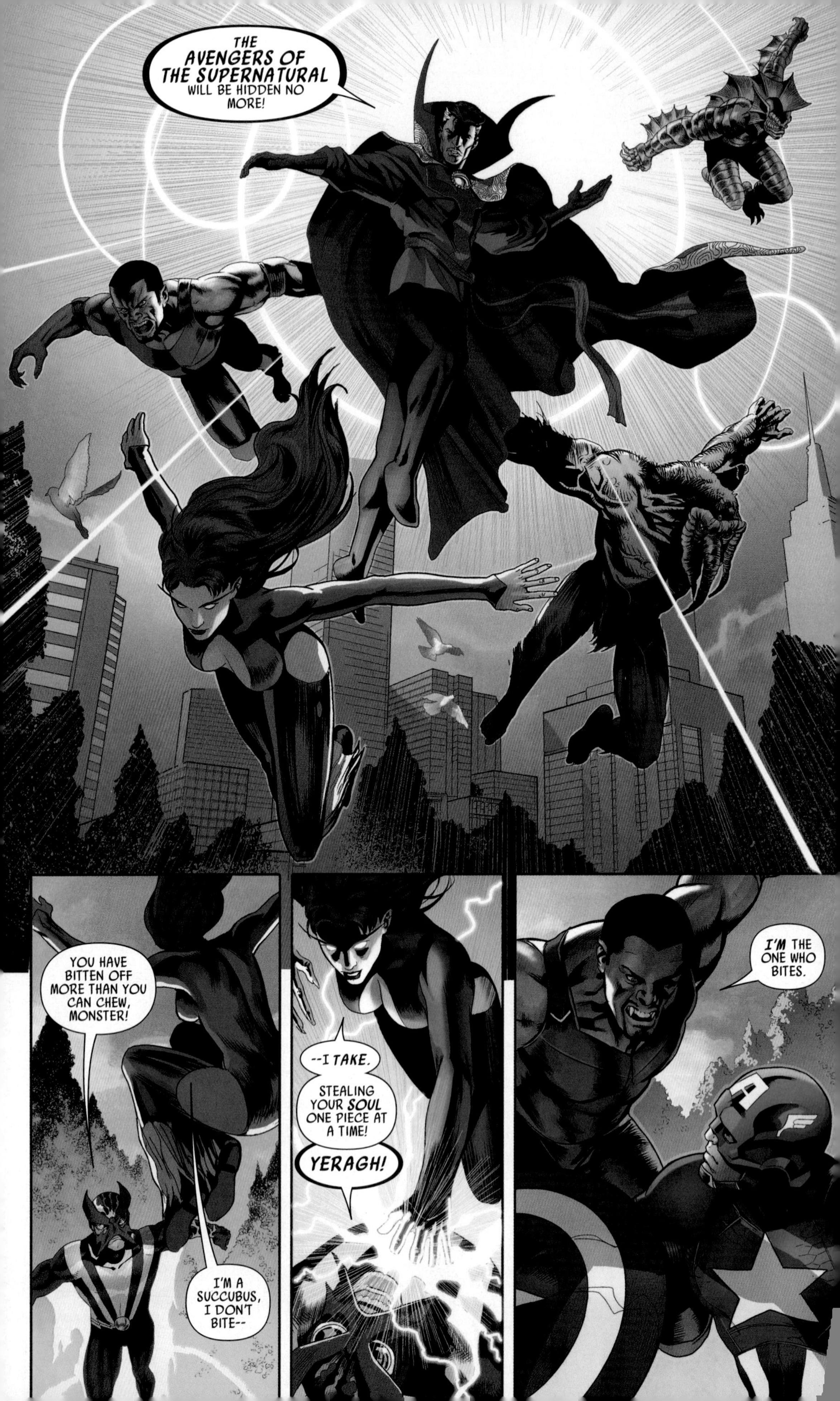
THE AVENGERS OF THE SUPERNATURAL WILL BE HIDDEN NO MORE!
YOU HAVE BITTEN OFF MORE THAN YOU CAN CHEW, MONSTER!
I'M A SUCCUBUS, I DON'T BITE--
--I TAKE.
STEALING YOUR SOUL ONE PIECE AT A TIME!
YERAGH!
I'M THE ONE WHO BITES.

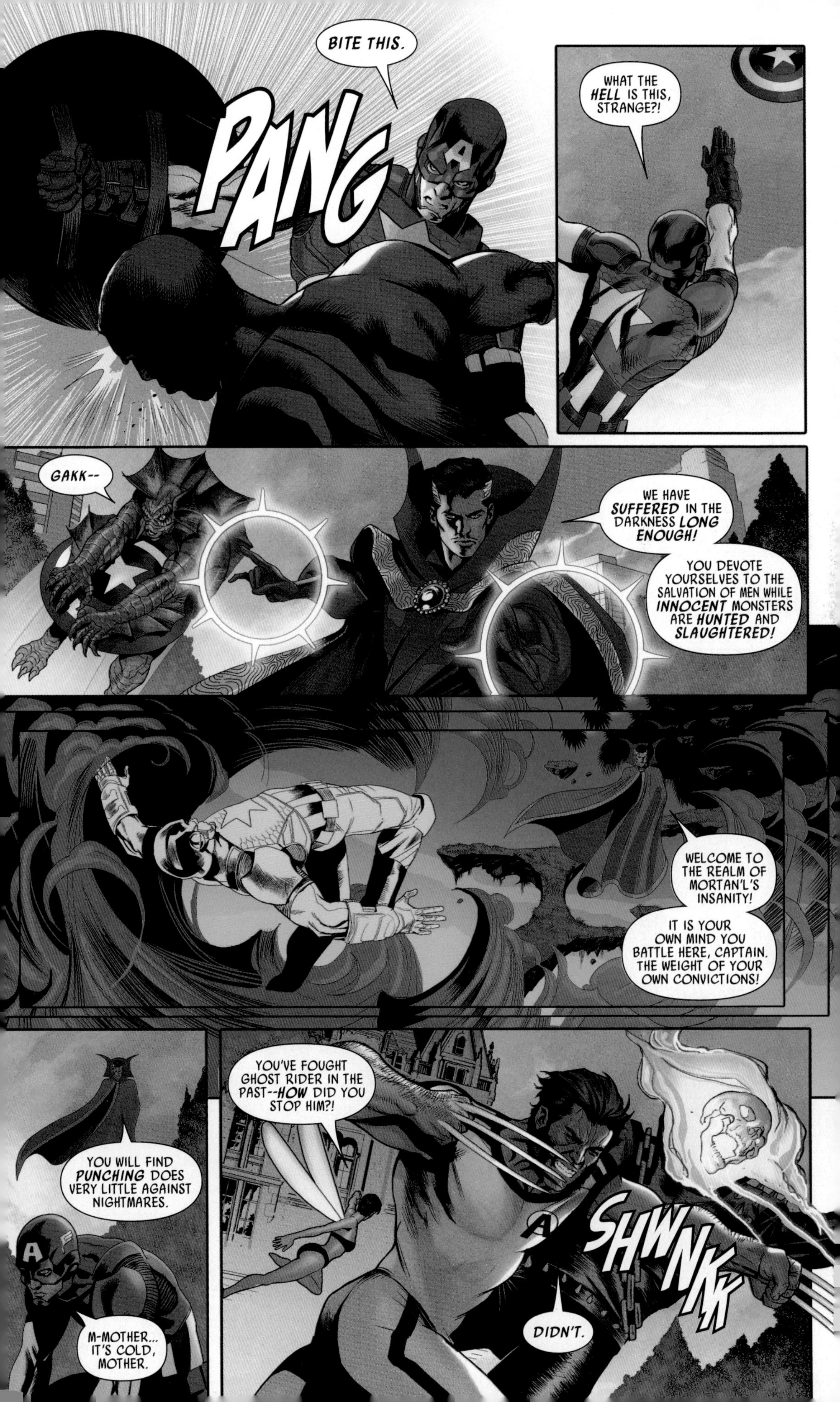

BITE THIS.
PANG
WHAT THE HELL IS THIS, STRANGE?!
GAKK--
WE HAVE SUFFERED IN THE DARKNESS LONG ENOUGH!
YOU DEVOTE YOURSELVES TO THE SALVATION OF MEN WHILE INNOCENT MONSTERS ARE HUNTED AND SLAUGHTERED!
WELCOME TO THE REALM OF MORTAN'L'S INSANITY!
IT IS YOUR OWN MIND YOU BATTLE HERE, CAPTAIN. THE WEIGHT OF YOUR OWN CONVICTIONS!
YOU WILL FIND PUNCHING DOES VERY LITTLE AGAINST NIGHTMARES.
M-MOTHER... IT'S COLD, MOTHER.
YOU'VE FOUGHT GHOST RIDER IN THE PAST--HOW DID YOU STOP HIM?!
SHWNKK
DIDN'T.

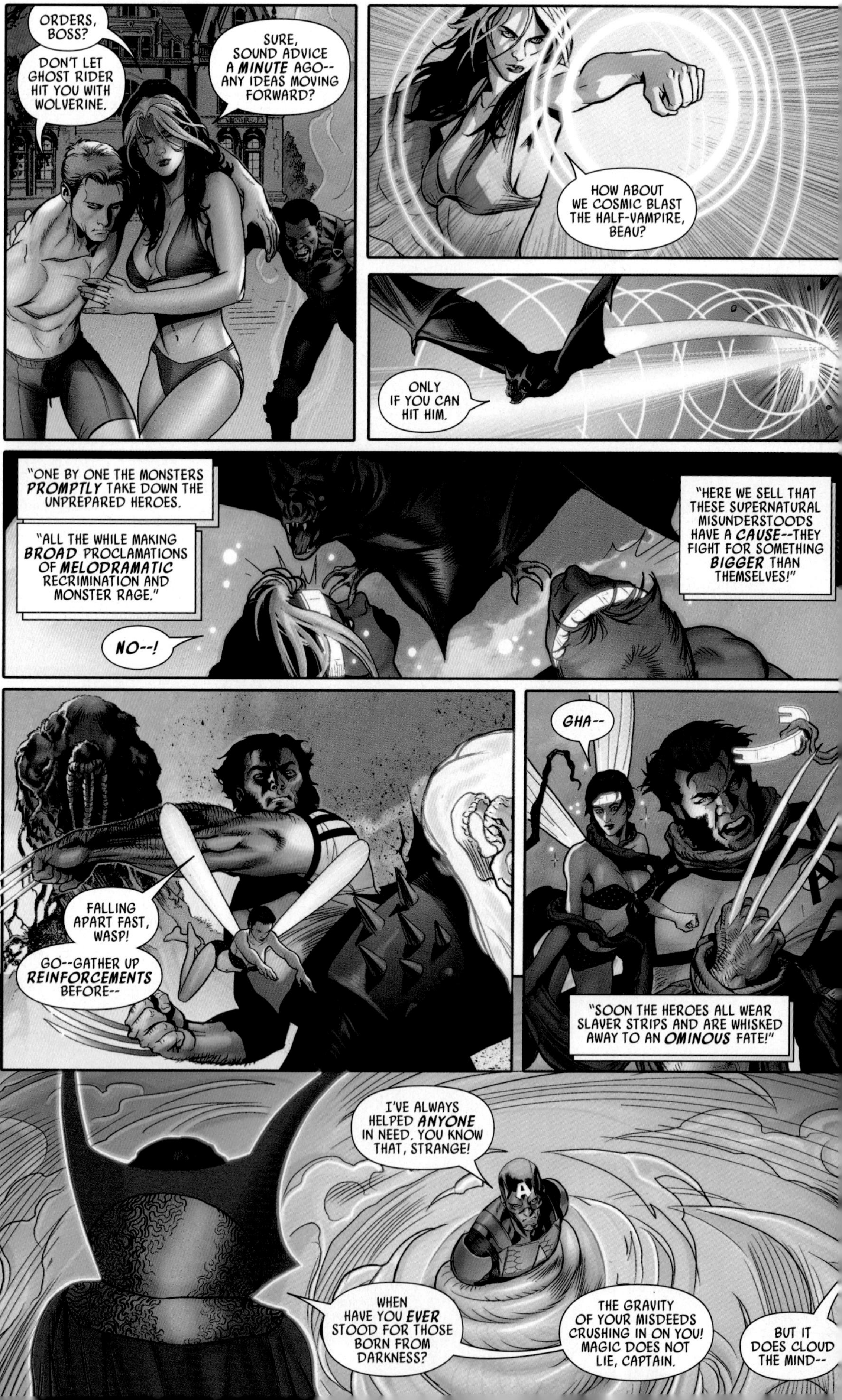

ORDERS, BOSS?
DON'T LET GHOST RIDER HIT YOU WITH WOLVERINE.
SURE, SOUND ADVICE A *MINUTE* AGO-- ANY IDEAS MOVING FORWARD?
HOW ABOUT WE COSMIC BLAST THE HALF-VAMPIRE, BEAU?
ONLY IF YOU CAN HIT HIM.
"ONE BY ONE THE MONSTERS *PROMPTLY* TAKE DOWN THE UNPREPARED HEROES.
"ALL THE WHILE MAKING *BROAD* PROCLAMATIONS OF *MELODRAMATIC* RECRIMINATION AND MONSTER RAGE."
NO--!
"HERE WE SELL THAT THESE SUPERNATURAL MISUNDERSTOODS HAVE A *CAUSE*--THEY FIGHT FOR SOMETHING *BIGGER* THAN THEMSELVES!"
FALLING APART FAST, WASP!
GO--GATHER UP *REINFORCEMENTS* BEFORE--
GHA--
"SOON THE HEROES ALL WEAR SLAVER STRIPS AND ARE WHISKED AWAY TO AN *OMINOUS* FATE!"
I'VE ALWAYS HELPED *ANYONE* IN NEED. YOU KNOW THAT, STRANGE!
WHEN HAVE YOU *EVER* STOOD FOR THOSE BORN FROM DARKNESS?
THE GRAVITY OF YOUR MISDEEDS CRUSHING IN ON YOU! MAGIC DOES NOT LIE, CAPTAIN.
BUT IT DOES CLOUD THE MIND--

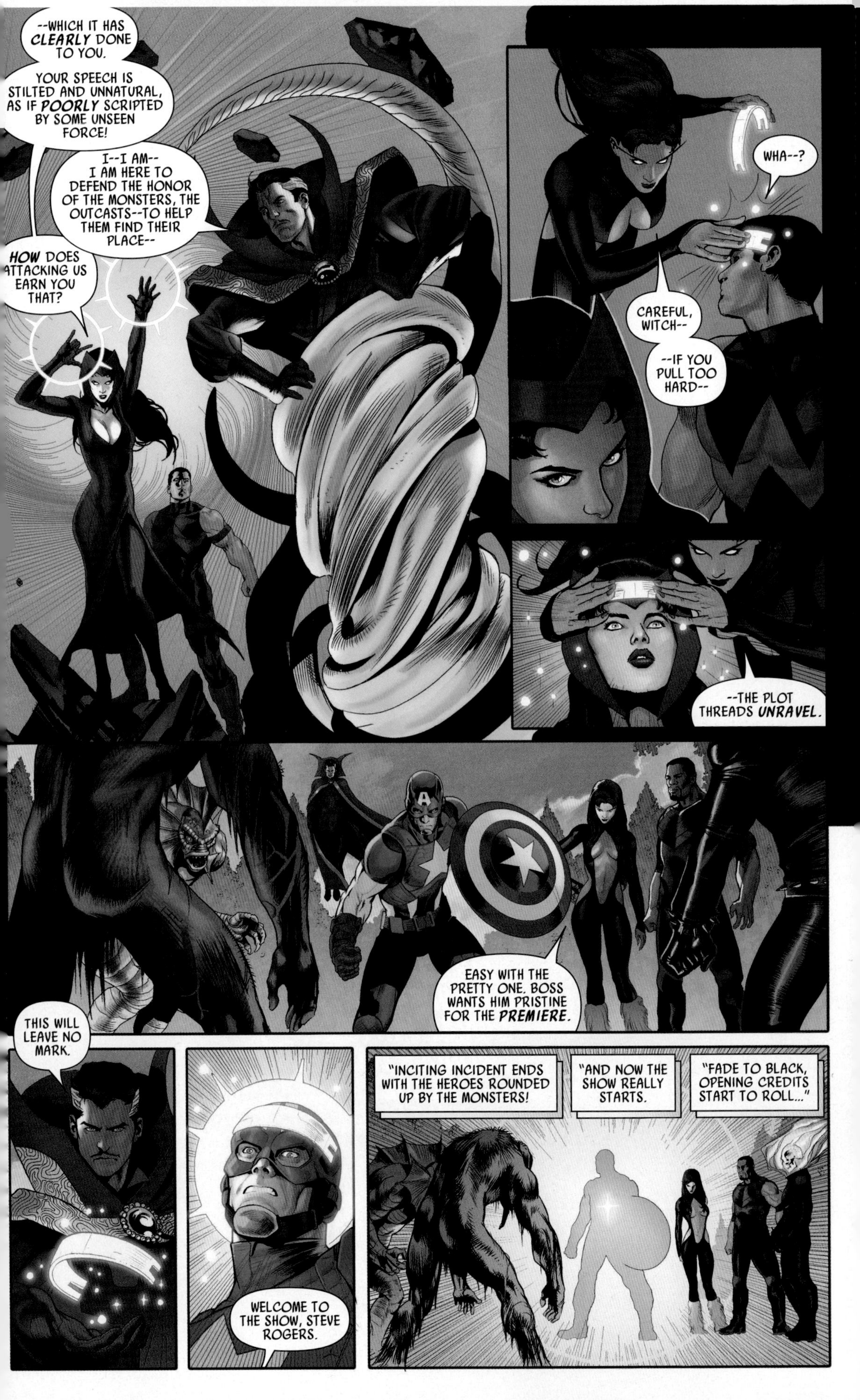
--WHICH IT HAS CLEARLY DONE TO YOU.
YOUR SPEECH IS STILTED AND UNNATURAL, AS IF POORLY SCRIPTED BY SOME UNSEEN FORCE!
I--I AM-- I AM HERE TO DEFEND THE HONOR OF THE MONSTERS, THE OUTCASTS--TO HELP THEM FIND THEIR PLACE--
HOW DOES ATTACKING US EARN YOU THAT?
WHA--?
CAREFUL, WITCH--
--IF YOU PULL TOO HARD--
--THE PLOT THREADS UNRAVEL.
EASY WITH THE PRETTY ONE. BOSS WANTS HIM PRISTINE FOR THE PREMIERE.
THIS WILL LEAVE NO MARK.
WELCOME TO THE SHOW, STEVE ROGERS.
"INCITING INCIDENT ENDS WITH THE HEROES ROUNDED UP BY THE MONSTERS!
"AND NOW THE SHOW REALLY STARTS.
"FADE TO BLACK, OPENING CREDITS START TO ROLL..."

Mojo/PLAN M Productions presents:

MARTIAN TRANSYLVANIA SUPER HERO MUTANT MONSTER HUNTER

HIGH SCHOOL

Starring

CAPTAIN AMERICA
DR. STRANGE
ROGUE
HAVOK
SUNFIRE
MAN-THING
GHOST RIDER
MANPHIBIAN
SCARLET WITCH
WONDER MAN
BLADE
WOLVERINE
WASP
THOR

and featuring
SATANA
as "The Succubus"

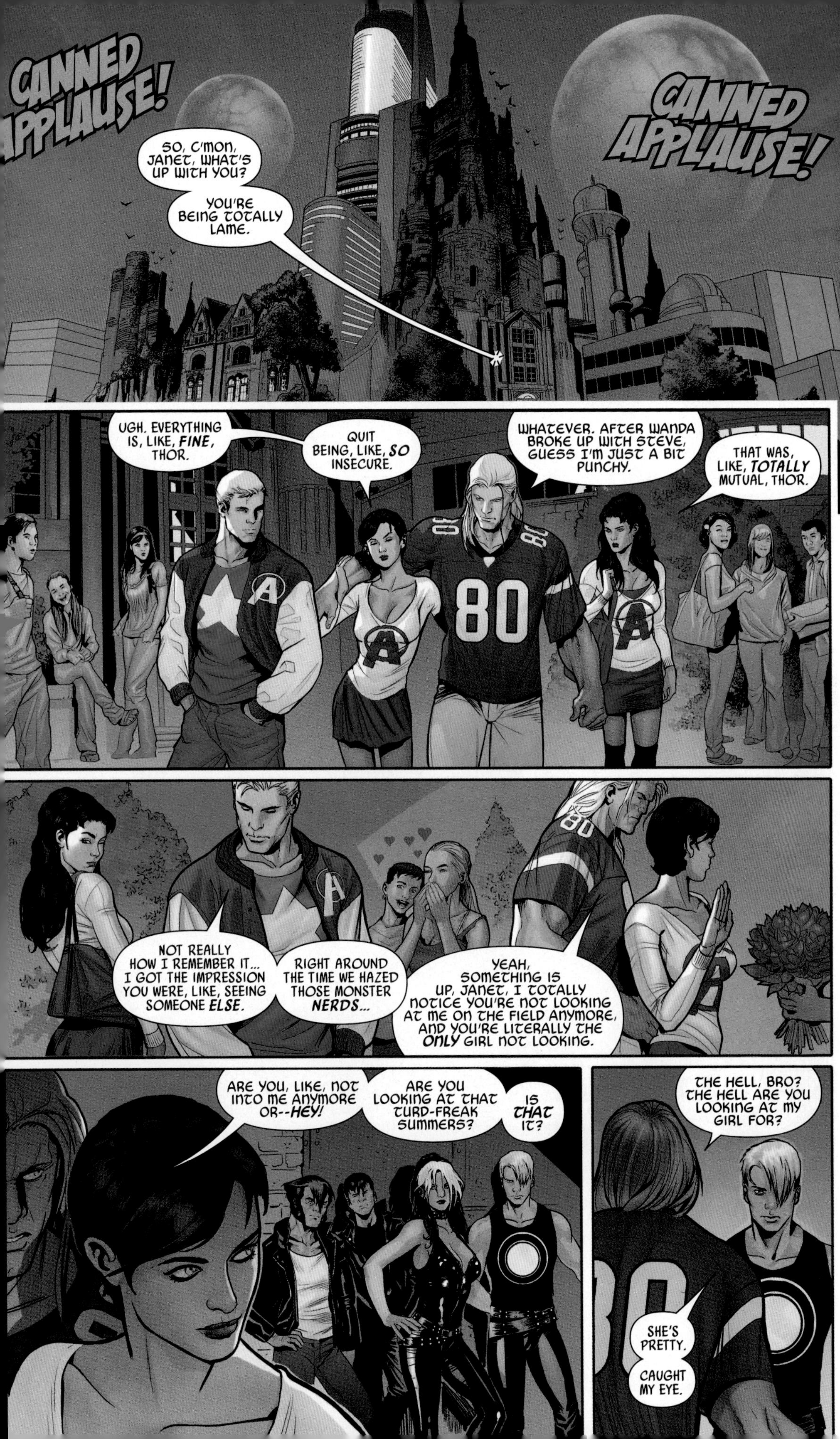
CANNED APPLAUSE!
CANNED APPLAUSE!
SO, C'MON, JANET, WHAT'S UP WITH YOU?
YOU'RE BEING TOTALLY LAME.
UGH. EVERYTHING IS, LIKE, FINE, THOR.
QUIT BEING, LIKE, SO INSECURE.
WHATEVER. AFTER WANDA BROKE UP WITH STEVE, GUESS I'M JUST A BIT PUNCHY.
THAT WAS, LIKE, TOTALLY MUTUAL, THOR.
NOT REALLY HOW I REMEMBER IT... I GOT THE IMPRESSION YOU WERE, LIKE, SEEING SOMEONE ELSE.
RIGHT AROUND THE TIME WE HAZED THOSE MONSTER NERDS...
YEAH, SOMETHING IS UP, JANET, I TOTALLY NOTICE YOU'RE NOT LOOKING AT ME ON THE FIELD ANYMORE, AND YOU'RE LITERALLY THE ONLY GIRL NOT LOOKING.
ARE YOU, LIKE, NOT INTO ME ANYMORE OR--HEY!
ARE YOU LOOKING AT THAT TURD-FREAK SUMMERS?
IS THAT IT?
THE HELL, BRO? THE HELL ARE YOU LOOKING AT MY GIRL FOR?
SHE'S PRETTY.
CAUGHT MY EYE.

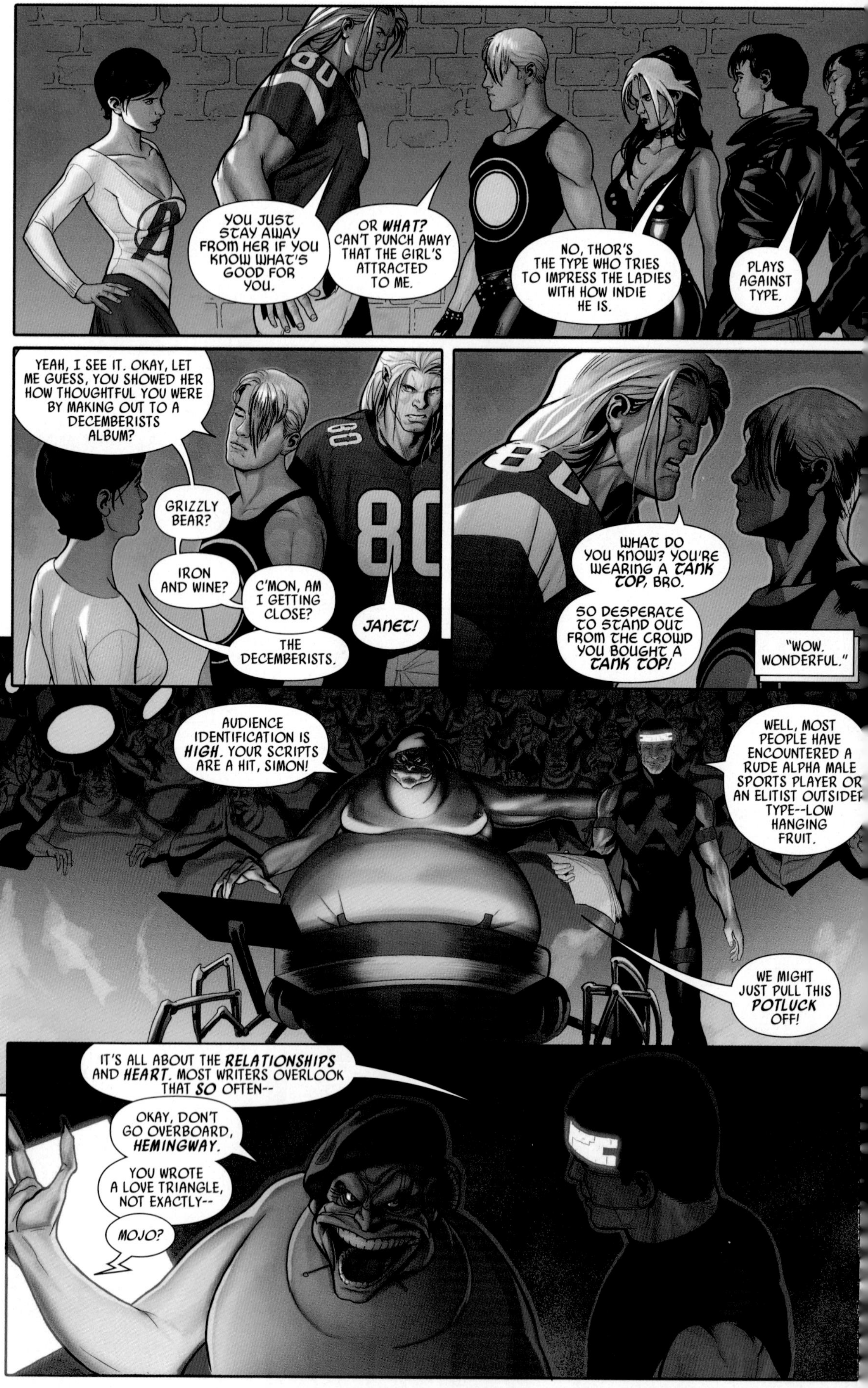

YOU JUST STAY AWAY FROM HER IF YOU KNOW WHAT'S GOOD FOR YOU.
OR WHAT? CAN'T PUNCH AWAY THAT THE GIRL'S ATTRACTED TO ME.
NO, THOR'S THE TYPE WHO TRIES TO IMPRESS THE LADIES WITH HOW INDIE HE IS.
PLAYS AGAINST TYPE.
YEAH, I SEE IT. OKAY, LET ME GUESS, YOU SHOWED HER HOW THOUGHTFUL YOU WERE BY MAKING OUT TO A DECEMBERISTS ALBUM?
GRIZZLY BEAR?
IRON AND WINE?
C'MON, AM I GETTING CLOSE?
THE DECEMBERISTS.
JANET!
WHAT DO YOU KNOW? YOU'RE WEARING A TANK TOP, BRO.
SO DESPERATE TO STAND OUT FROM THE CROWD YOU BOUGHT A TANK TOP!
"WOW. WONDERFUL."
AUDIENCE IDENTIFICATION IS HIGH. YOUR SCRIPTS ARE A HIT, SIMON!
WELL, MOST PEOPLE HAVE ENCOUNTERED A RUDE ALPHA MALE SPORTS PLAYER OR AN ELITIST OUTSIDER TYPE--LOW HANGING FRUIT.
WE MIGHT JUST PULL THIS POTLUCK OFF!
IT'S ALL ABOUT THE RELATIONSHIPS AND HEART. MOST WRITERS OVERLOOK THAT SO OFTEN--
OKAY, DON'T GO OVERBOARD, HEMINGWAY.
YOU WROTE A LOVE TRIANGLE, NOT EXACTLY--
MOJO?

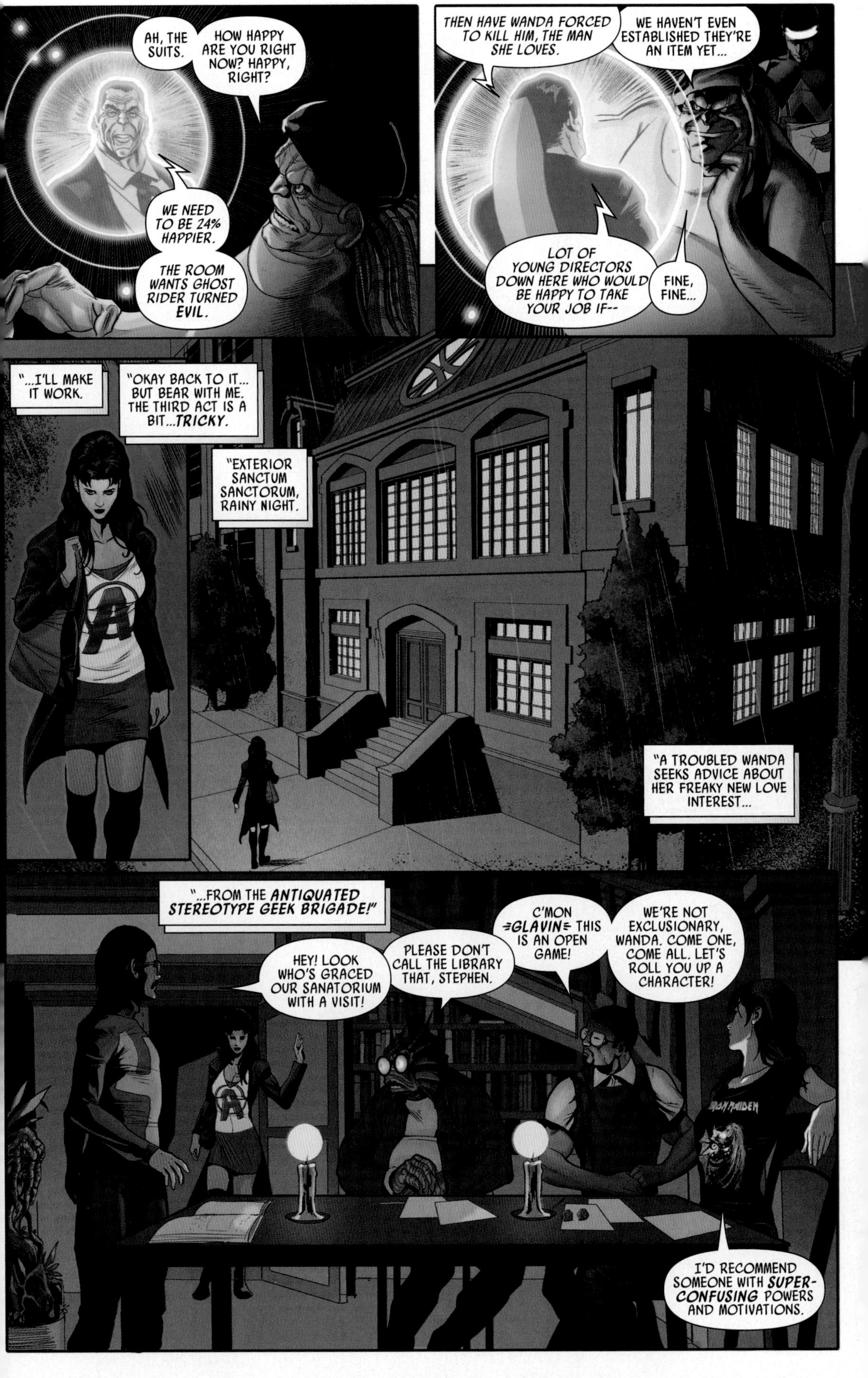
AH, THE SUITS.
HOW HAPPY ARE YOU RIGHT NOW? HAPPY, RIGHT?
WE NEED TO BE 24% HAPPIER.
THE ROOM WANTS GHOST RIDER TURNED EVIL.
THEN HAVE WANDA FORCED TO KILL HIM, THE MAN SHE LOVES.
WE HAVEN'T EVEN ESTABLISHED THEY'RE AN ITEM YET...
LOT OF YOUNG DIRECTORS DOWN HERE WHO WOULD BE HAPPY TO TAKE YOUR JOB IF--
FINE, FINE...
"...I'LL MAKE IT WORK.
"OKAY BACK TO IT... BUT BEAR WITH ME. THE THIRD ACT IS A BIT...TRICKY.
"EXTERIOR SANCTUM SANCTORUM, RAINY NIGHT.
"A TROUBLED WANDA SEEKS ADVICE ABOUT HER FREAKY NEW LOVE INTEREST...
"...FROM THE ANTIQUATED STEREOTYPE GEEK BRIGADE!"
HEY! LOOK WHO'S GRACED OUR SANATORIUM WITH A VISIT!
PLEASE DON'T CALL THE LIBRARY THAT, STEPHEN.
C'MON GLAVIN THIS IS AN OPEN GAME!
WE'RE NOT EXCLUSIONARY, WANDA. COME ONE, COME ALL. LET'S ROLL YOU UP A CHARACTER!
I'D RECOMMEND SOMEONE WITH SUPER-CONFUSING POWERS AND MOTIVATIONS.
IRON MAIDEN

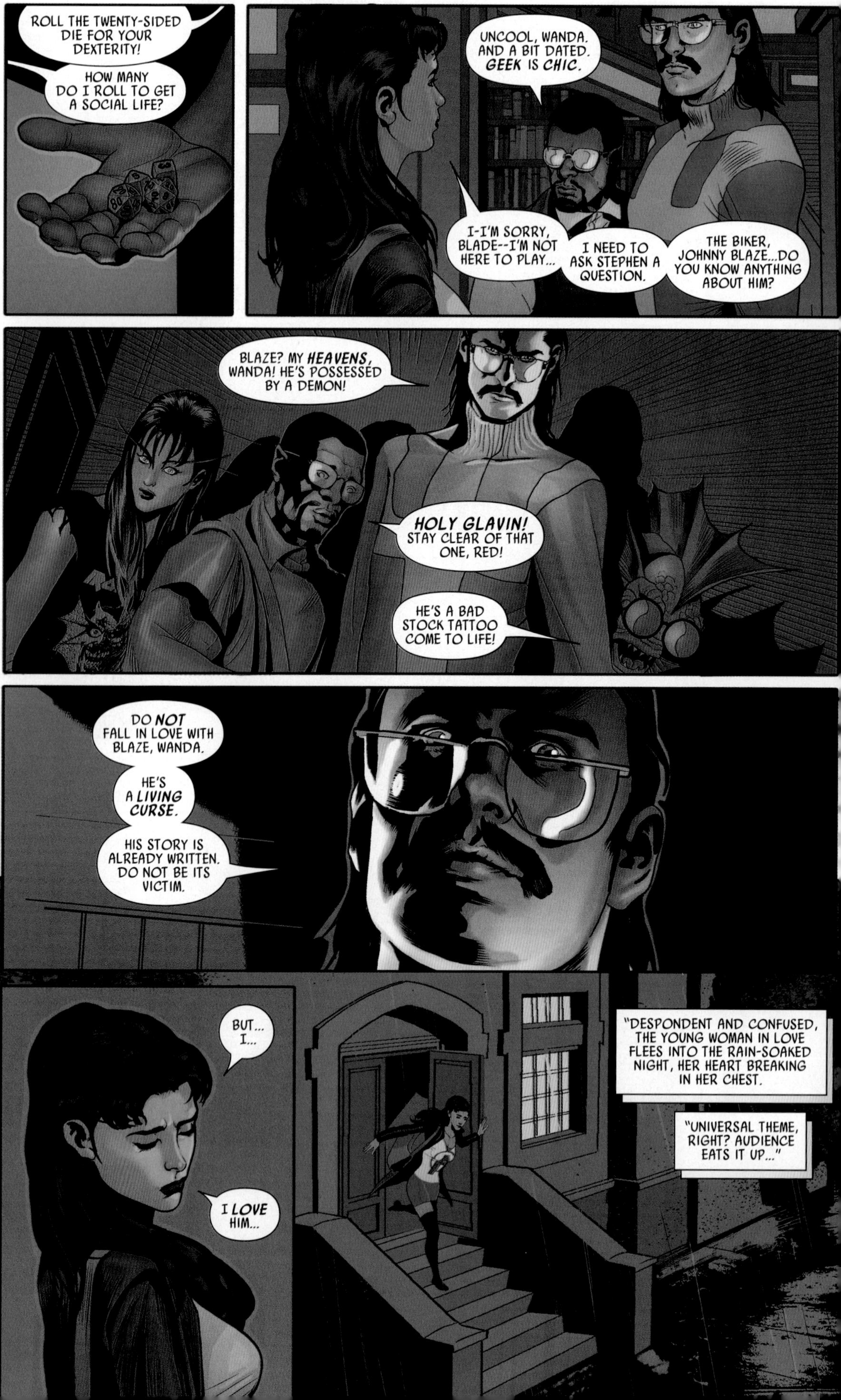

ROLL THE TWENTY-SIDED DIE FOR YOUR DEXTERITY!
HOW MANY DO I ROLL TO GET A SOCIAL LIFE?
UNCOOL, WANDA. AND A BIT DATED. GEEK IS CHIC.
I-I'M SORRY, BLADE--I'M NOT HERE TO PLAY...
I NEED TO ASK STEPHEN A QUESTION.
THE BIKER, JOHNNY BLAZE...DO YOU KNOW ANYTHING ABOUT HIM?
BLAZE? MY HEAVENS, WANDA! HE'S POSSESSED BY A DEMON!
HOLY GLAVIN! STAY CLEAR OF THAT ONE, RED!
HE'S A BAD STOCK TATTOO COME TO LIFE!
DO NOT FALL IN LOVE WITH BLAZE, WANDA.
HE'S A LIVING CURSE.
HIS STORY IS ALREADY WRITTEN. DO NOT BE ITS VICTIM.
BUT... I...
I LOVE HIM...
"DESPONDENT AND CONFUSED, THE YOUNG WOMAN IN LOVE FLEES INTO THE RAIN-SOAKED NIGHT, HER HEART BREAKING IN HER CHEST.
"UNIVERSAL THEME, RIGHT? AUDIENCE EATS IT UP..."

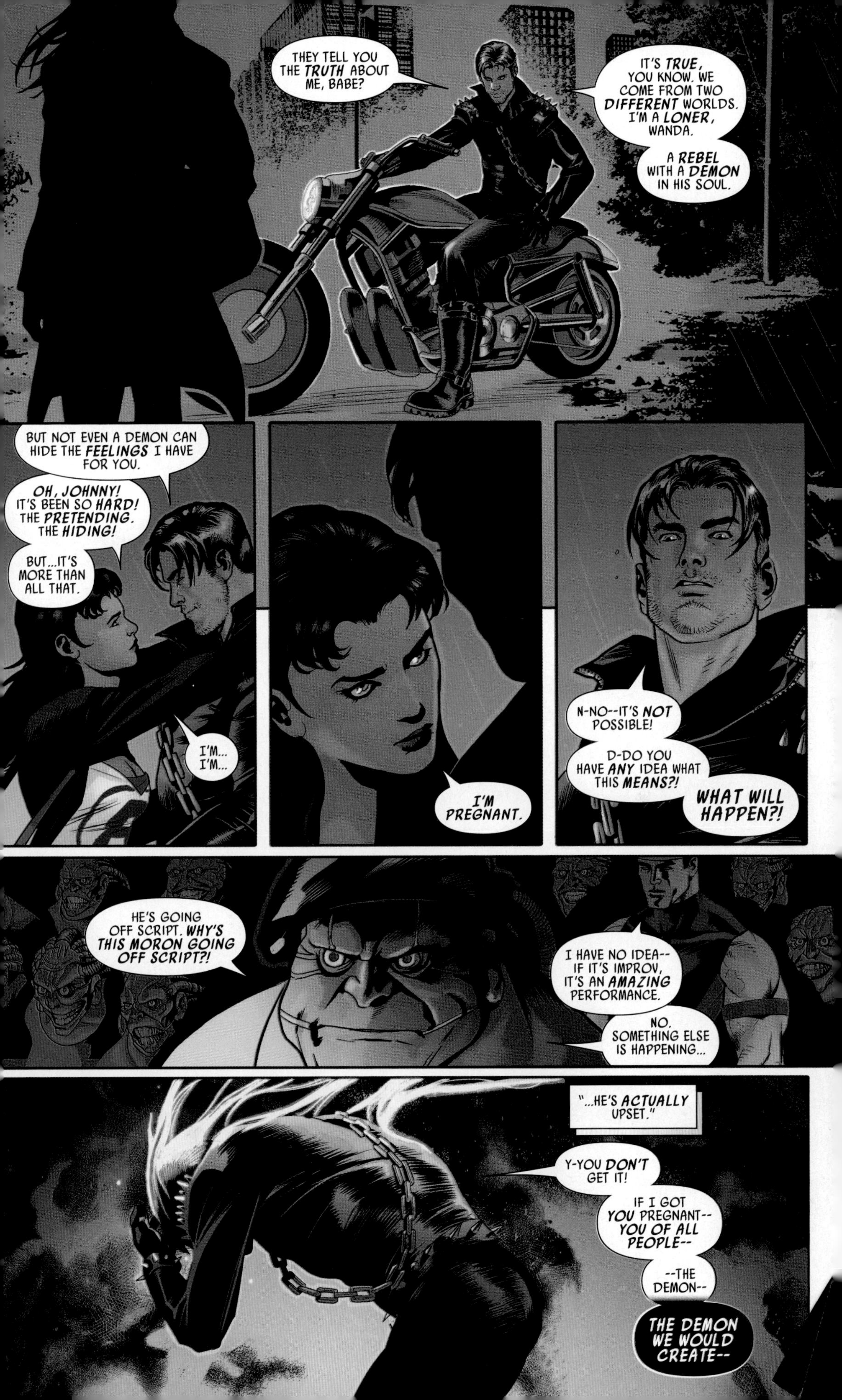

THEY TELL YOU THE TRUTH ABOUT ME, BABE?
IT'S TRUE, YOU KNOW. WE COME FROM TWO DIFFERENT WORLDS. I'M A LONER, WANDA.
A REBEL WITH A DEMON IN HIS SOUL.
BUT NOT EVEN A DEMON CAN HIDE THE FEELINGS I HAVE FOR YOU.
OH, JOHNNY! IT'S BEEN SO HARD! THE PRETENDING. THE HIDING!
BUT...IT'S MORE THAN ALL THAT.
I'M... I'M...
I'M PREGNANT.
N-NO--IT'S NOT POSSIBLE!
D-DO YOU HAVE ANY IDEA WHAT THIS MEANS?!
WHAT WILL HAPPEN?!
HE'S GOING OFF SCRIPT. WHY'S THIS MORON GOING OFF SCRIPT?!
I HAVE NO IDEA-- IF IT'S IMPROV, IT'S AN AMAZING PERFORMANCE.
NO. SOMETHING ELSE IS HAPPENING...
"...HE'S ACTUALLY UPSET."
Y-YOU DON'T GET IT!
IF I GOT YOU PREGNANT-- YOU OF ALL PEOPLE--
--THE DEMON--
THE DEMON WE WOULD CREATE--

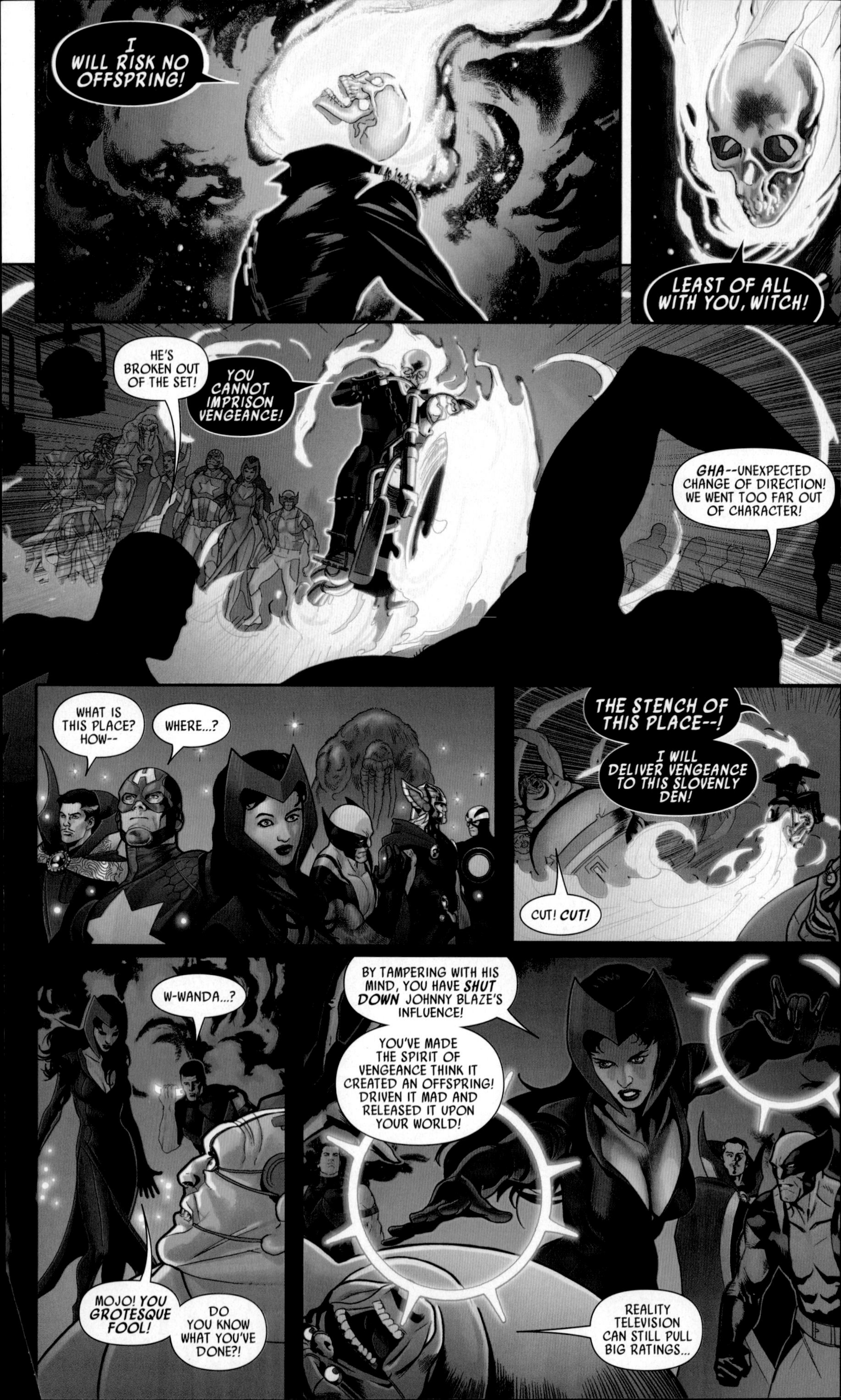
I WILL RISK NO OFFSPRING!
LEAST OF ALL WITH YOU, WITCH!
HE'S BROKEN OUT OF THE SET!
YOU CANNOT IMPRISON VENGEANCE!
GHA--UNEXPECTED CHANGE OF DIRECTION! WE WENT TOO FAR OUT OF CHARACTER!
WHAT IS THIS PLACE? HOW--
WHERE...?
THE STENCH OF THIS PLACE--!
I WILL DELIVER VENGEANCE TO THIS SLOVENLY DEN!
CUT! CUT!
W-WANDA...?
MOJO! YOU GROTESQUE FOOL!
DO YOU KNOW WHAT YOU'VE DONE?!
BY TAMPERING WITH HIS MIND, YOU HAVE SHUT DOWN JOHNNY BLAZE'S INFLUENCE!
YOU'VE MADE THE SPIRIT OF VENGEANCE THINK IT CREATED AN OFFSPRING! DRIVEN IT MAD AND RELEASED IT UPON YOUR WORLD!
REALITY TELEVISION CAN STILL PULL BIG RATINGS...

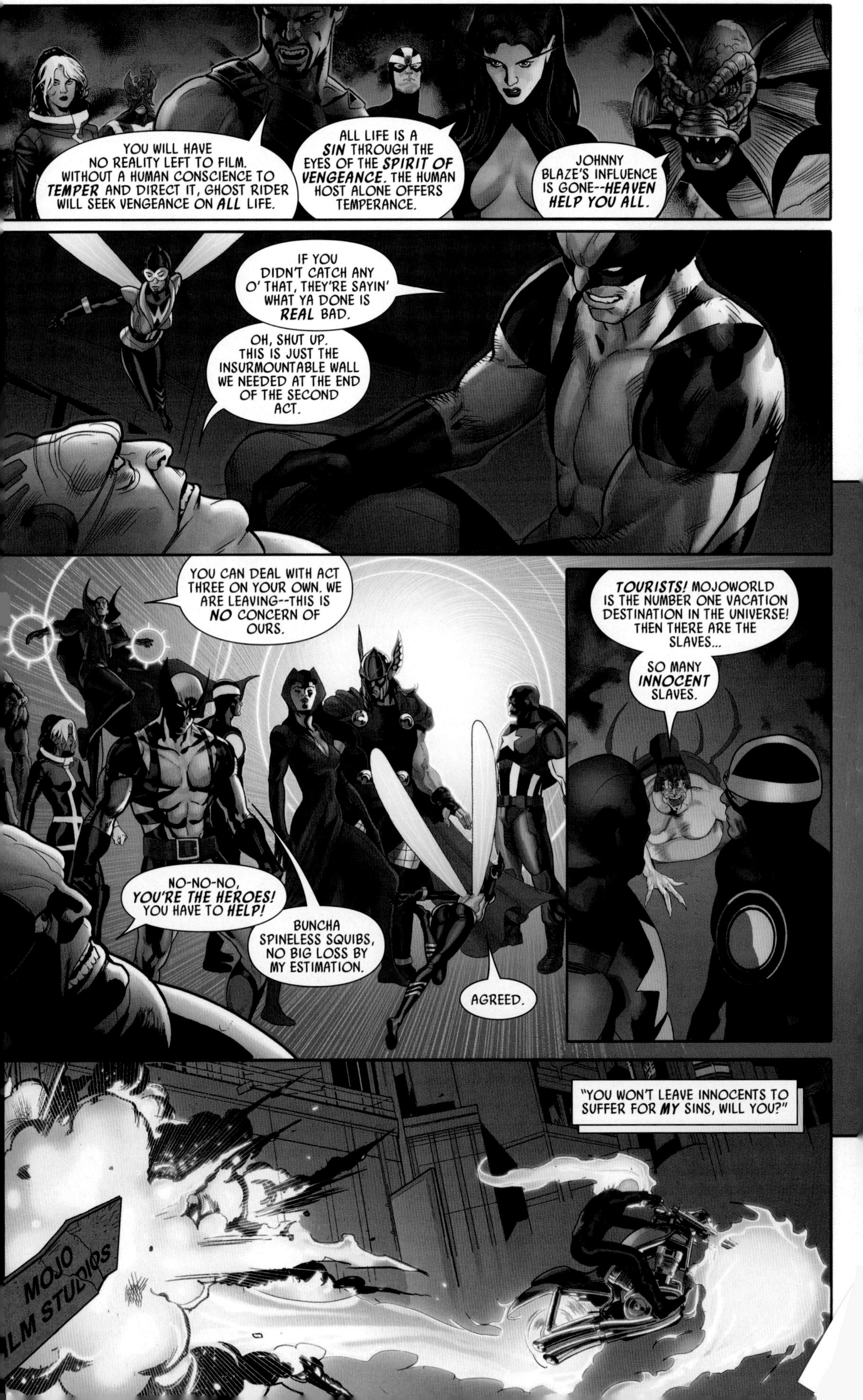
YOU WILL HAVE NO REALITY LEFT TO FILM. WITHOUT A HUMAN CONSCIENCE TO TEMPER AND DIRECT IT, GHOST RIDER WILL SEEK VENGEANCE ON ALL LIFE.
ALL LIFE IS A SIN THROUGH THE EYES OF THE SPIRIT OF VENGEANCE. THE HUMAN HOST ALONE OFFERS TEMPERANCE.
JOHNNY BLAZE'S INFLUENCE IS GONE--HEAVEN HELP YOU ALL.
IF YOU DIDN'T CATCH ANY O' THAT, THEY'RE SAYIN' WHAT YA DONE IS REAL BAD.
OH, SHUT UP. THIS IS JUST THE INSURMOUNTABLE WALL WE NEEDED AT THE END OF THE SECOND ACT.
YOU CAN DEAL WITH ACT THREE ON YOUR OWN. WE ARE LEAVING--THIS IS NO CONCERN OF OURS.
NO-NO-NO, YOU'RE THE HEROES! YOU HAVE TO HELP!
BUNCHA SPINELESS SQUIBS, NO BIG LOSS BY MY ESTIMATION.
AGREED.
TOURISTS! MOJOWORLD IS THE NUMBER ONE VACATION DESTINATION IN THE UNIVERSE! THEN THERE ARE THE SLAVES...
SO MANY INNOCENT SLAVES.
"YOU WON'T LEAVE INNOCENTS TO SUFFER FOR MY SINS, WILL YOU?"
MOJO
LM STUDIOS

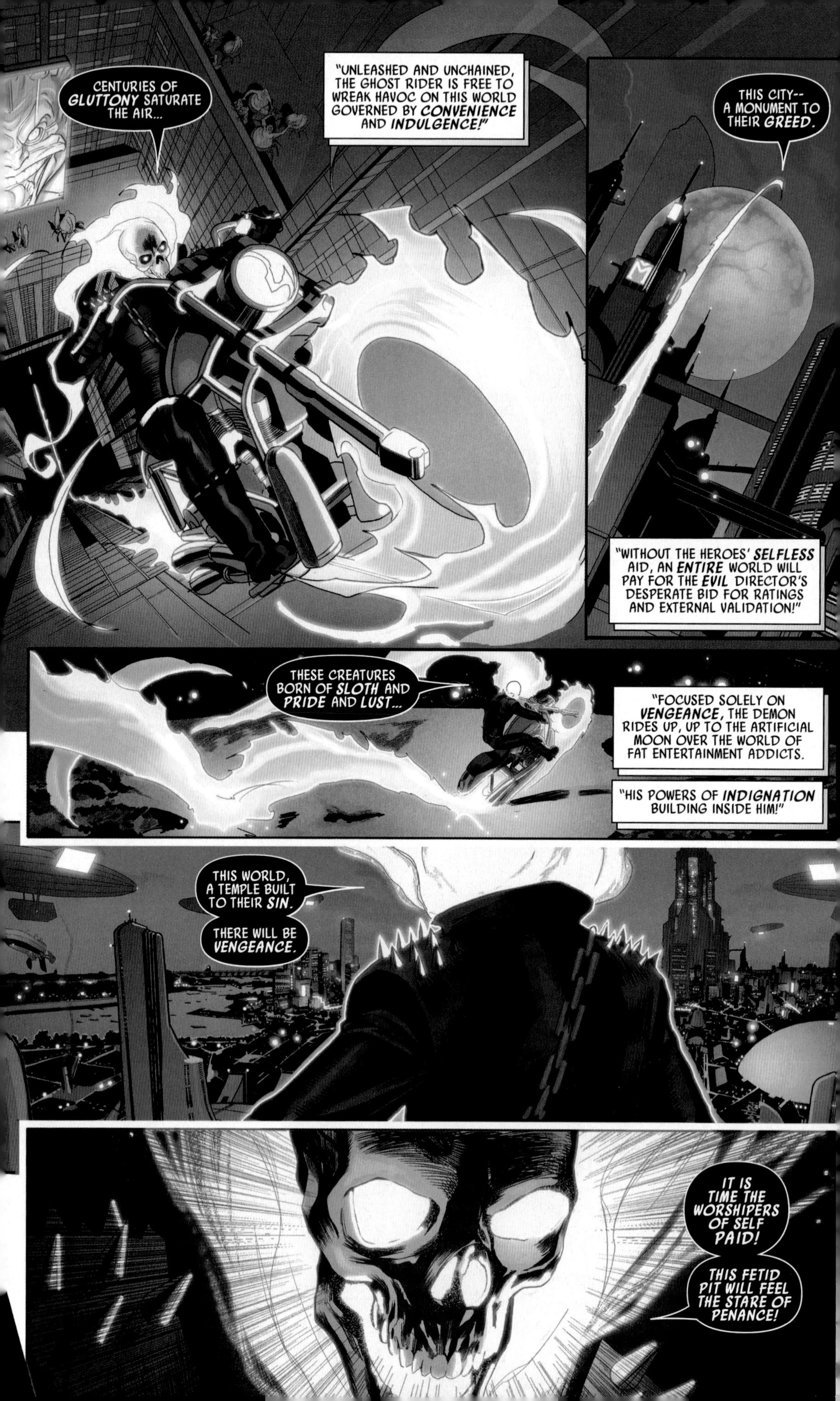
"UNLEASHED AND UNCHAINED, THE GHOST RIDER IS FREE TO WREAK HAVOC ON THIS WORLD GOVERNED BY CONVENIENCE AND INDULGENCE!"
CENTURIES OF GLUTTONY SATURATE THE AIR...
THIS CITY-- A MONUMENT TO THEIR GREED.
"WITHOUT THE HEROES' SELFLESS AID, AN ENTIRE WORLD WILL PAY FOR THE EVIL DIRECTOR'S DESPERATE BID FOR RATINGS AND EXTERNAL VALIDATION!"
THESE CREATURES BORN OF SLOTH AND PRIDE AND LUST...
"FOCUSED SOLELY ON VENGEANCE, THE DEMON RIDES UP, UP TO THE ARTIFICIAL MOON OVER THE WORLD OF FAT ENTERTAINMENT ADDICTS.
"HIS POWERS OF INDIGNATION BUILDING INSIDE HIM!"
THIS WORLD, A TEMPLE BUILT TO THEIR SIN.
THERE WILL BE VENGEANCE.
IT IS TIME THE WORSHIPERS OF SELF PAID!
THIS FETID PIT WILL FEEL THE STARE OF PENANCE!

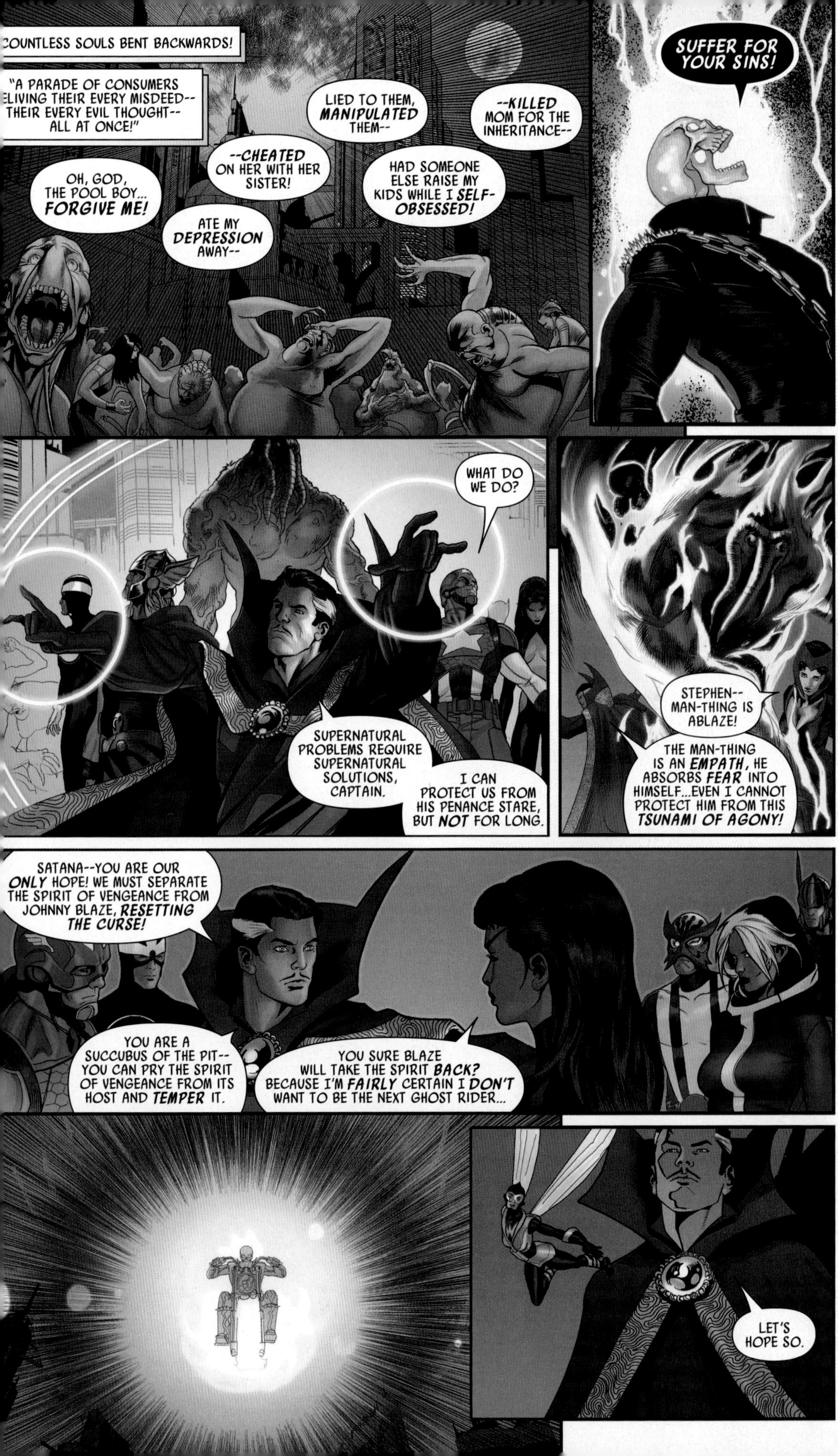
COUNTLESS SOULS BENT BACKWARDS!
"A PARADE OF CONSUMERS RELIVING THEIR EVERY MISDEED--THEIR EVERY EVIL THOUGHT--ALL AT ONCE!"
OH, GOD, THE POOL BOY... FORGIVE ME!
ATE MY DEPRESSION AWAY--
--CHEATED ON HER WITH HER SISTER!
LIED TO THEM, MANIPULATED THEM--
HAD SOMEONE ELSE RAISE MY KIDS WHILE I SELF-OBSESSED!
--KILLED MOM FOR THE INHERITANCE--
SUFFER FOR YOUR SINS!
WHAT DO WE DO?
SUPERNATURAL PROBLEMS REQUIRE SUPERNATURAL SOLUTIONS, CAPTAIN.
I CAN PROTECT US FROM HIS PENANCE STARE, BUT NOT FOR LONG.
STEPHEN--MAN-THING IS ABLAZE!
THE MAN-THING IS AN EMPATH, HE ABSORBS FEAR INTO HIMSELF...EVEN I CANNOT PROTECT HIM FROM THIS TSUNAMI OF AGONY!
SATANA--YOU ARE OUR ONLY HOPE! WE MUST SEPARATE THE SPIRIT OF VENGEANCE FROM JOHNNY BLAZE, RESETTING THE CURSE!
YOU ARE A SUCCUBUS OF THE PIT--YOU CAN PRY THE SPIRIT OF VENGEANCE FROM ITS HOST AND TEMPER IT.
YOU SURE BLAZE WILL TAKE THE SPIRIT BACK? BECAUSE I'M FAIRLY CERTAIN I DON'T WANT TO BE THE NEXT GHOST RIDER...
LET'S HOPE SO.

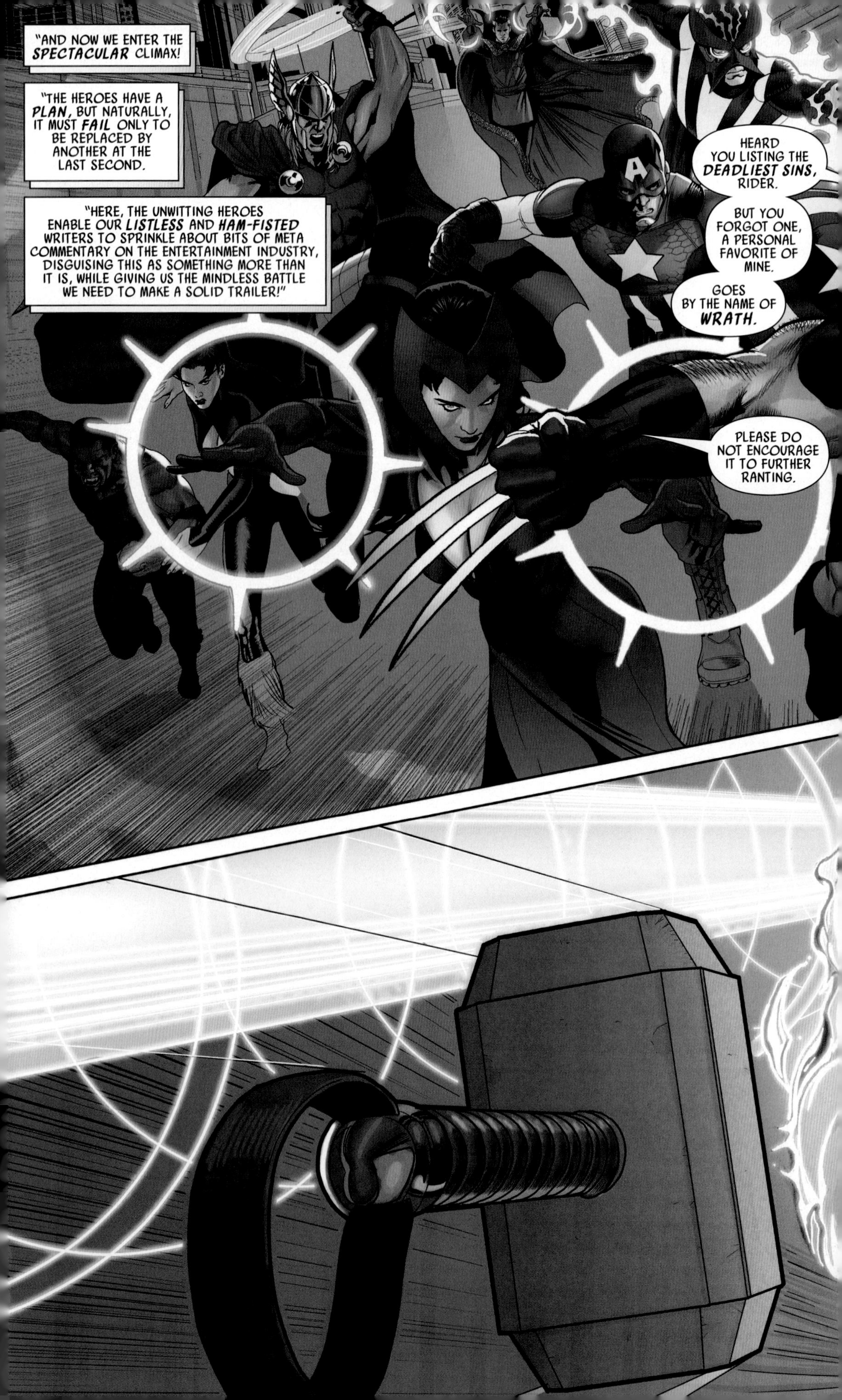

"AND NOW WE ENTER THE SPECTACULAR CLIMAX!
"THE HEROES HAVE A PLAN, BUT NATURALLY, IT MUST FAIL ONLY TO BE REPLACED BY ANOTHER AT THE LAST SECOND.
"HERE, THE UNWITTING HEROES ENABLE OUR LISTLESS AND HAM-FISTED WRITERS TO SPRINKLE ABOUT BITS OF META COMMENTARY ON THE ENTERTAINMENT INDUSTRY, DISGUISING THIS AS SOMETHING MORE THAN IT IS, WHILE GIVING US THE MINDLESS BATTLE WE NEED TO MAKE A SOLID TRAILER!"
HEARD YOU LISTING THE DEADLIEST SINS, RIDER.
BUT YOU FORGOT ONE, A PERSONAL FAVORITE OF MINE.
GOES BY THE NAME OF WRATH.
PLEASE DO NOT ENCOURAGE IT TO FURTHER RANTING.

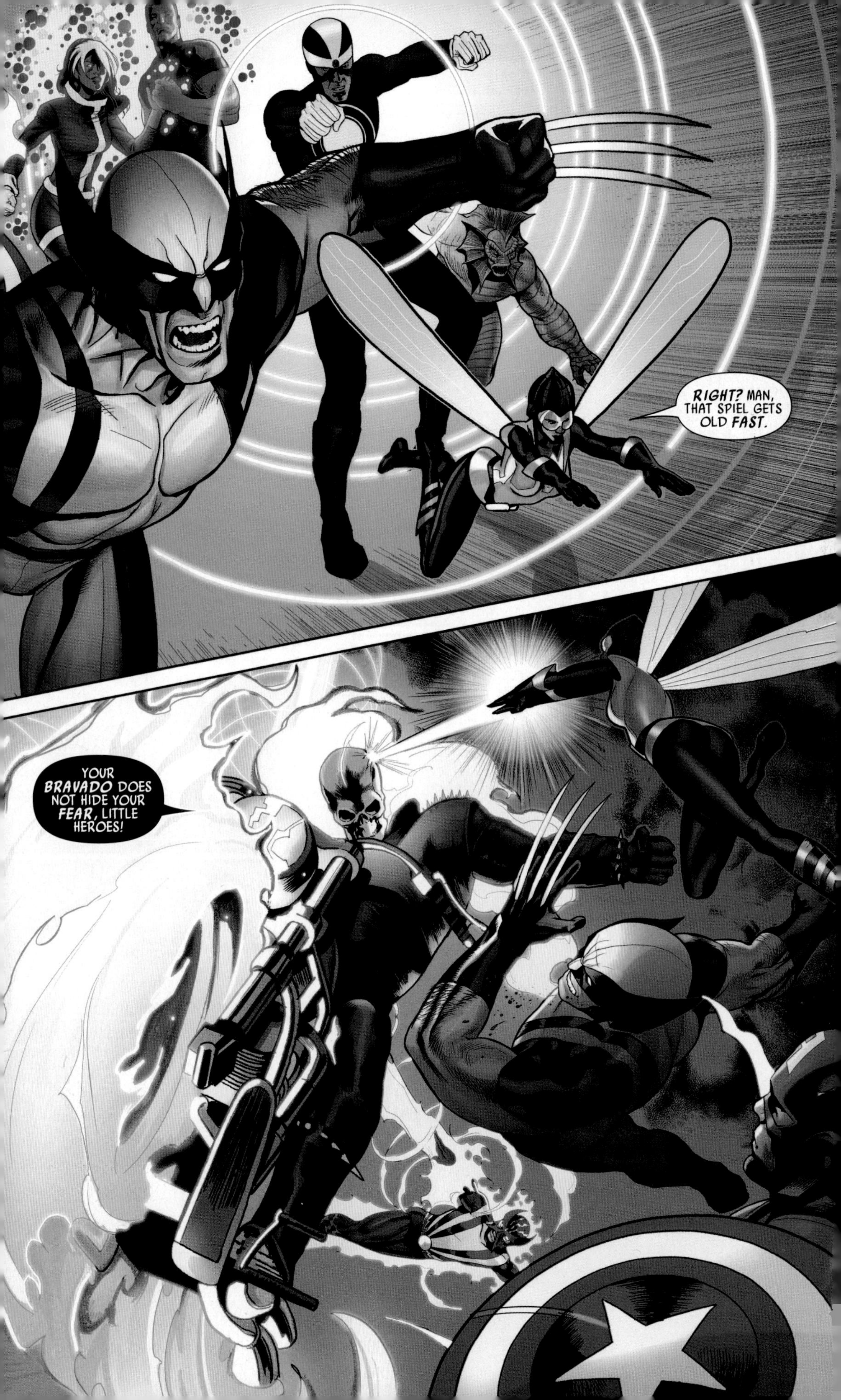
RIGHT? MAN, THAT SPIEL GETS OLD FAST.
YOUR BRAVADO DOES NOT HIDE YOUR FEAR, LITTLE HEROES!

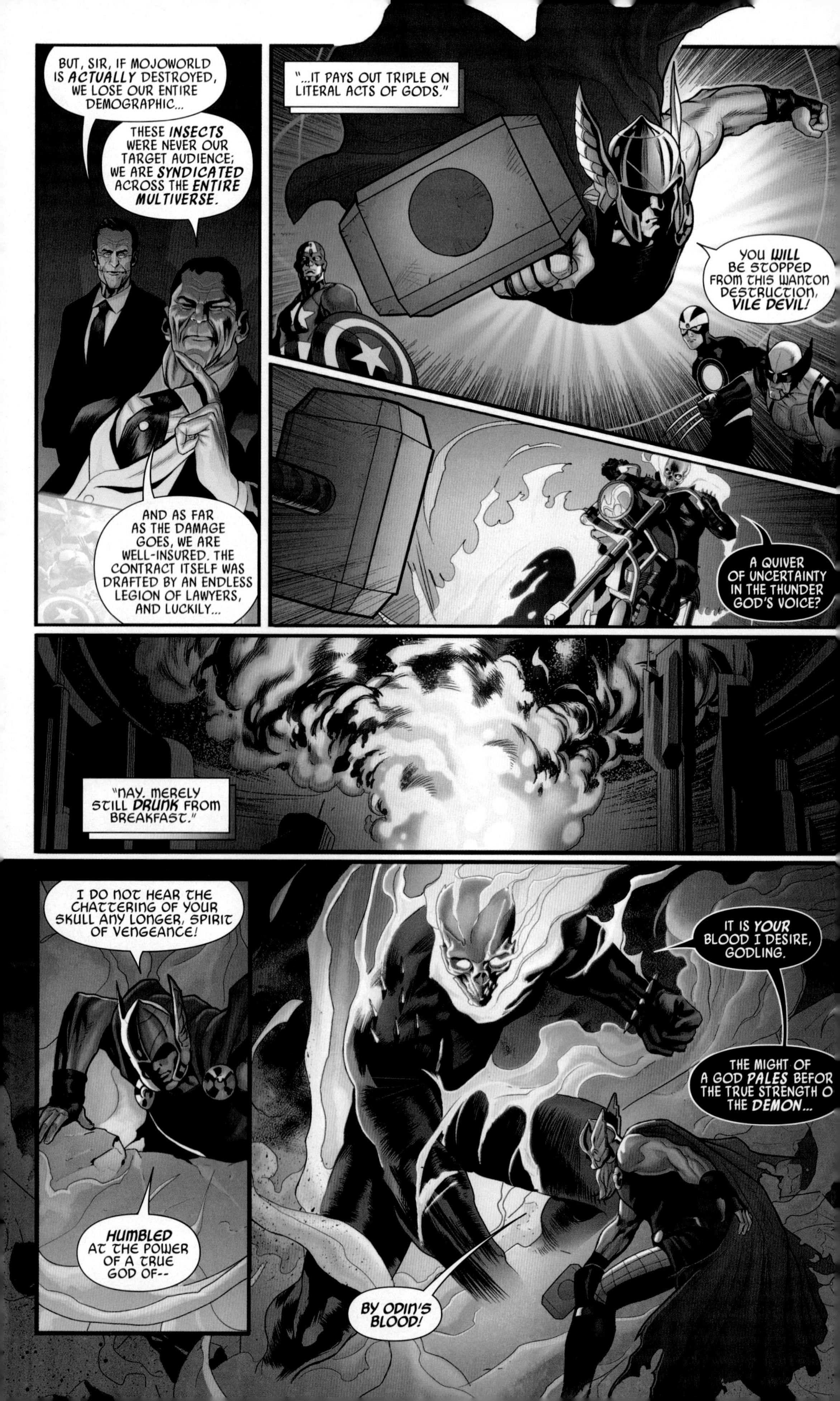

BUT, SIR, IF MOJOWORLD IS ACTUALLY DESTROYED, WE LOSE OUR ENTIRE DEMOGRAPHIC...
THESE INSECTS WERE NEVER OUR TARGET AUDIENCE; WE ARE SYNDICATED ACROSS THE ENTIRE MULTIVERSE.
AND AS FAR AS THE DAMAGE GOES, WE ARE WELL-INSURED. THE CONTRACT ITSELF WAS DRAFTED BY AN ENDLESS LEGION OF LAWYERS, AND LUCKILY...
"...IT PAYS OUT TRIPLE ON LITERAL ACTS OF GODS."
YOU WILL BE STOPPED FROM THIS WANTON DESTRUCTION, VILE DEVIL!
A QUIVER OF UNCERTAINTY IN THE THUNDER GOD'S VOICE?
"NAY. MERELY STILL DRUNK FROM BREAKFAST."
I DO NOT HEAR THE CHATTERING OF YOUR SKULL ANY LONGER, SPIRIT OF VENGEANCE!
IT IS YOUR BLOOD I DESIRE, GODLING.
THE MIGHT OF A GOD PALES BEFOR THE TRUE STRENGTH O THE DEMON...
HUMBLED AT THE POWER OF A TRUE GOD OF--
BY ODIN'S BLOOD!

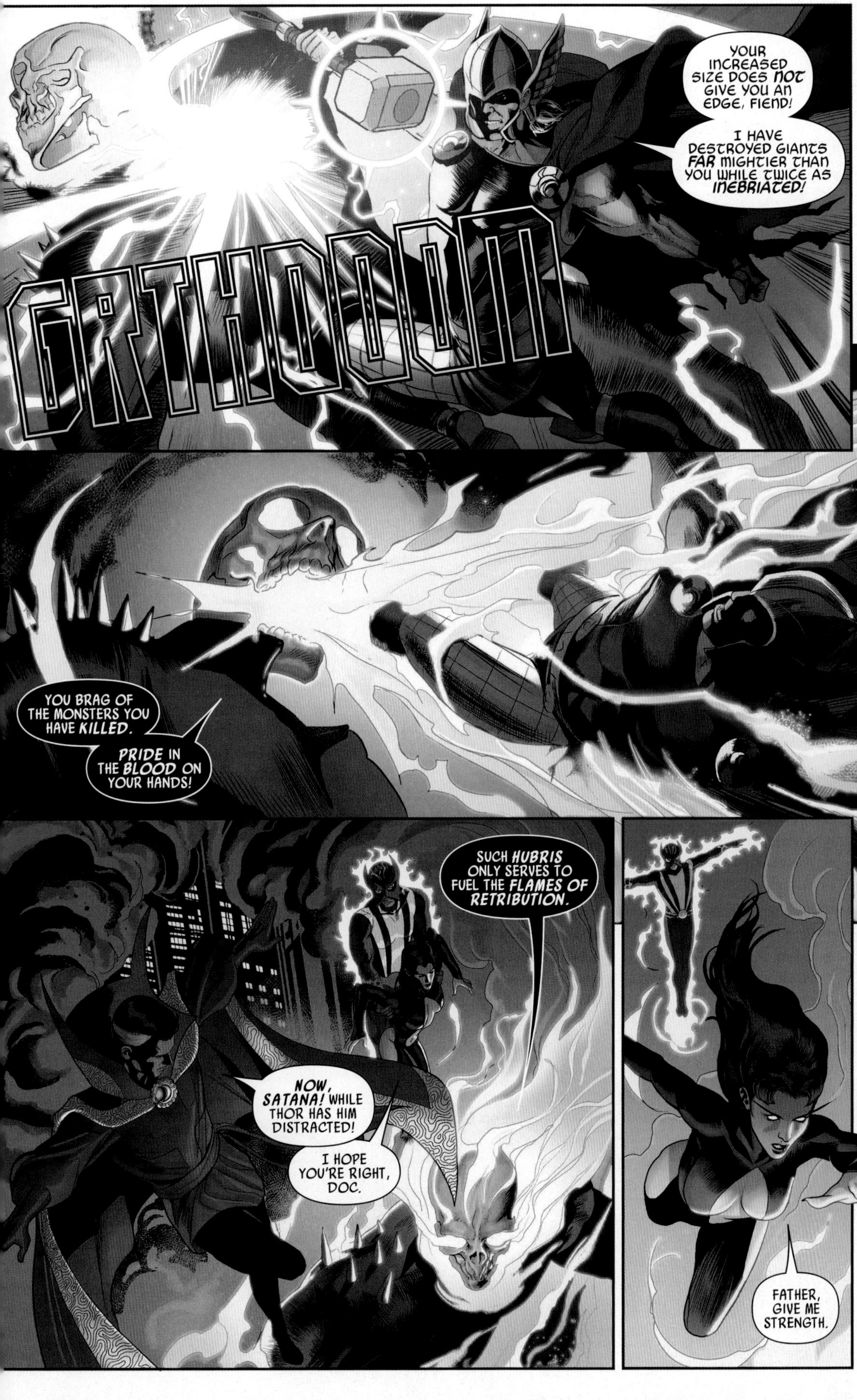
YOUR INCREASED SIZE DOES NOT GIVE YOU AN EDGE, FIEND!
I HAVE DESTROYED GIANTS FAR MIGHTIER THAN YOU WHILE TWICE AS INEBRIATED!
GRTHOOOM
YOU BRAG OF THE MONSTERS YOU HAVE KILLED.
PRIDE IN THE BLOOD ON YOUR HANDS!
SUCH HUBRIS ONLY SERVES TO FUEL THE FLAMES OF RETRIBUTION.
NOW, SATANA! WHILE THOR HAS HIM DISTRACTED!
I HOPE YOU'RE RIGHT, DOC.
FATHER, GIVE ME STRENGTH.

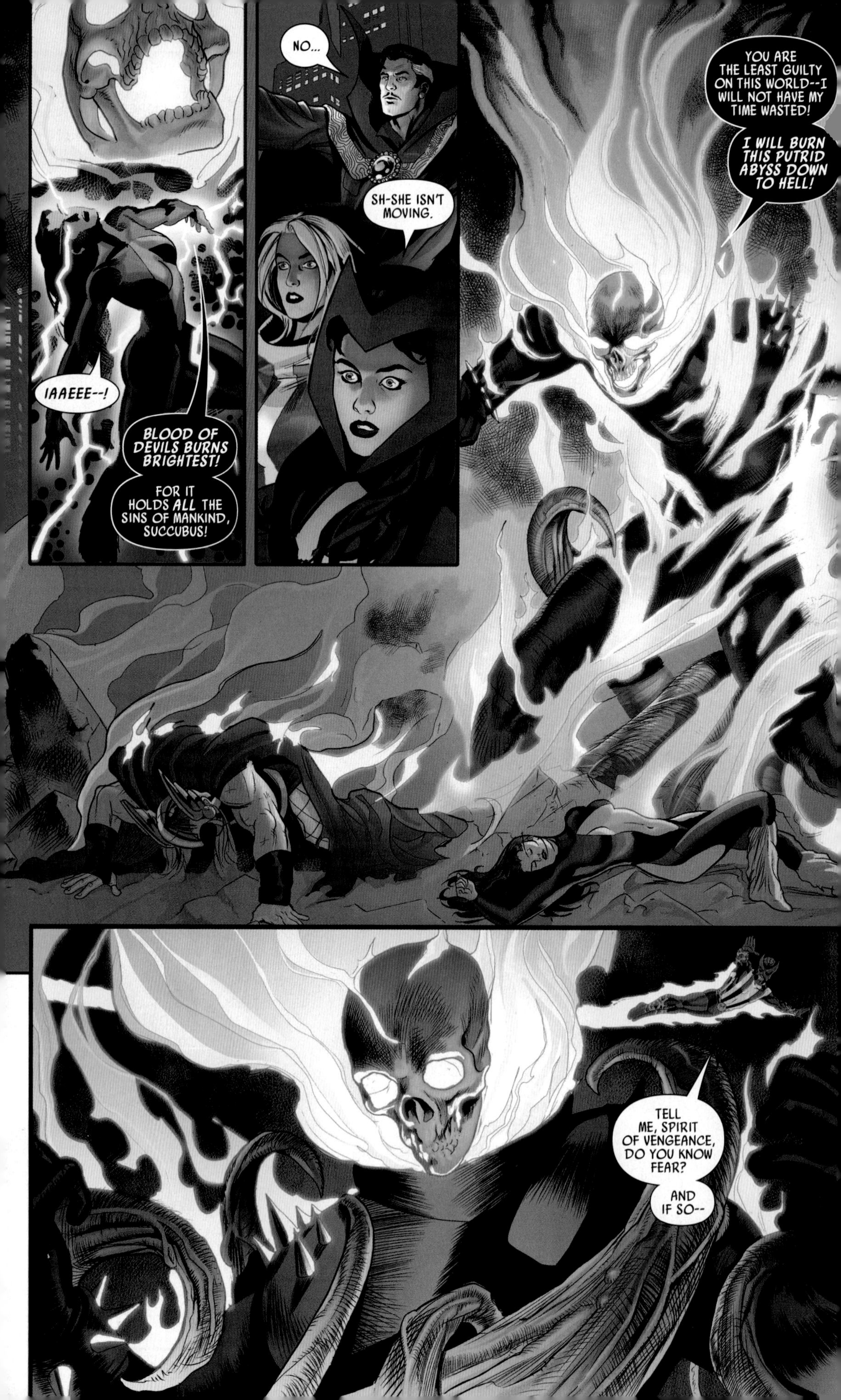

IAAEEE--!
BLOOD OF DEVILS BURNS BRIGHTEST!
FOR IT HOLDS ALL THE SINS OF MANKIND, SUCCUBUS!
NO...
SH-SHE ISN'T MOVING.
YOU ARE THE LEAST GUILTY ON THIS WORLD--I WILL NOT HAVE MY TIME WASTED!
I WILL BURN THIS PUTRID ABYSS DOWN TO HELL!
TELL ME, SPIRIT OF VENGEANCE, DO YOU KNOW FEAR?
AND IF SO--

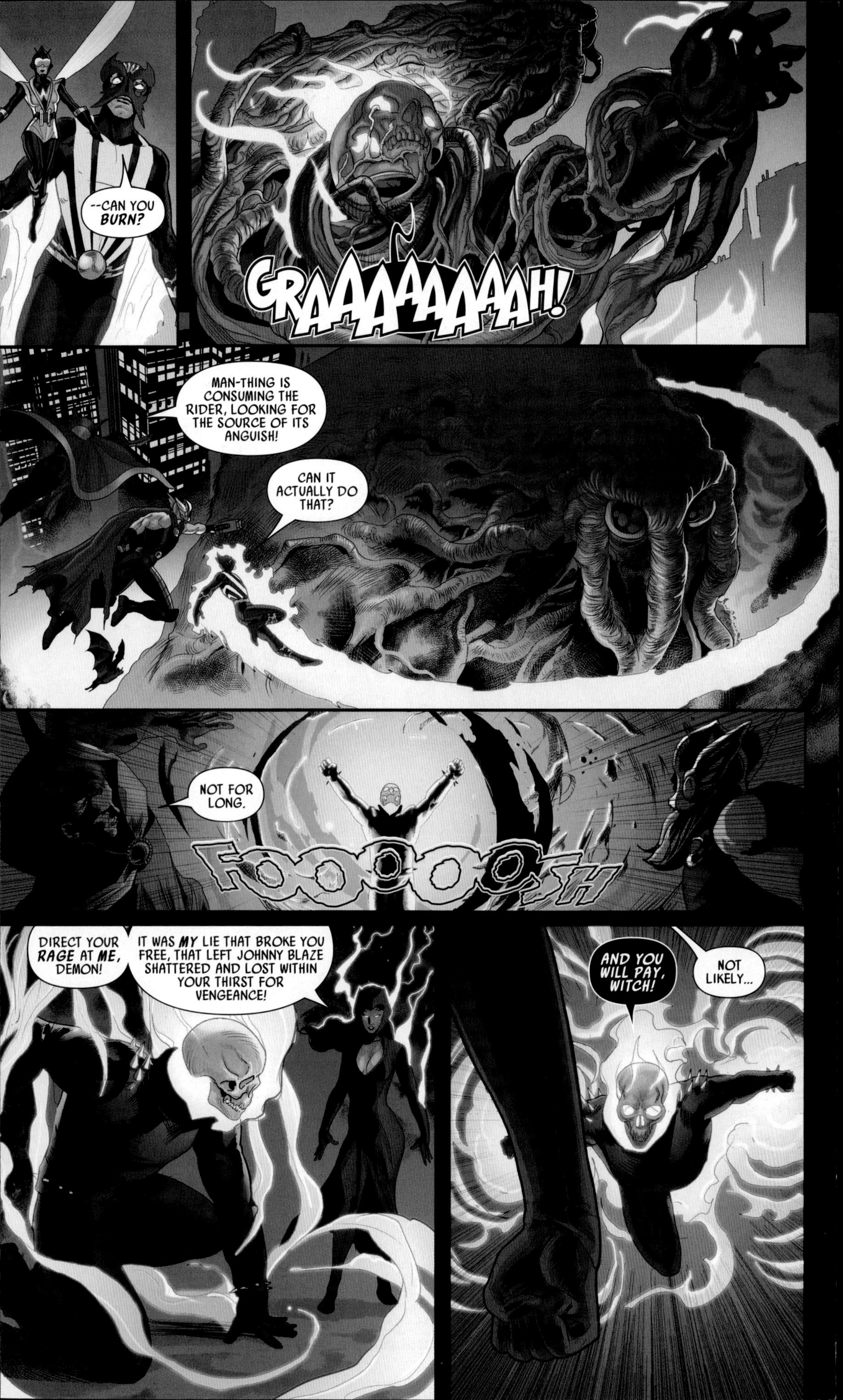
--CAN YOU BURN?
GRAAAAAAAAH!
MAN-THING IS CONSUMING THE RIDER, LOOKING FOR THE SOURCE OF ITS ANGUISH!
CAN IT ACTUALLY DO THAT?
NOT FOR LONG.
FOOOOOSH
DIRECT YOUR RAGE AT ME, DEMON!
IT WAS MY LIE THAT BROKE YOU FREE, THAT LEFT JOHNNY BLAZE SHATTERED AND LOST WITHIN YOUR THIRST FOR VENGEANCE!
AND YOU WILL PAY, WITCH!
NOT LIKELY...

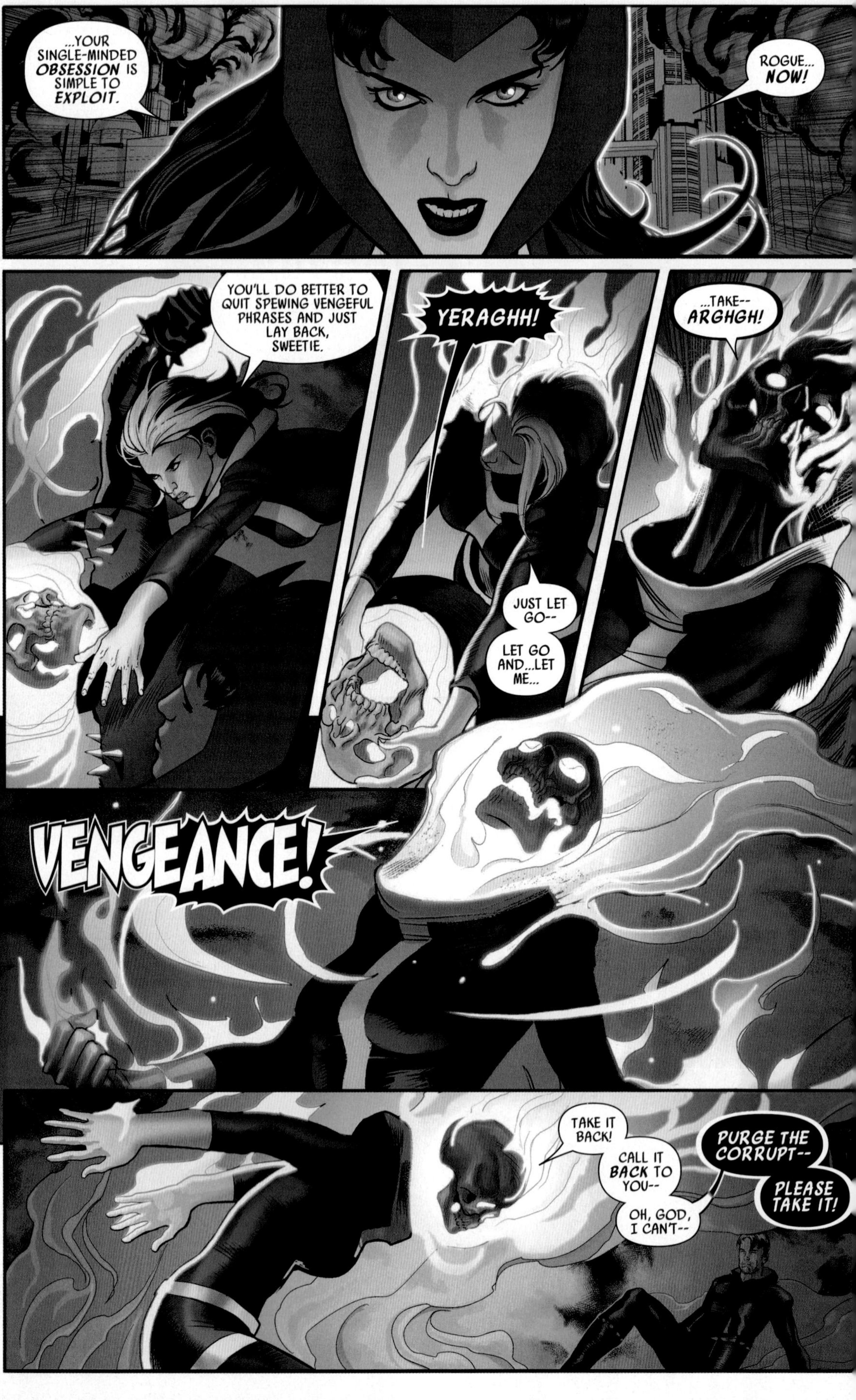

...YOUR SINGLE-MINDED OBSESSION IS SIMPLE TO EXPLOIT.
ROGUE... NOW!
YOU'LL DO BETTER TO QUIT SPEWING VENGEFUL PHRASES AND JUST LAY BACK, SWEETIE.
YERAGHH!
JUST LET GO--
LET GO AND...LET ME...
...TAKE-- ARGHGH!
VENGEANCE!
TAKE IT BACK!
CALL IT BACK TO YOU--
OH, GOD, I CAN'T--
PURGE THE CORRUPT--
PLEASE TAKE IT!

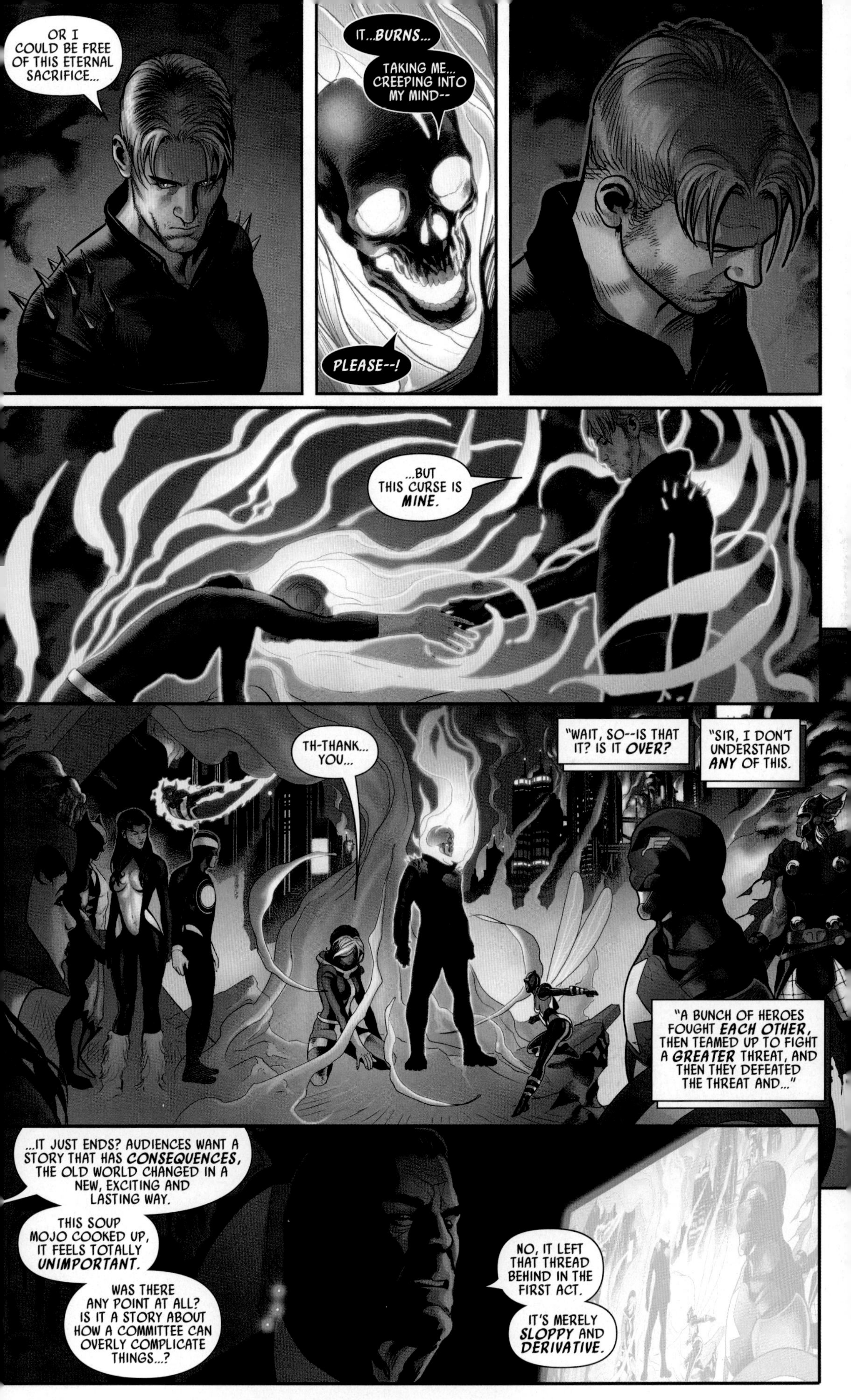

OR I COULD BE FREE OF THIS ETERNAL SACRIFICE...
IT...BURNS...
TAKING ME... CREEPING INTO MY MIND--
PLEASE--!
...BUT THIS CURSE IS MINE.
TH-THANK... YOU...
"WAIT, SO--IS THAT IT? IS IT OVER?
"SIR, I DON'T UNDERSTAND ANY OF THIS.
"A BUNCH OF HEROES FOUGHT EACH OTHER, THEN TEAMED UP TO FIGHT A GREATER THREAT, AND THEN THEY DEFEATED THE THREAT AND..."
...IT JUST ENDS? AUDIENCES WANT A STORY THAT HAS CONSEQUENCES, THE OLD WORLD CHANGED IN A NEW, EXCITING AND LASTING WAY.
THIS SOUP MOJO COOKED UP, IT FEELS TOTALLY UNIMPORTANT.
WAS THERE ANY POINT AT ALL? IS IT A STORY ABOUT HOW A COMMITTEE CAN OVERLY COMPLICATE THINGS...?
NO, IT LEFT THAT THREAD BEHIND IN THE FIRST ACT.
IT'S MERELY SLOPPY AND DERIVATIVE.

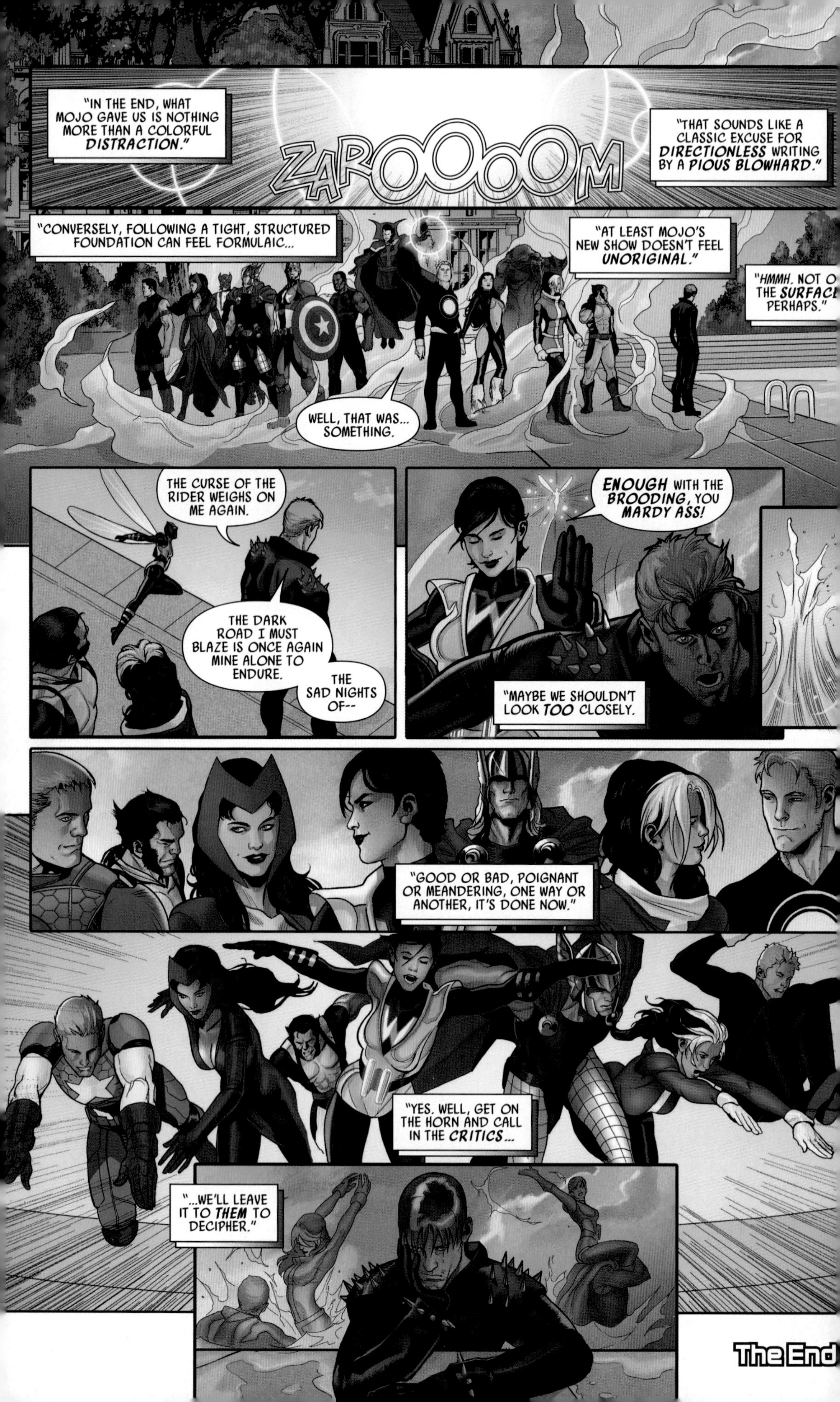
"IN THE END, WHAT MOJO GAVE US IS NOTHING MORE THAN A COLORFUL DISTRACTION."
ZAROOOoOM
"THAT SOUNDS LIKE A CLASSIC EXCUSE FOR DIRECTIONLESS WRITING BY A PIOUS BLOWHARD."
"CONVERSELY, FOLLOWING A TIGHT, STRUCTURED FOUNDATION CAN FEEL FORMULAIC...
"AT LEAST MOJO'S NEW SHOW DOESN'T FEEL UNORIGINAL."
"HMMH. NOT O THE SURFAC PERHAPS."
WELL, THAT WAS... SOMETHING.
THE CURSE OF THE RIDER WEIGHS ON ME AGAIN.
THE DARK ROAD I MUST BLAZE IS ONCE AGAIN MINE ALONE TO ENDURE.
THE SAD NIGHTS OF--
ENOUGH WITH THE BROODING, YOU MARDY ASS!
"MAYBE WE SHOULDN'T LOOK TOO CLOSELY.
"GOOD OR BAD, POIGNANT OR MEANDERING, ONE WAY OR ANOTHER, IT'S DONE NOW."
"YES. WELL, GET ON THE HORN AND CALL IN THE CRITICS...
"...WE'LL LEAVE IT TO THEM TO DECIPHER."
The End

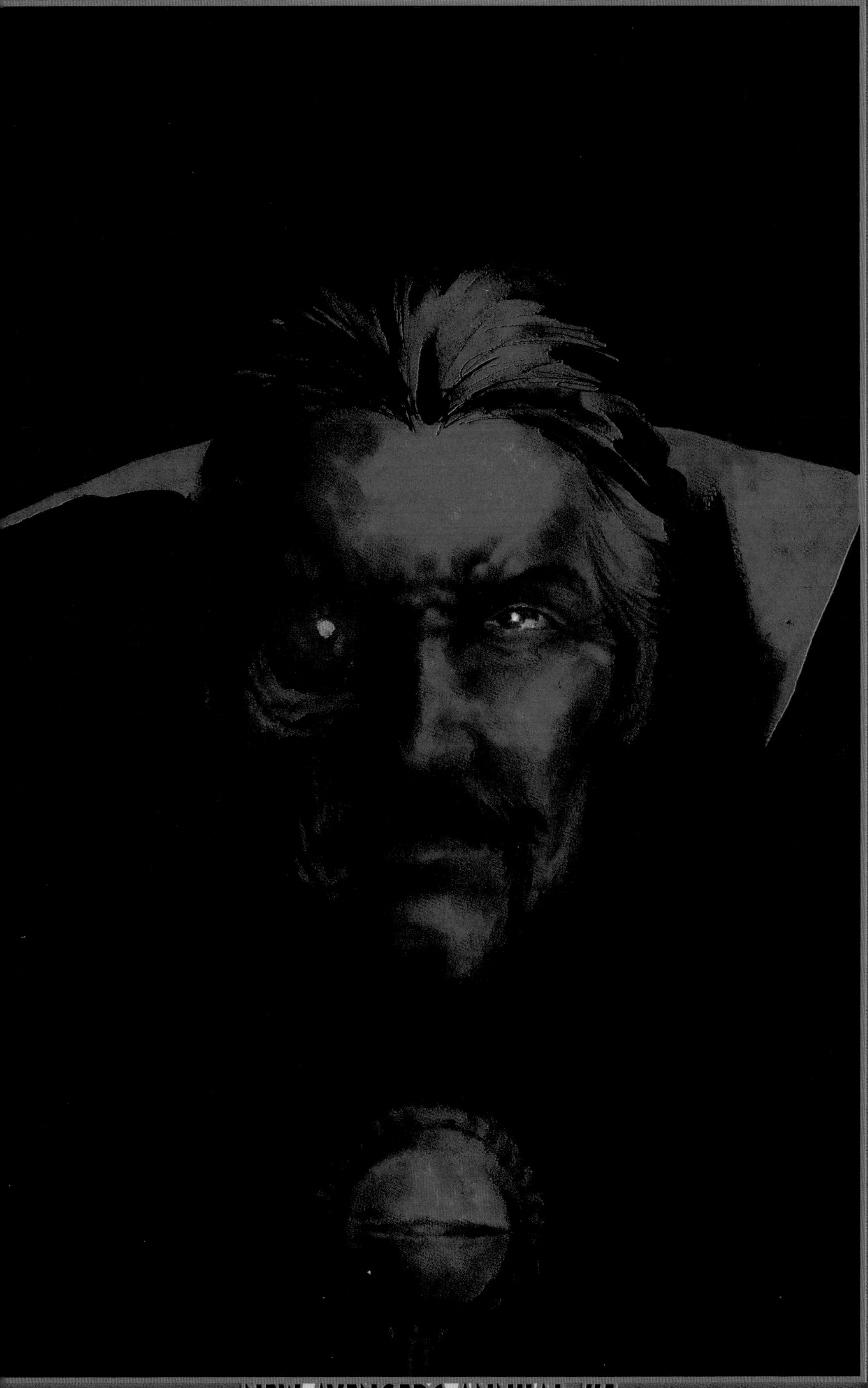

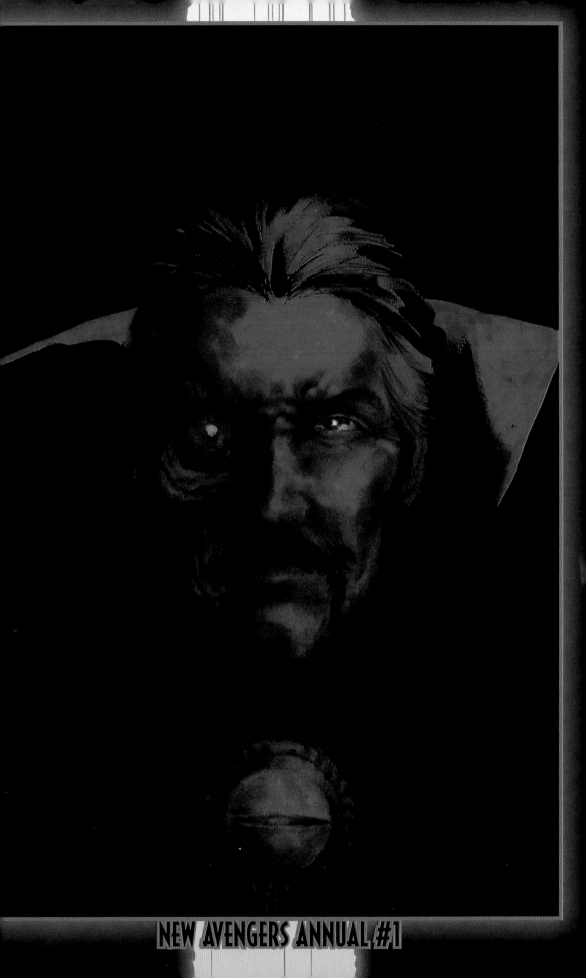

NEW AVENGERS ANNUAL #1

STEPHEN STRANGE was a brilliant neurosurgeon whose exceptional skills nearly matched his ego. When a car accident caused nerve damage in his hands, Strange scoured the globe looking for a cure to his condition. His search led him to Tibet, where he found THE ANCIENT ONE. Although he refused to cure Strange's condition, the Ancient One revealed to him a world of magic and power that humbled the brilliant doctor. Strange gave himself over to being the Ancient One's protégé, eventually mastering the mystic arts and becoming…

DOCTOR STRANGE

IN

SORCERER SUPREME

SELF-SURGERY

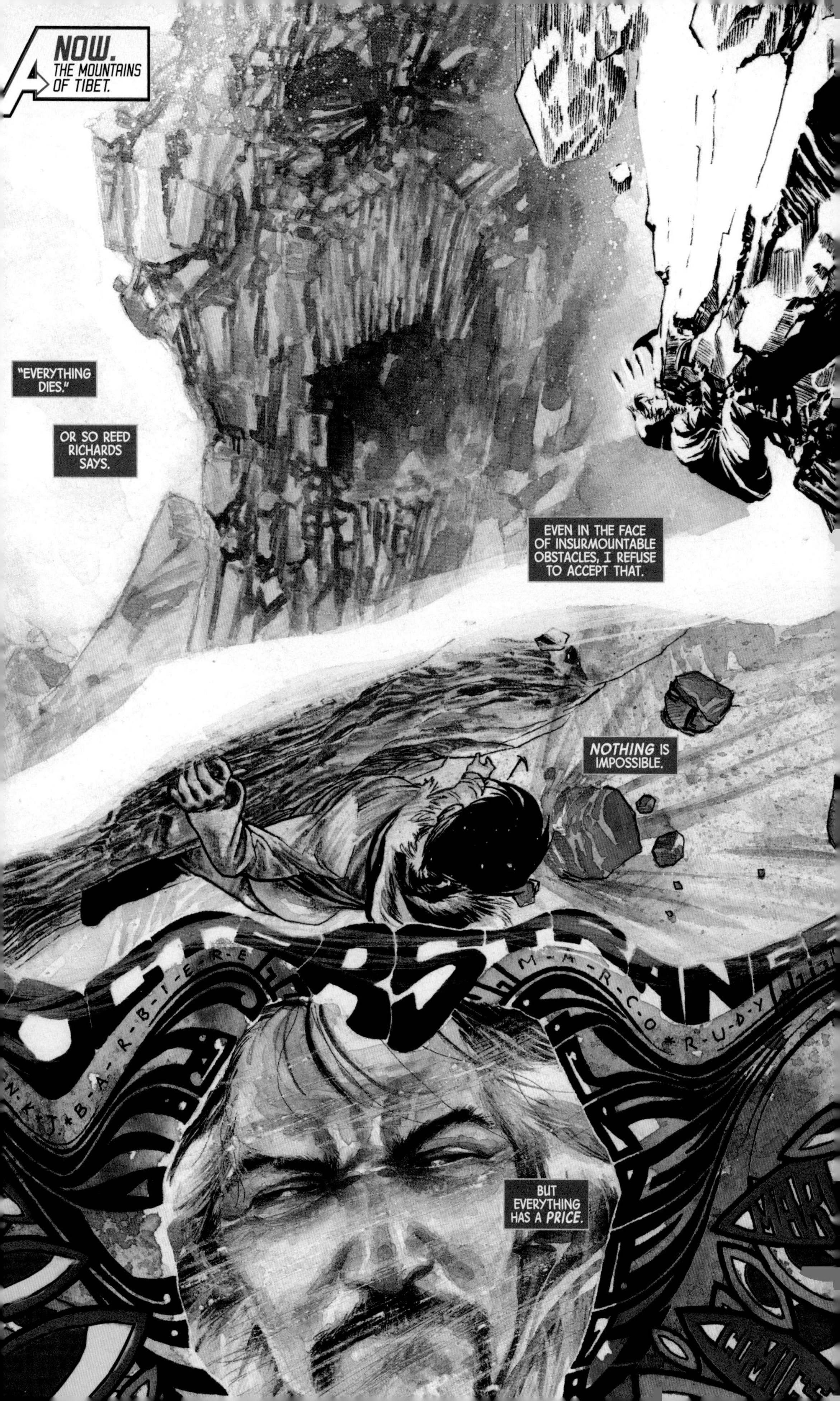
NOW.
THE MOUNTAINS OF TIBET.
"EVERYTHING DIES."
OR SO REED RICHARDS SAYS.
EVEN IN THE FACE OF INSURMOUNTABLE OBSTACLES, I REFUSE TO ACCEPT THAT.
NOTHING IS IMPOSSIBLE.
BUT EVERYTHING HAS A PRICE.

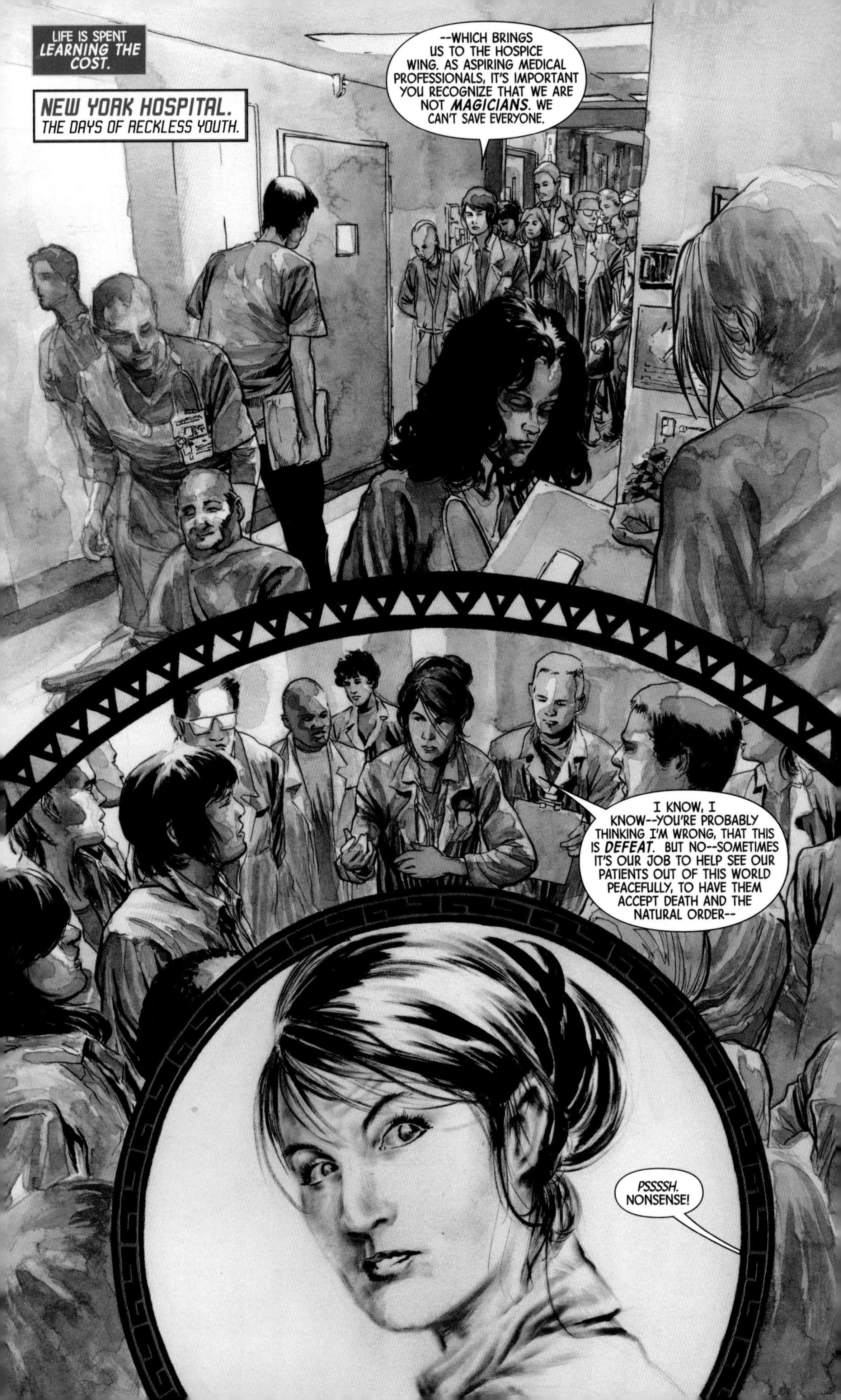
LIFE IS SPENT LEARNING THE COST.
NEW YORK HOSPITAL. THE DAYS OF RECKLESS YOUTH.
--WHICH BRINGS US TO THE HOSPICE WING. AS ASPIRING MEDICAL PROFESSIONALS, IT'S IMPORTANT YOU RECOGNIZE THAT WE ARE NOT MAGICIANS. WE CAN'T SAVE EVERYONE.
I KNOW, I KNOW--YOU'RE PROBABLY THINKING I'M WRONG, THAT THIS IS DEFEAT. BUT NO--SOMETIMES IT'S OUR JOB TO HELP SEE OUR PATIENTS OUT OF THIS WORLD PEACEFULLY, TO HAVE THEM ACCEPT DEATH AND THE NATURAL ORDER--
PSSSSH. NONSENSE!

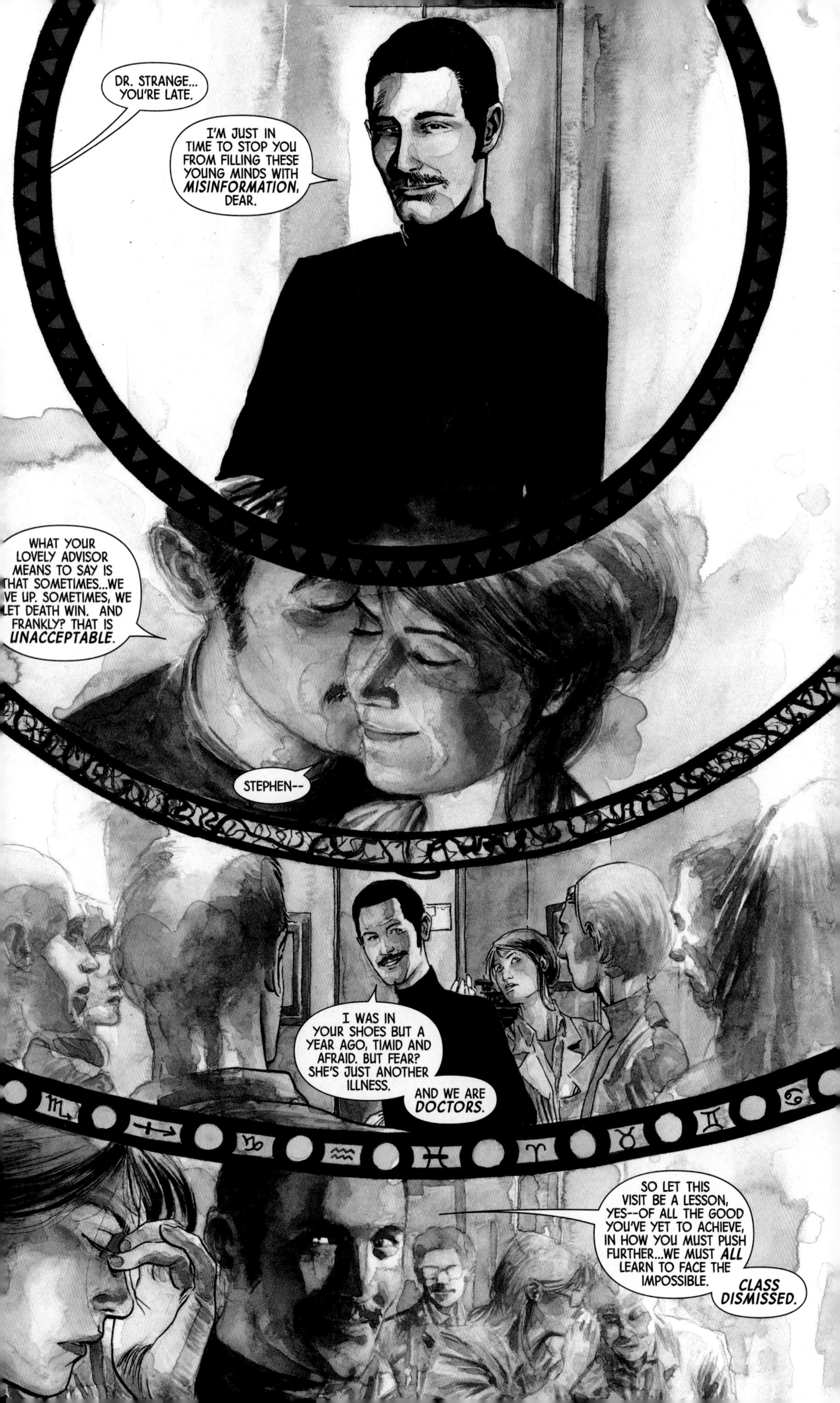

DR. STRANGE... YOU'RE LATE.
I'M JUST IN TIME TO STOP YOU FROM FILLING THESE YOUNG MINDS WITH MISINFORMATION, DEAR.
WHAT YOUR LOVELY ADVISOR MEANS TO SAY IS THAT SOMETIMES...WE VE UP. SOMETIMES, WE LET DEATH WIN. AND FRANKLY? THAT IS UNACCEPTABLE.
STEPHEN--
I WAS IN YOUR SHOES BUT A YEAR AGO, TIMID AND AFRAID. BUT FEAR? SHE'S JUST ANOTHER ILLNESS.
AND WE ARE DOCTORS.
SO LET THIS VISIT BE A LESSON, YES--OF ALL THE GOOD YOU'VE YET TO ACHIEVE, IN HOW YOU MUST PUSH FURTHER...WE MUST ALL LEARN TO FACE THE IMPOSSIBLE.
CLASS DISMISSED.

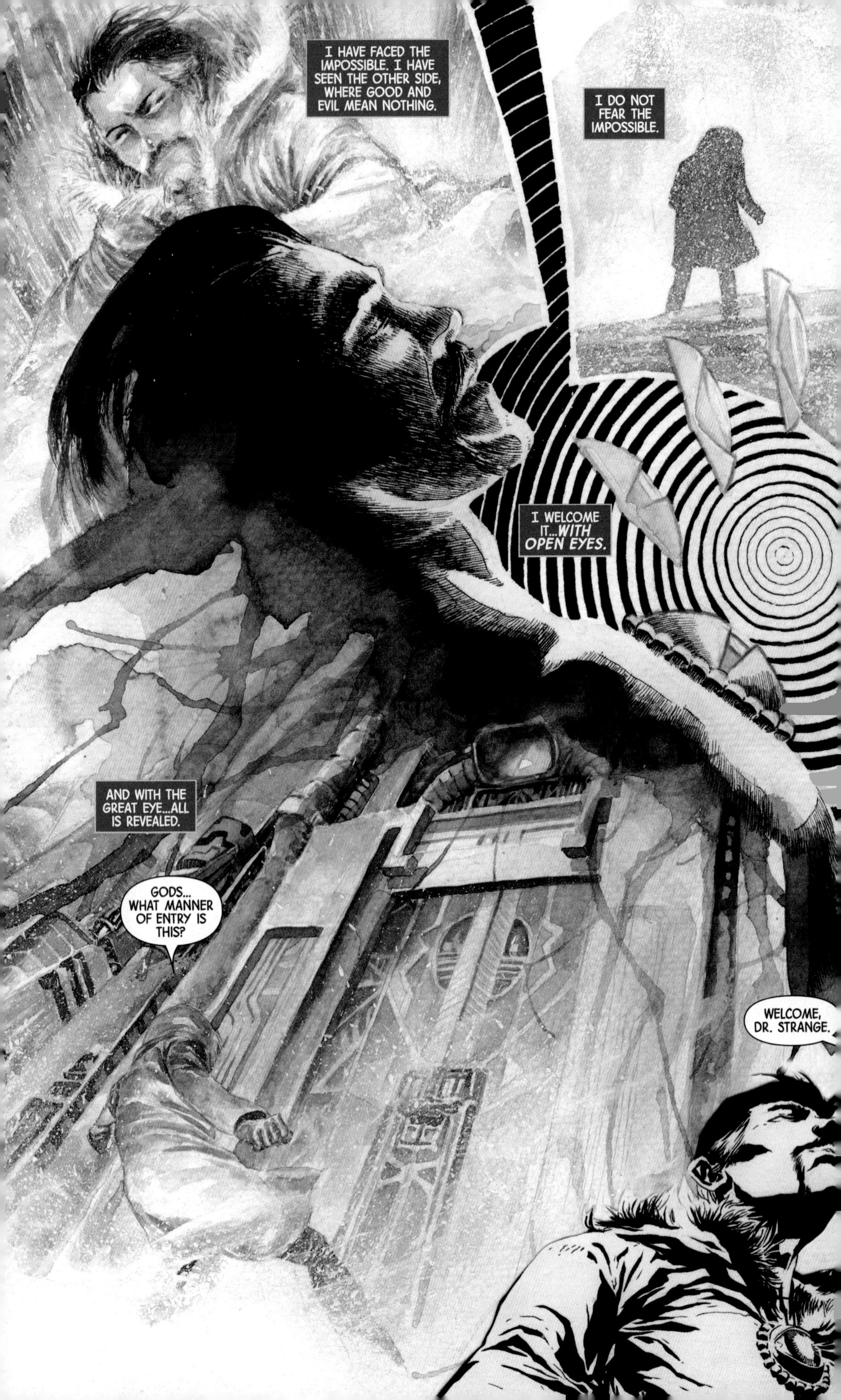

I HAVE FACED THE IMPOSSIBLE. I HAVE SEEN THE OTHER SIDE, WHERE GOOD AND EVIL MEAN NOTHING.
I DO NOT FEAR THE IMPOSSIBLE.
I WELCOME IT...*WITH OPEN EYES.*
AND WITH THE GREAT EYE...ALL IS REVEALED.
GODS... WHAT MANNER OF ENTRY IS THIS?
WELCOME, DR. STRANGE.

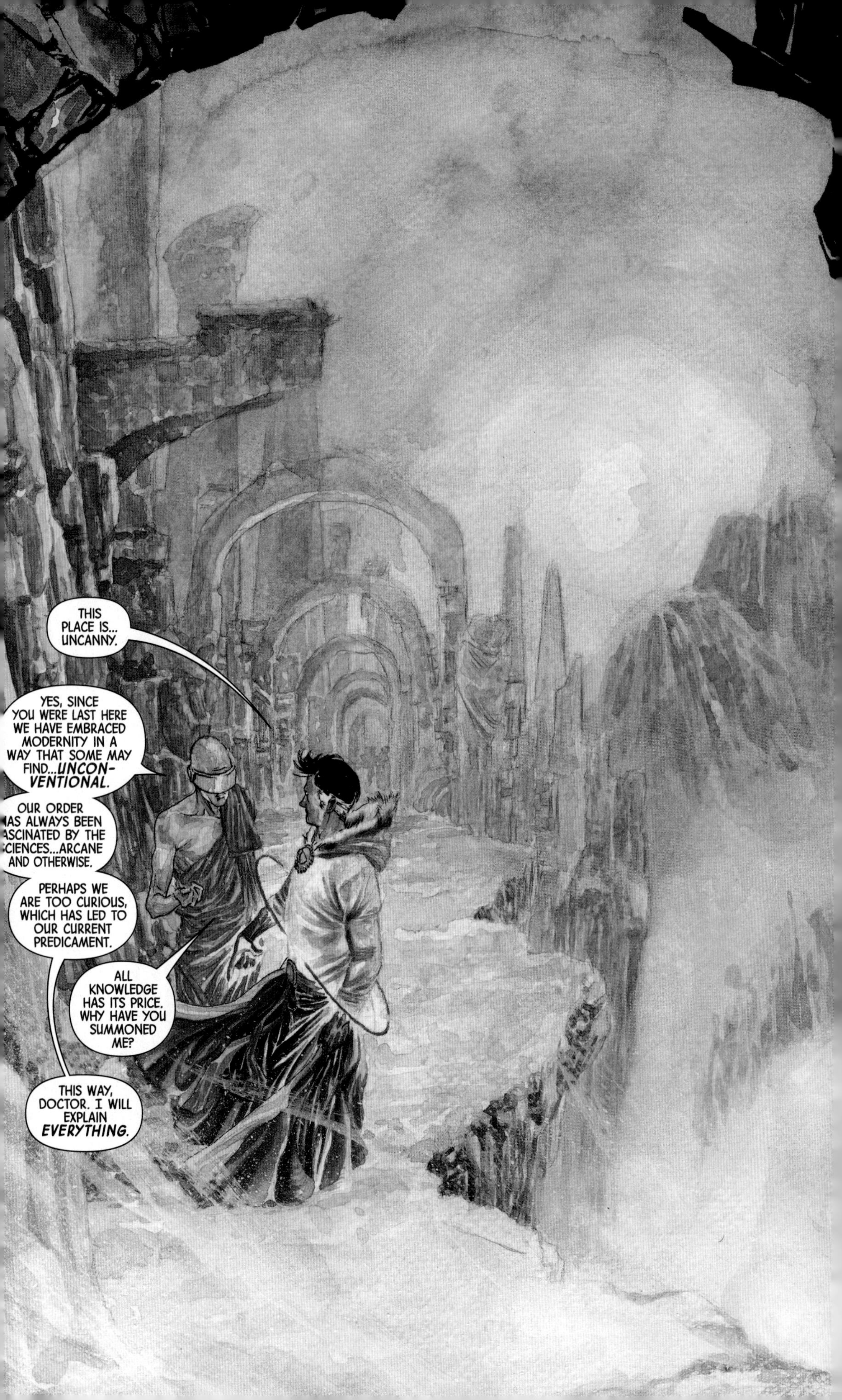

THIS PLACE IS... UNCANNY.
YES, SINCE YOU WERE LAST HERE WE HAVE EMBRACED MODERNITY IN A WAY THAT SOME MAY FIND...UNCONVENTIONAL.
OUR ORDER HAS ALWAYS BEEN FASCINATED BY THE SCIENCES...ARCANE AND OTHERWISE.
PERHAPS WE ARE TOO CURIOUS, WHICH HAS LED TO OUR CURRENT PREDICAMENT.
ALL KNOWLEDGE HAS ITS PRICE. WHY HAVE YOU SUMMONED ME?
THIS WAY, DOCTOR. I WILL EXPLAIN EVERYTHING.

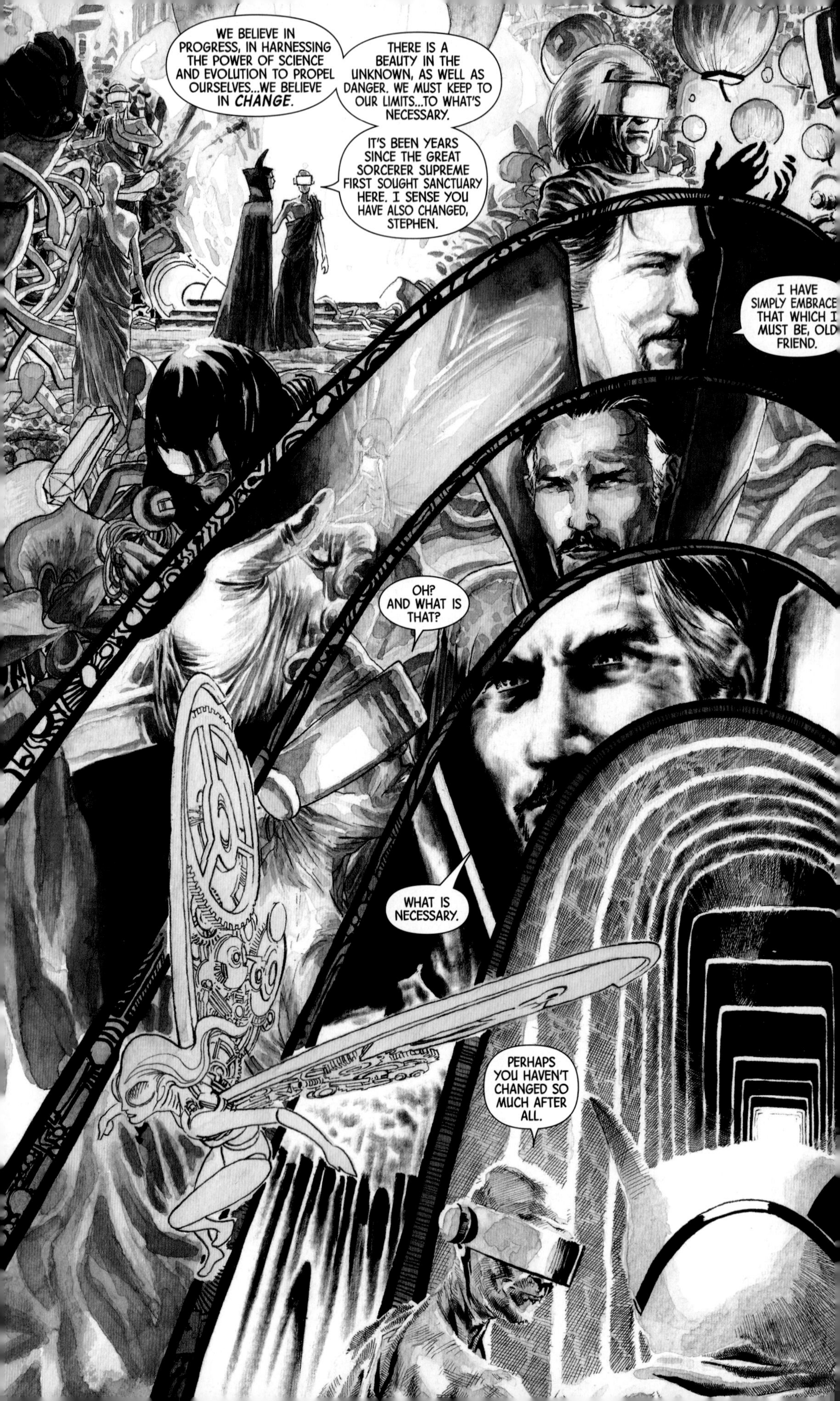
WE BELIEVE IN PROGRESS, IN HARNESSING THE POWER OF SCIENCE AND EVOLUTION TO PROPEL OURSELVES...WE BELIEVE IN *CHANGE*.
THERE IS A BEAUTY IN THE UNKNOWN, AS WELL AS DANGER. WE MUST KEEP TO OUR LIMITS...TO WHAT'S NECESSARY.
IT'S BEEN YEARS SINCE THE GREAT SORCERER SUPREME FIRST SOUGHT SANCTUARY HERE. I SENSE YOU HAVE ALSO CHANGED, STEPHEN.
I HAVE SIMPLY EMBRACE THAT WHICH I MUST BE, OLD FRIEND.
OH? AND WHAT IS THAT?
WHAT IS NECESSARY.
PERHAPS YOU HAVEN'T CHANGED SO MUCH AFTER ALL.

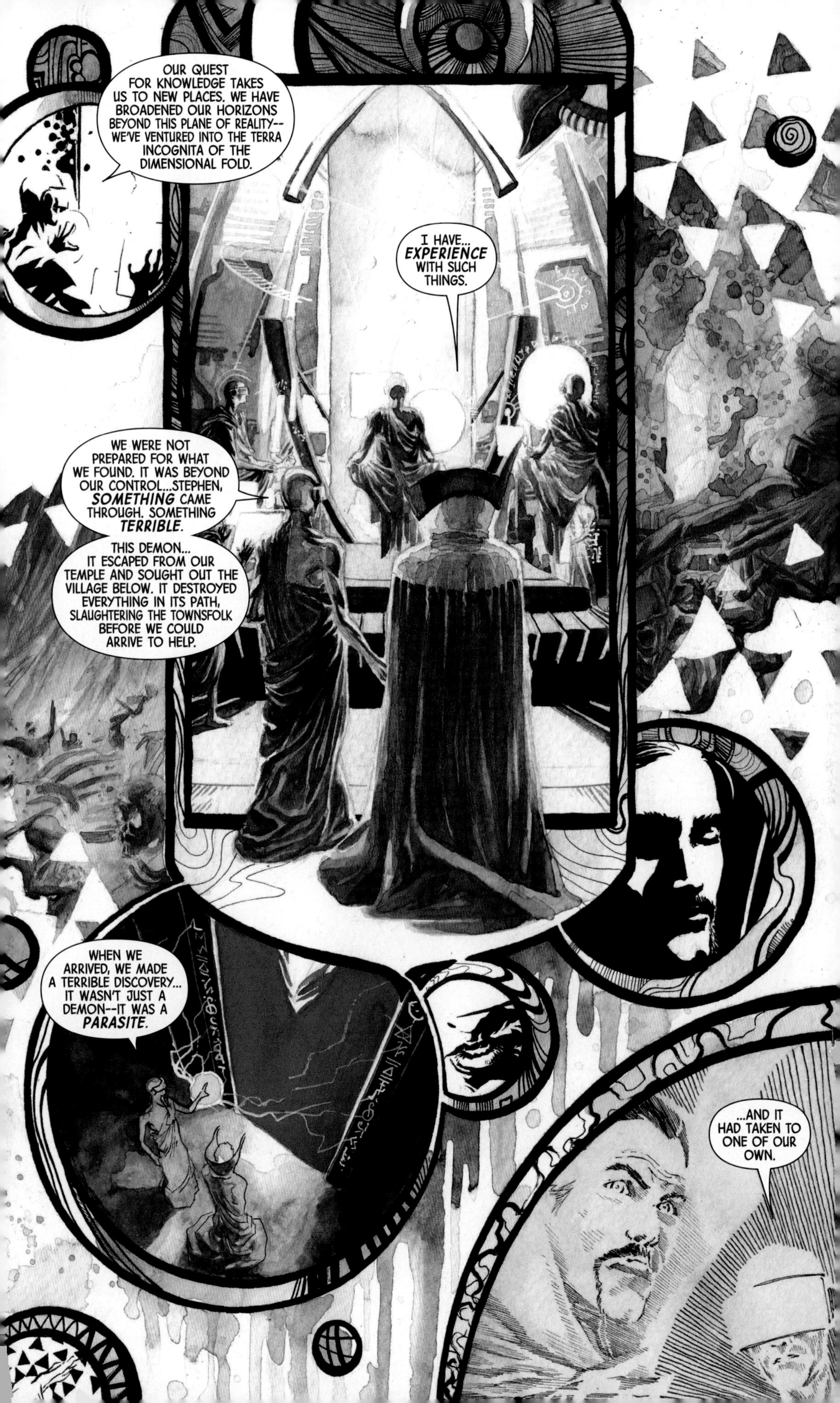
OUR QUEST FOR KNOWLEDGE TAKES US TO NEW PLACES. WE HAVE BROADENED OUR HORIZONS BEYOND THIS PLANE OF REALITY-- WE'VE VENTURED INTO THE TERRA INCOGNITA OF THE DIMENSIONAL FOLD.
I HAVE... EXPERIENCE WITH SUCH THINGS.
WE WERE NOT PREPARED FOR WHAT WE FOUND. IT WAS BEYOND OUR CONTROL...STEPHEN, SOMETHING CAME THROUGH. SOMETHING TERRIBLE.
THIS DEMON... IT ESCAPED FROM OUR TEMPLE AND SOUGHT OUT THE VILLAGE BELOW. IT DESTROYED EVERYTHING IN ITS PATH, SLAUGHTERING THE TOWNSFOLK BEFORE WE COULD ARRIVE TO HELP.
WHEN WE ARRIVED, WE MADE A TERRIBLE DISCOVERY... IT WASN'T JUST A DEMON--IT WAS A PARASITE.
...AND IT HAD TAKEN TO ONE OF OUR OWN.

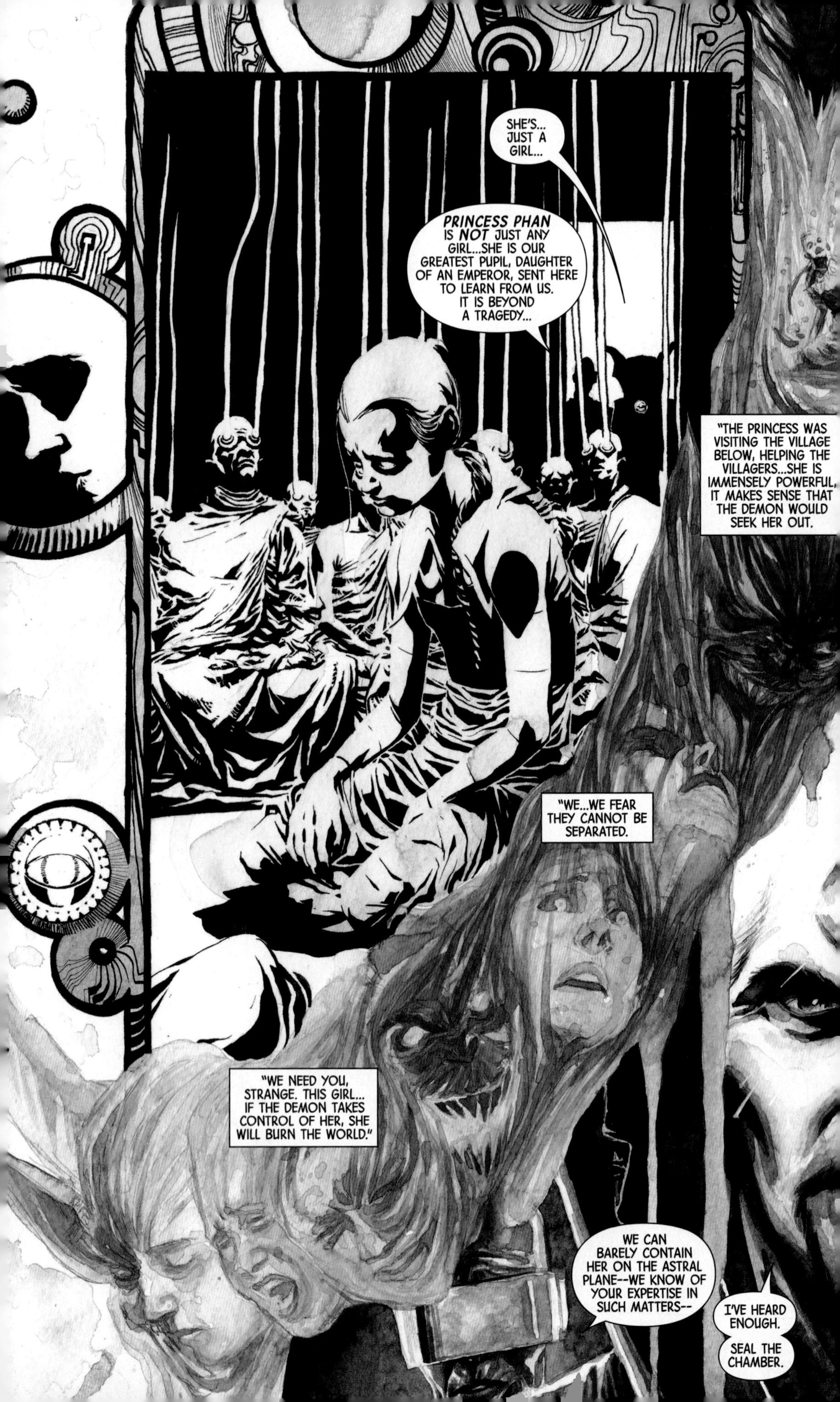
SHE'S... JUST A GIRL...
PRINCESS PHAN IS NOT JUST ANY GIRL...SHE IS OUR GREATEST PUPIL, DAUGHTER OF AN EMPEROR, SENT HERE TO LEARN FROM US. IT IS BEYOND A TRAGEDY...
"THE PRINCESS WAS VISITING THE VILLAGE BELOW, HELPING THE VILLAGERS...SHE IS IMMENSELY POWERFUL, IT MAKES SENSE THAT THE DEMON WOULD SEEK HER OUT.
"WE...WE FEAR THEY CANNOT BE SEPARATED.
"WE NEED YOU, STRANGE. THIS GIRL... IF THE DEMON TAKES CONTROL OF HER, SHE WILL BURN THE WORLD."
WE CAN BARELY CONTAIN HER ON THE ASTRAL PLANE--WE KNOW OF YOUR EXPERTISE IN SUCH MATTERS--
I'VE HEARD ENOUGH.
SEAL THE CHAMBER.

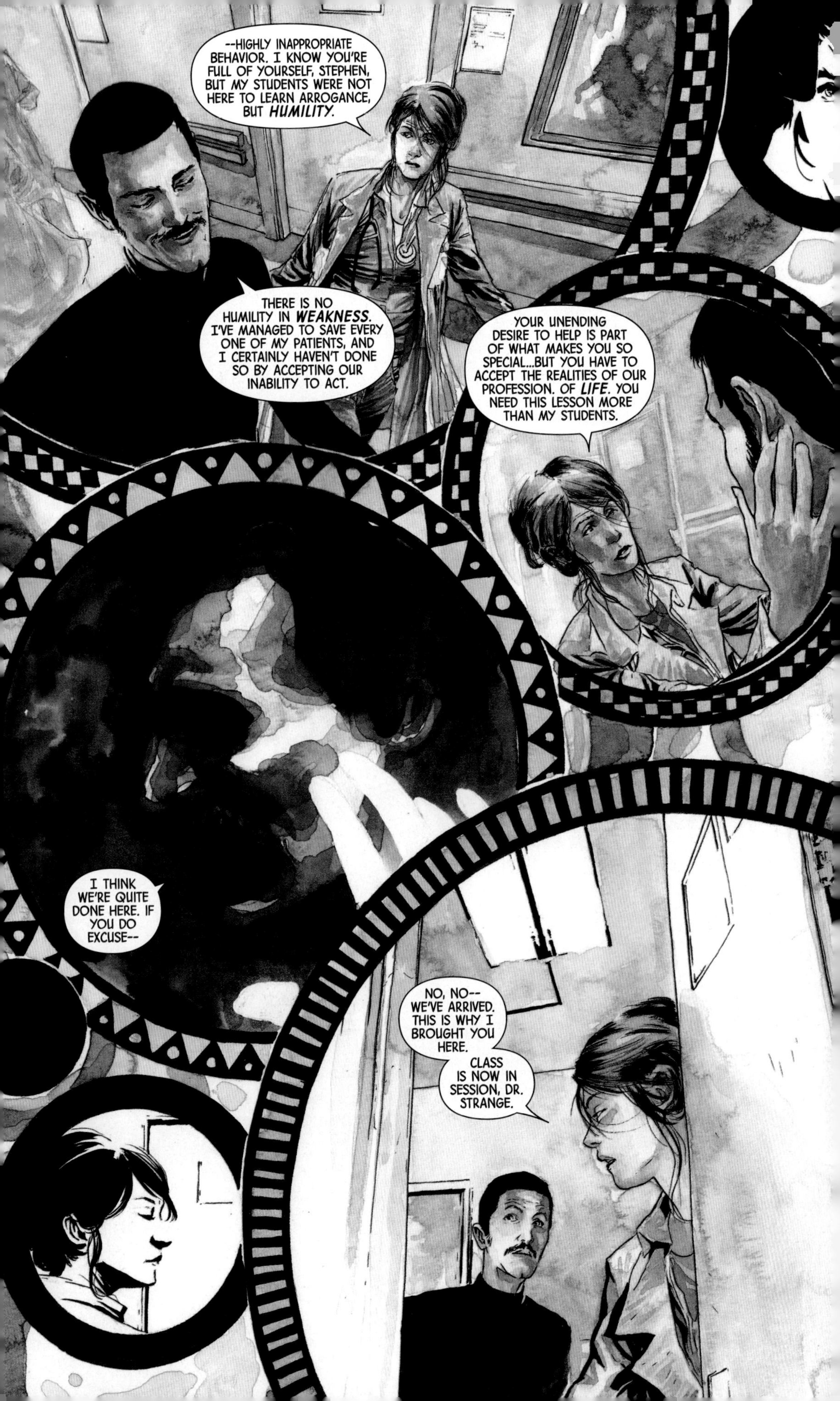
--HIGHLY INAPPROPRIATE BEHAVIOR. I KNOW YOU'RE FULL OF YOURSELF, STEPHEN, BUT MY STUDENTS WERE NOT HERE TO LEARN ARROGANCE, BUT HUMILITY.
THERE IS NO HUMILITY IN WEAKNESS. I'VE MANAGED TO SAVE EVERY ONE OF MY PATIENTS, AND I CERTAINLY HAVEN'T DONE SO BY ACCEPTING OUR INABILITY TO ACT.
YOUR UNENDING DESIRE TO HELP IS PART OF WHAT MAKES YOU SO SPECIAL...BUT YOU HAVE TO ACCEPT THE REALITIES OF OUR PROFESSION. OF LIFE. YOU NEED THIS LESSON MORE THAN MY STUDENTS.
I THINK WE'RE QUITE DONE HERE. IF YOU DO EXCUSE--
NO, NO-- WE'VE ARRIVED. THIS IS WHY I BROUGHT YOU HERE.
CLASS IS NOW IN SESSION, DR. STRANGE.

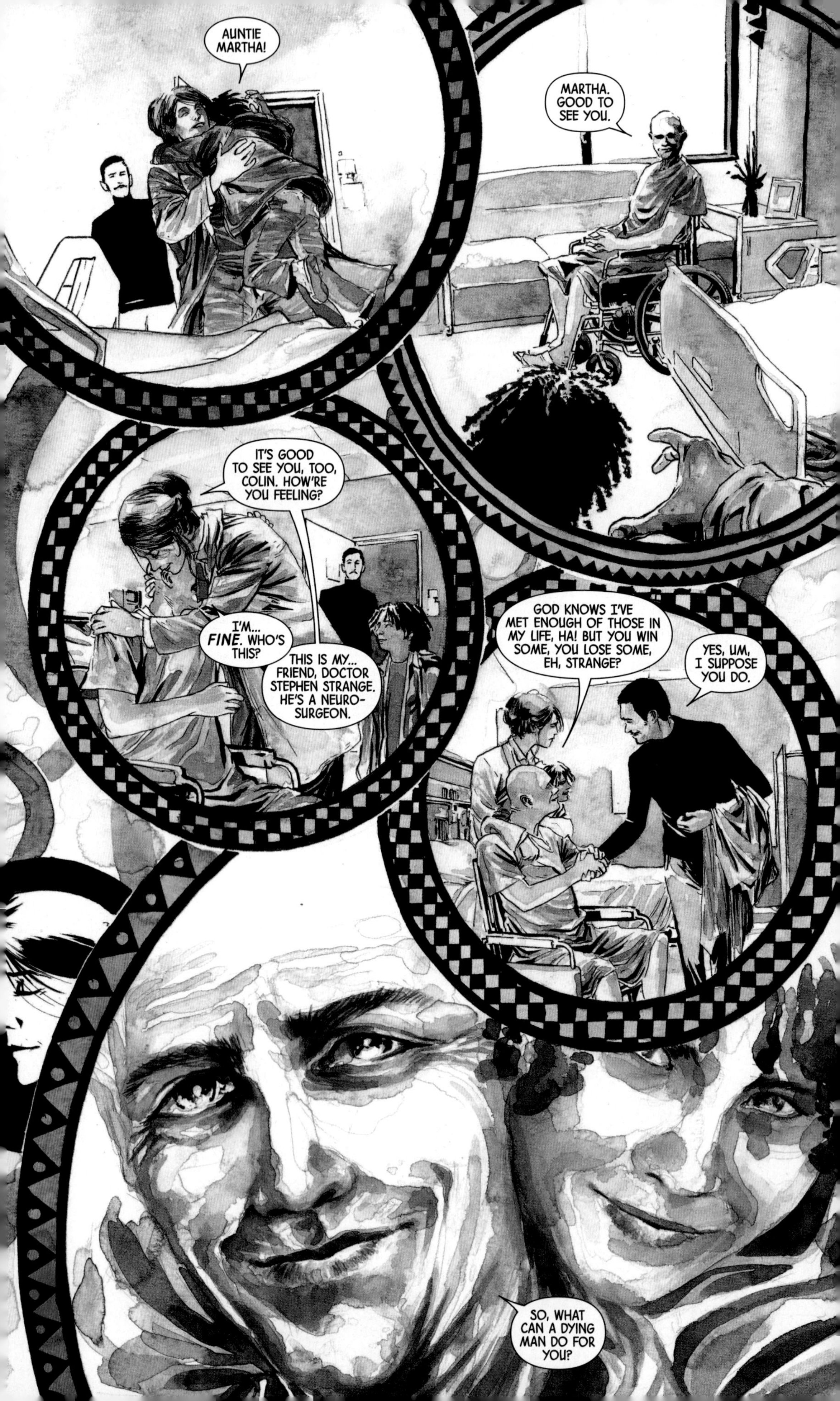
AUNTIE MARTHA!
MARTHA. GOOD TO SEE YOU.
IT'S GOOD TO SEE YOU, TOO, COLIN. HOW'RE YOU FEELING?
I'M... *FINE*. WHO'S THIS?
THIS IS MY... FRIEND, DOCTOR STEPHEN STRANGE. HE'S A NEURO-SURGEON.
GOD KNOWS I'VE MET ENOUGH OF THOSE IN MY LIFE, HA! BUT YOU WIN SOME, YOU LOSE SOME, EH, STRANGE?
YES, UM, I SUPPOSE YOU DO.
SO, WHAT CAN A DYING MAN DO FOR YOU?

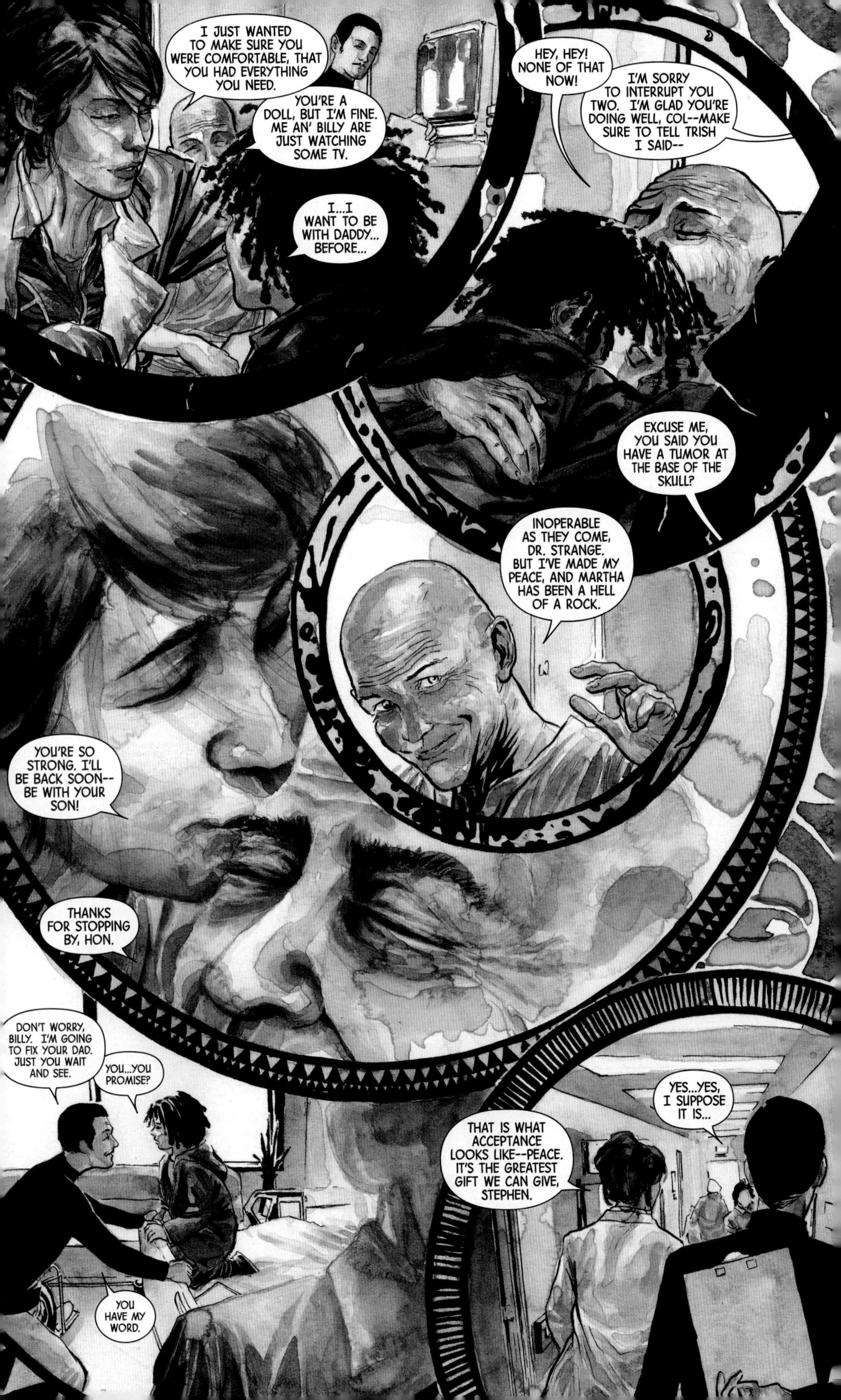
I JUST WANTED TO MAKE SURE YOU WERE COMFORTABLE, THAT YOU HAD EVERYTHING YOU NEED.
YOU'RE A DOLL, BUT I'M FINE. ME AN' BILLY ARE JUST WATCHING SOME TV.
I...I WANT TO BE WITH DADDY... BEFORE...
HEY, HEY! NONE OF THAT NOW!
I'M SORRY TO INTERRUPT YOU TWO. I'M GLAD YOU'RE DOING WELL, COL--MAKE SURE TO TELL TRISH I SAID--
EXCUSE ME, YOU SAID YOU HAVE A TUMOR AT THE BASE OF THE SKULL?
INOPERABLE AS THEY COME, DR. STRANGE. BUT I'VE MADE MY PEACE, AND MARTHA HAS BEEN A HELL OF A ROCK.
YOU'RE SO STRONG. I'LL BE BACK SOON--BE WITH YOUR SON!
THANKS FOR STOPPING BY, HON.
DON'T WORRY, BILLY. I'M GOING TO FIX YOUR DAD. JUST YOU WAIT AND SEE.
YOU...YOU PROMISE?
YOU HAVE MY WORD.
THAT IS WHAT ACCEPTANCE LOOKS LIKE--PEACE. IT'S THE GREATEST GIFT WE CAN GIVE, STEPHEN.
YES...YES, I SUPPOSE IT IS...

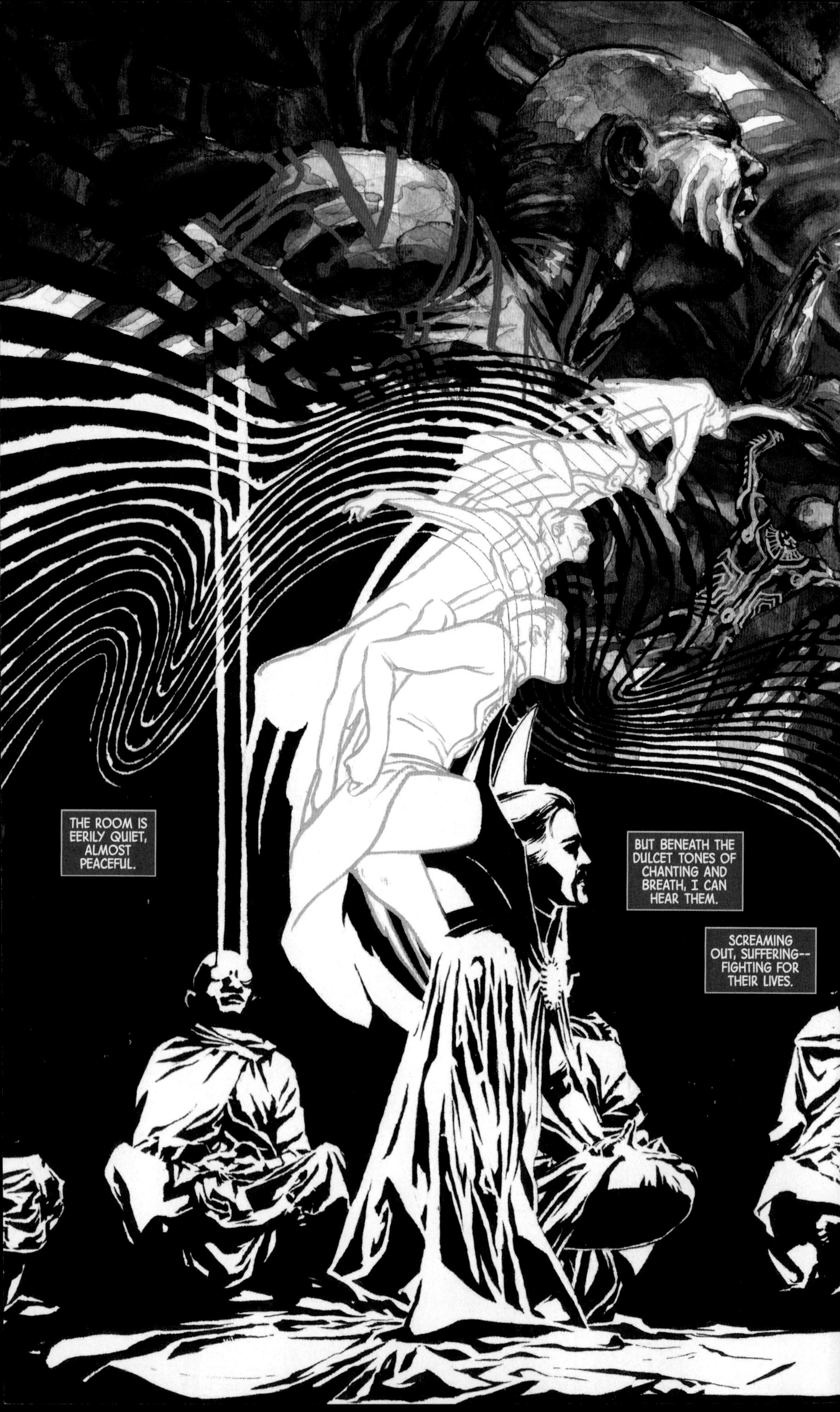
THE ROOM IS EERILY QUIET, ALMOST PEACEFUL.
BUT BENEATH THE DULCET TONES OF CHANTING AND BREATH, I CAN HEAR THEM.
SCREAMING OUT, SUFFERING-- FIGHTING FOR THEIR LIVES.

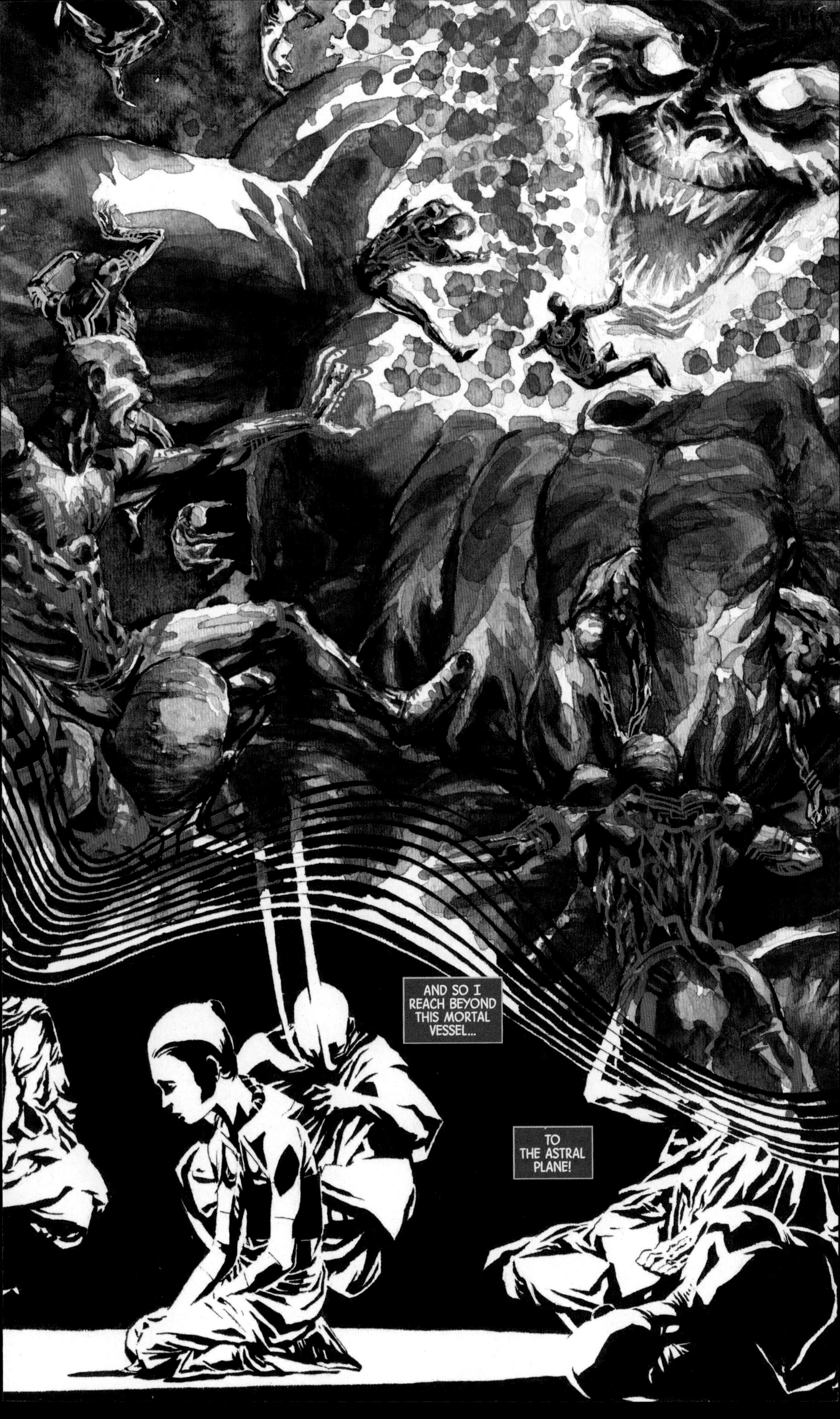
AND SO I REACH BEYOND THIS MORTAL VESSEL...
TO THE ASTRAL PLANE!

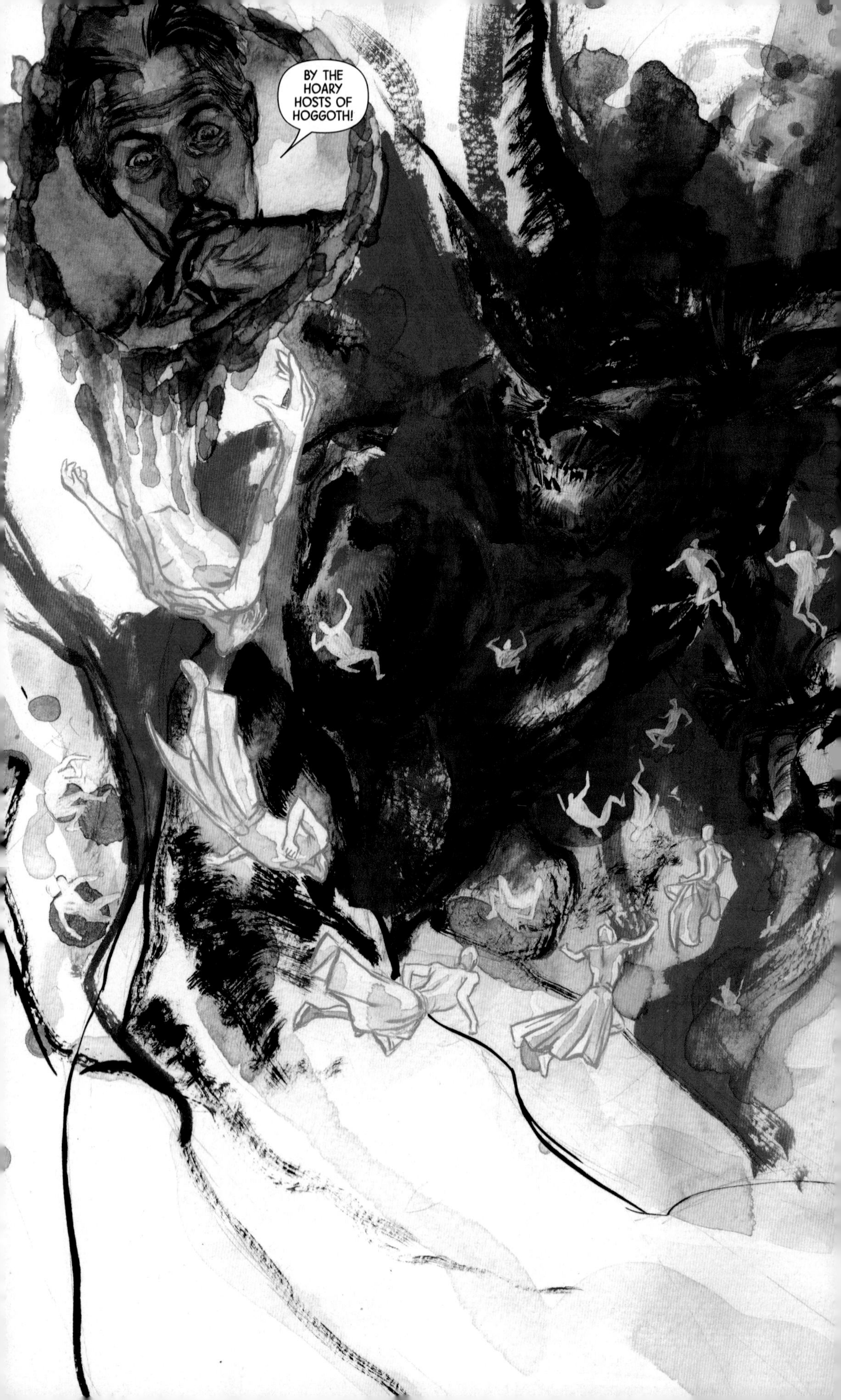
BY THE HOARY HOSTS OF HOGGOTH!

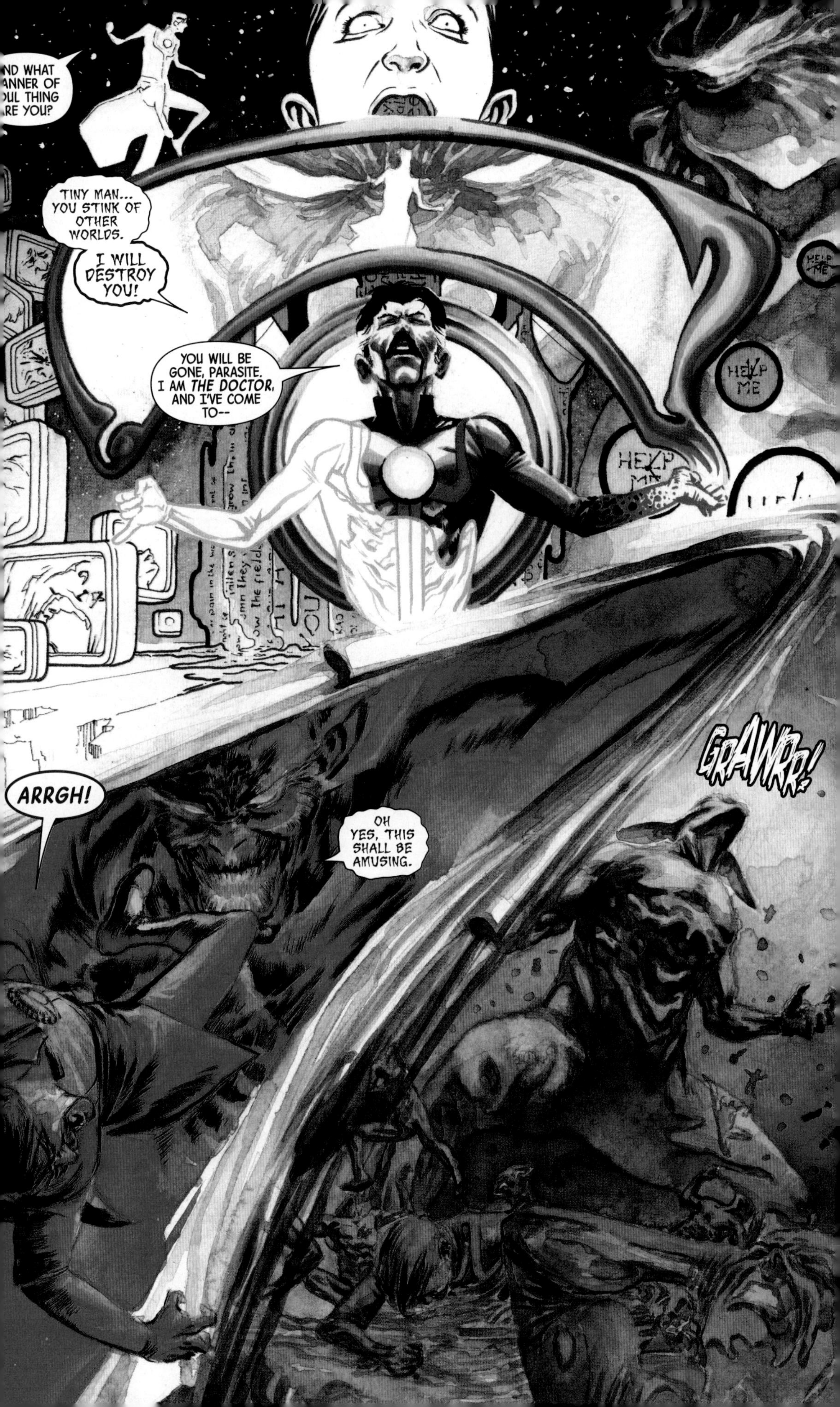
ND WHAT ANNER OF OUL THING RE YOU?
TINY MAN... YOU STINK OF OTHER WORLDS.
I WILL DESTROY YOU!
HELP ME
YOU WILL BE GONE, PARASITE. I AM *THE DOCTOR*, AND I'VE COME TO--
HELP ME
HELP ME
GRAWRR!
ARRGH!
OH YES, THIS SHALL BE AMUSING.

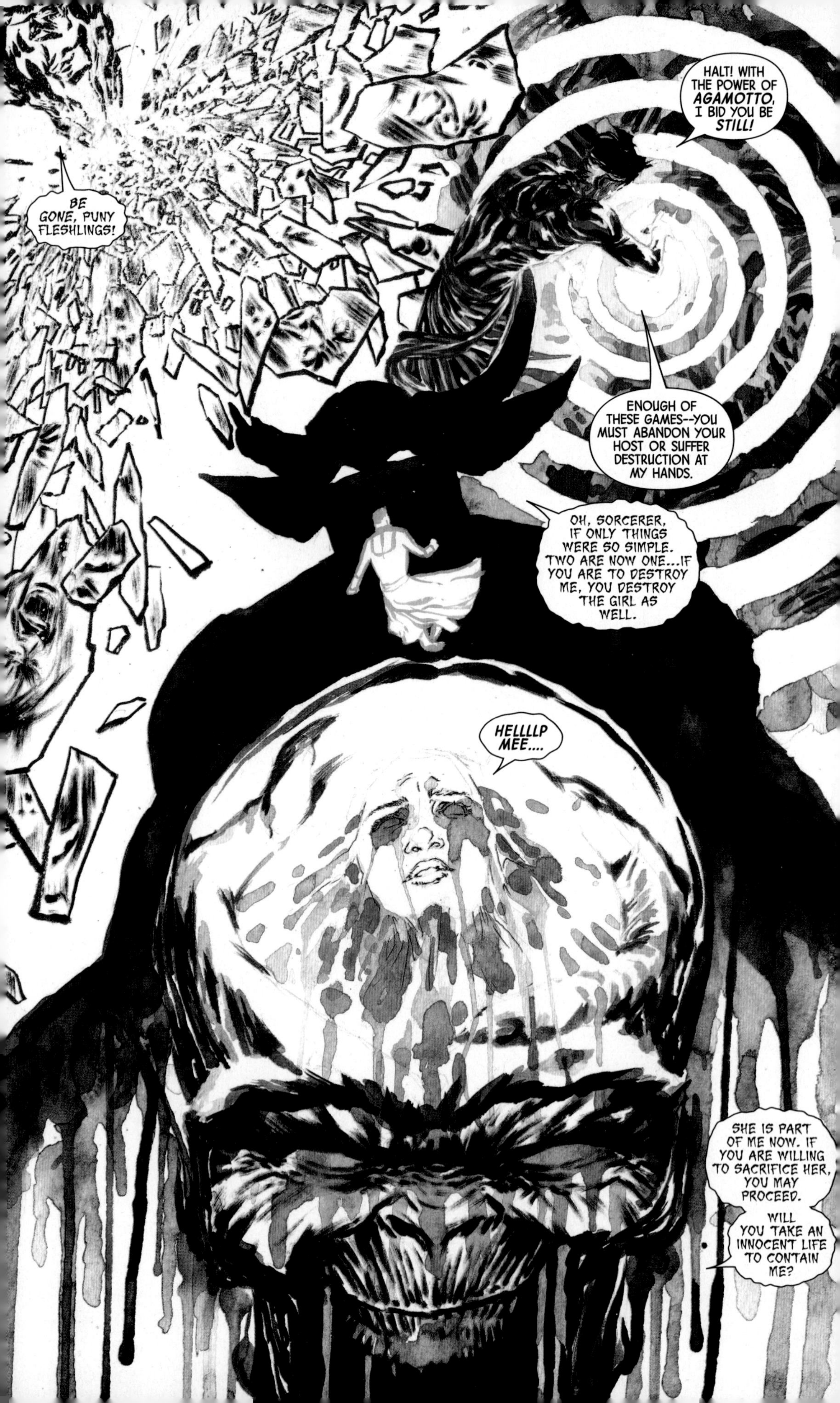
HALT! WITH THE POWER OF AGAMOTTO, I BID YOU BE STILL!
BE GONE, PUNY FLESHLINGS!
ENOUGH OF THESE GAMES--YOU MUST ABANDON YOUR HOST OR SUFFER DESTRUCTION AT MY HANDS.
OH, SORCERER, IF ONLY THINGS WERE SO SIMPLE. TWO ARE NOW ONE...IF YOU ARE TO DESTROY ME, YOU DESTROY THE GIRL AS WELL.
HELLLLP MEE....
SHE IS PART OF ME NOW. IF YOU ARE WILLING TO SACRIFICE HER, YOU MAY PROCEED.
WILL YOU TAKE AN INNOCENT LIFE TO CONTAIN ME?

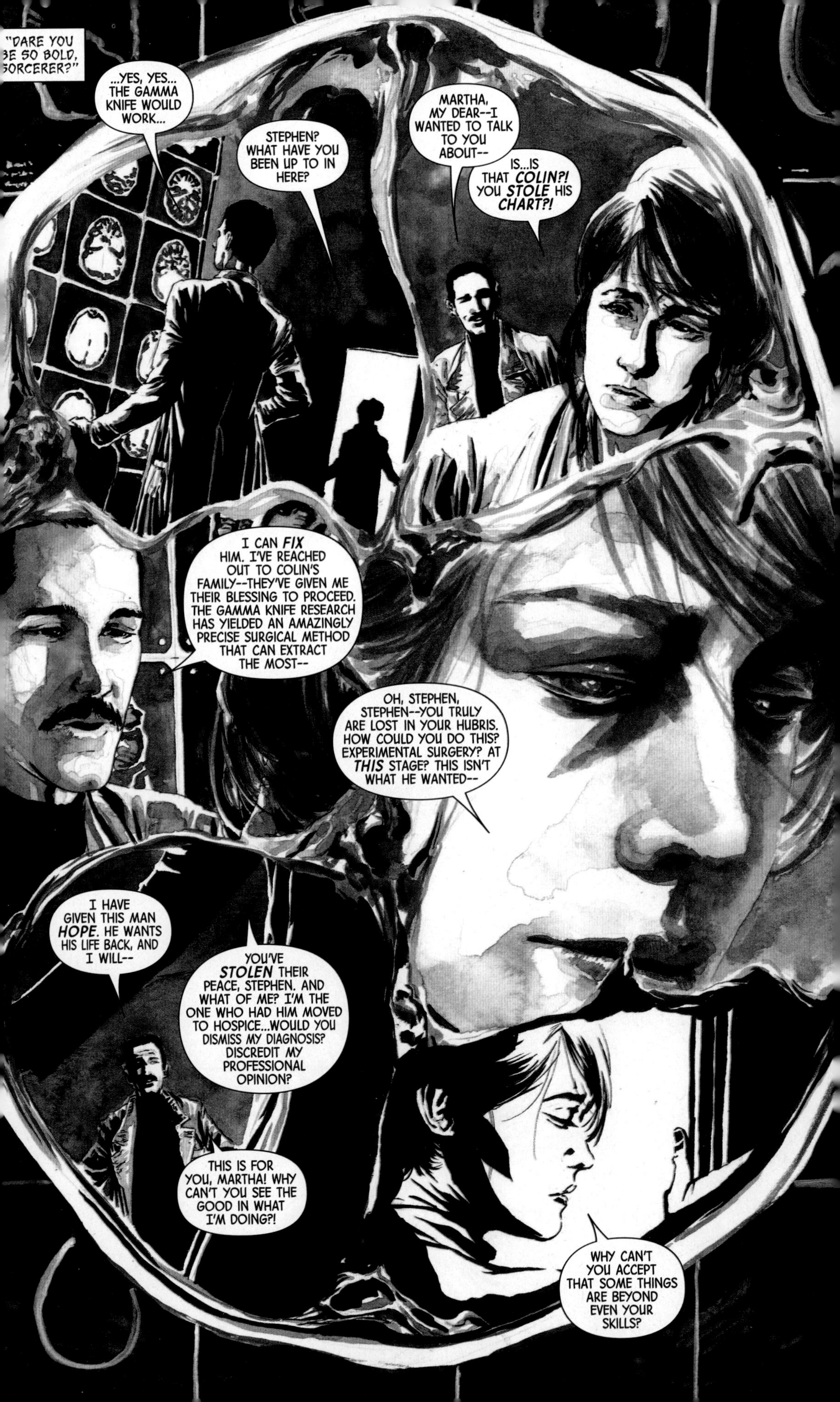
"DARE YOU BE SO BOLD, SORCERER?"
...YES, YES... THE GAMMA KNIFE WOULD WORK...
STEPHEN? WHAT HAVE YOU BEEN UP TO IN HERE?
MARTHA, MY DEAR--I WANTED TO TALK TO YOU ABOUT--
IS...IS THAT COLIN?! YOU STOLE HIS CHART?!
I CAN FIX HIM. I'VE REACHED OUT TO COLIN'S FAMILY--THEY'VE GIVEN ME THEIR BLESSING TO PROCEED. THE GAMMA KNIFE RESEARCH HAS YIELDED AN AMAZINGLY PRECISE SURGICAL METHOD THAT CAN EXTRACT THE MOST--
OH, STEPHEN, STEPHEN--YOU TRULY ARE LOST IN YOUR HUBRIS. HOW COULD YOU DO THIS? EXPERIMENTAL SURGERY? AT THIS STAGE? THIS ISN'T WHAT HE WANTED--
I HAVE GIVEN THIS MAN HOPE. HE WANTS HIS LIFE BACK, AND I WILL--
YOU'VE STOLEN THEIR PEACE, STEPHEN. AND WHAT OF ME? I'M THE ONE WHO HAD HIM MOVED TO HOSPICE...WOULD YOU DISMISS MY DIAGNOSIS? DISCREDIT MY PROFESSIONAL OPINION?
THIS IS FOR YOU, MARTHA! WHY CAN'T YOU SEE THE GOOD IN WHAT I'M DOING?!
WHY CAN'T YOU ACCEPT THAT SOME THINGS ARE BEYOND EVEN YOUR SKILLS?

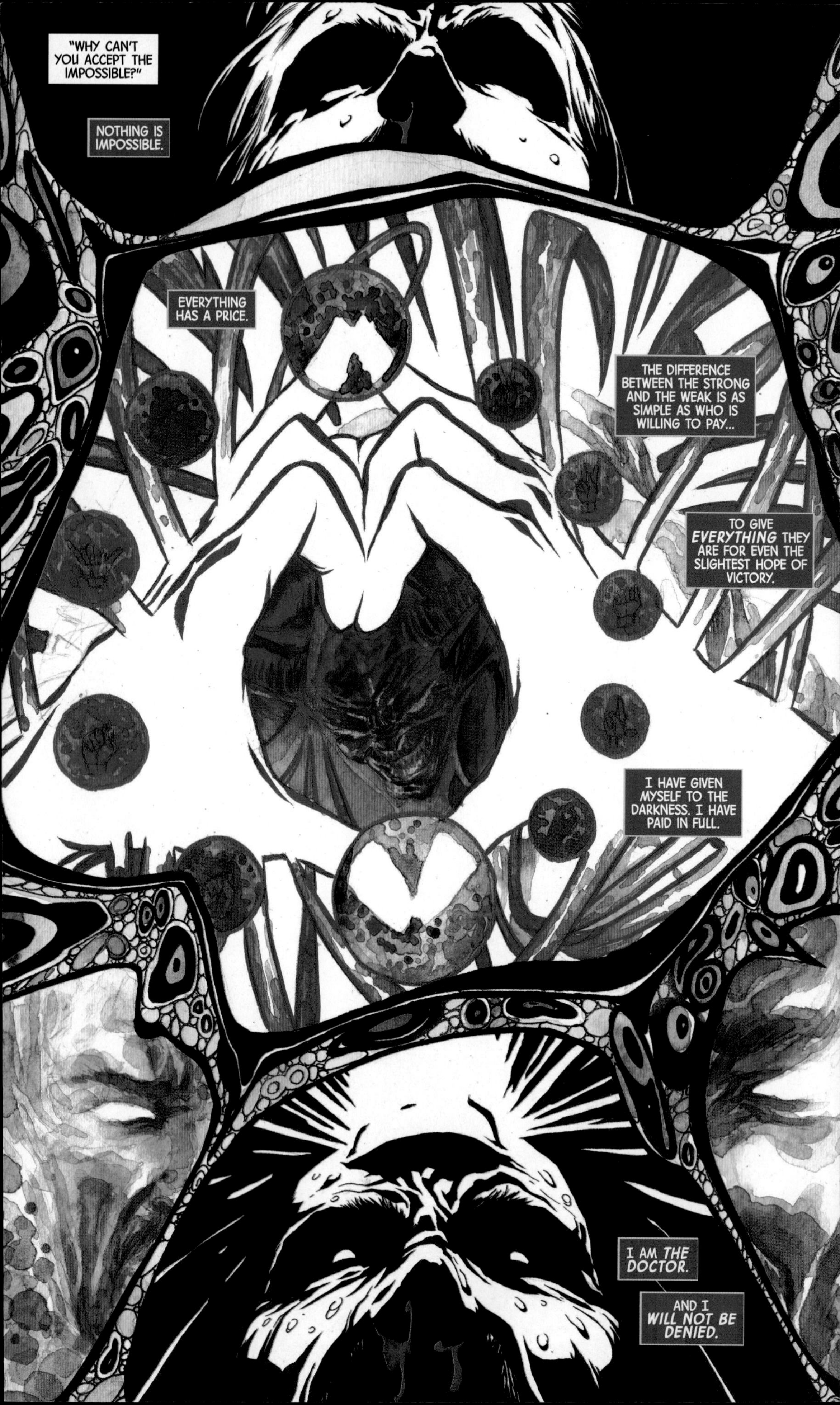
"WHY CAN'T YOU ACCEPT THE IMPOSSIBLE?"
NOTHING IS IMPOSSIBLE.
EVERYTHING HAS A PRICE.
THE DIFFERENCE BETWEEN THE STRONG AND THE WEAK IS AS SIMPLE AS WHO IS WILLING TO PAY...
TO GIVE *EVERYTHING* THEY ARE FOR EVEN THE SLIGHTEST HOPE OF VICTORY.
I HAVE GIVEN MYSELF TO THE DARKNESS. I HAVE PAID IN FULL.
I AM *THE DOCTOR.*
AND I *WILL NOT BE DENIED.*

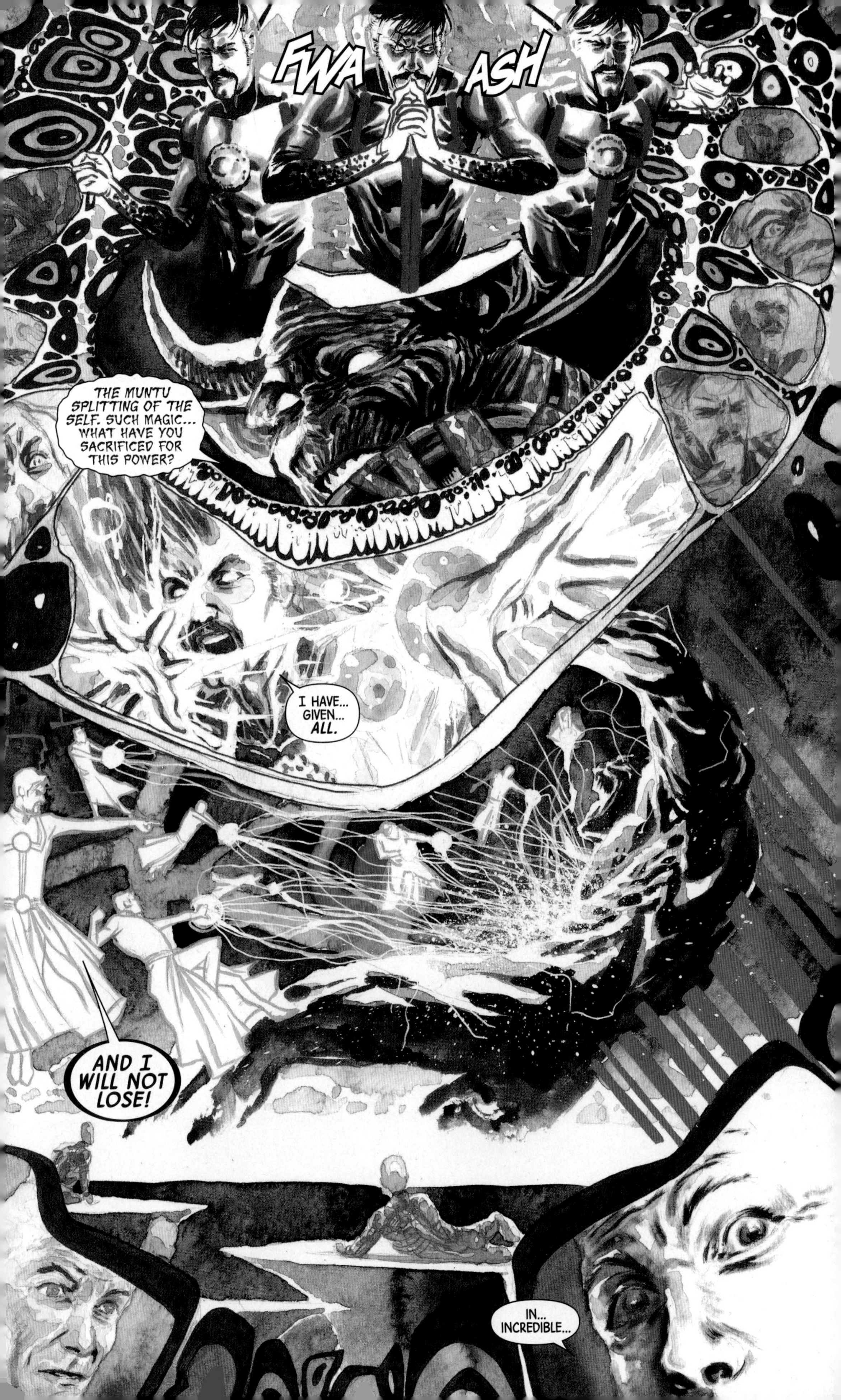
FWA ASH
THE MUNTU SPLITTING OF THE SELF. SUCH MAGIC... WHAT HAVE YOU SACRIFICED FOR THIS POWER?
I HAVE... GIVEN... ALL.
AND I WILL NOT LOSE!
IN... INCREDIBLE...

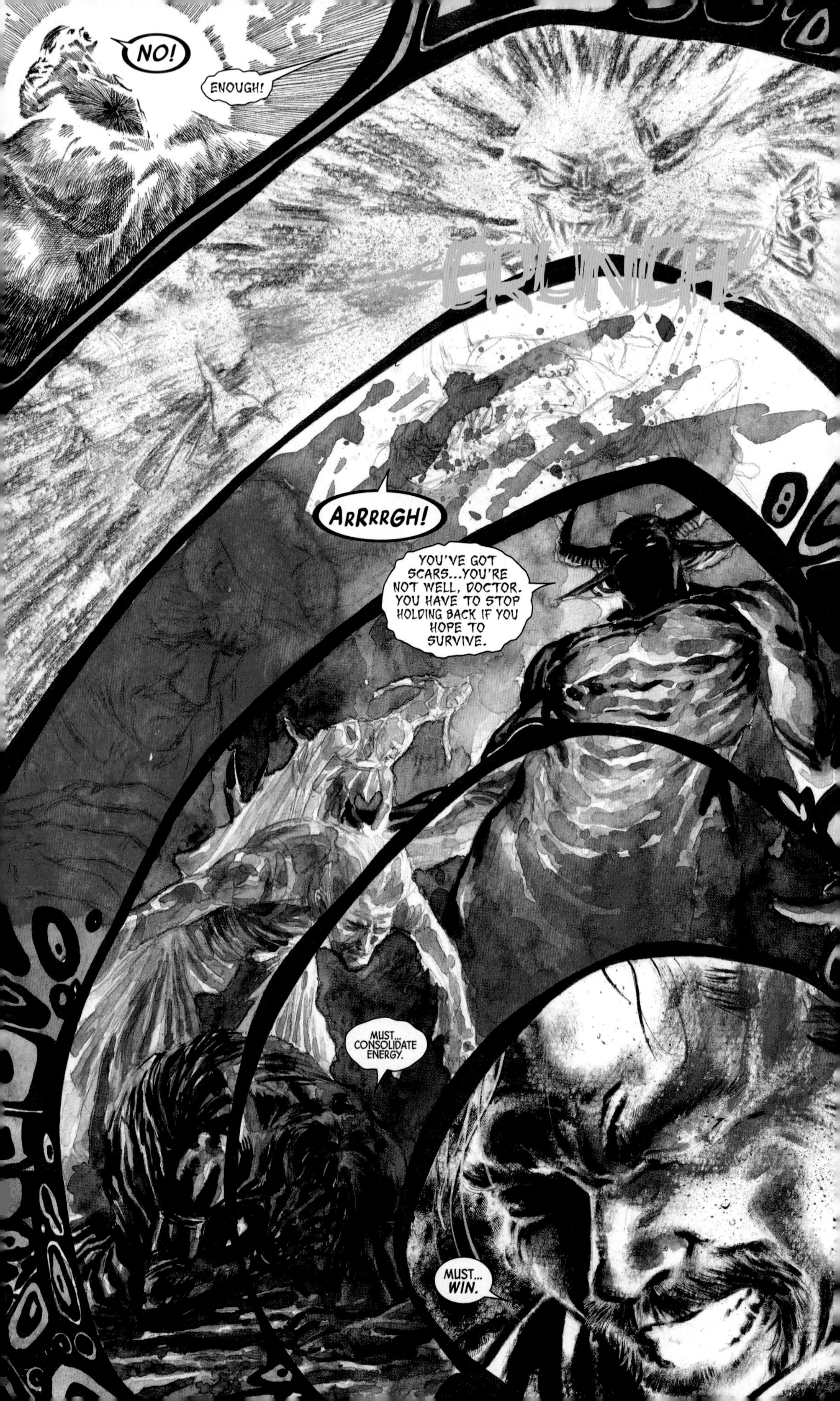
NO!
ENOUGH!
CRUNCH!
ARRRRGH!
YOU'VE GOT SCARS...YOU'RE NOT WELL, DOCTOR. YOU HAVE TO STOP HOLDING BACK IF YOU HOPE TO SURVIVE.
MUST... CONSOLIDATE ENERGY.
MUST... WIN.

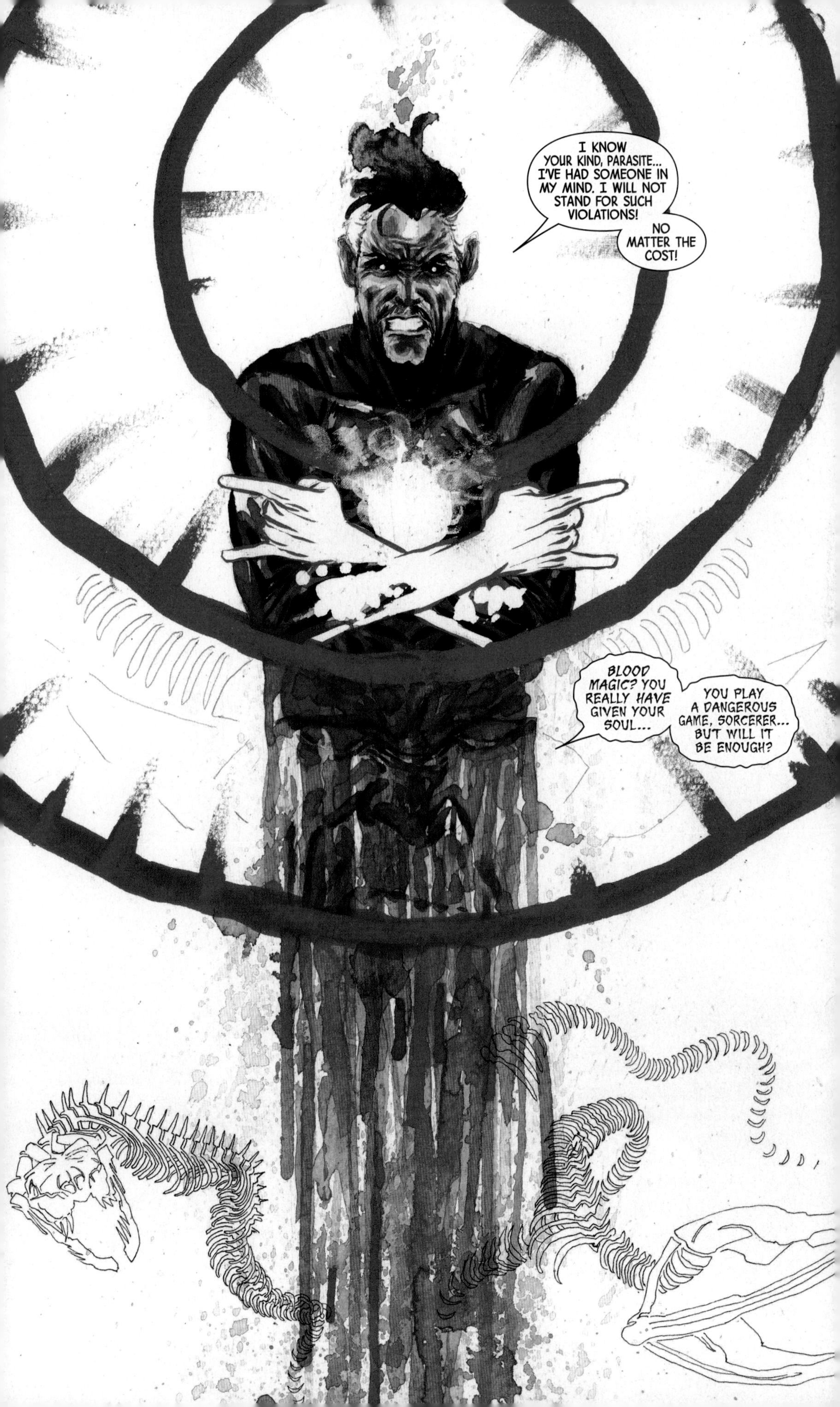
I KNOW YOUR KIND, PARASITE... I'VE HAD SOMEONE IN MY MIND. I WILL NOT STAND FOR SUCH VIOLATIONS!
NO MATTER THE COST!
BLOOD MAGIC? YOU REALLY HAVE GIVEN YOUR SOUL...
YOU PLAY A DANGEROUS GAME, SORCERER... BUT WILL IT BE ENOUGH?

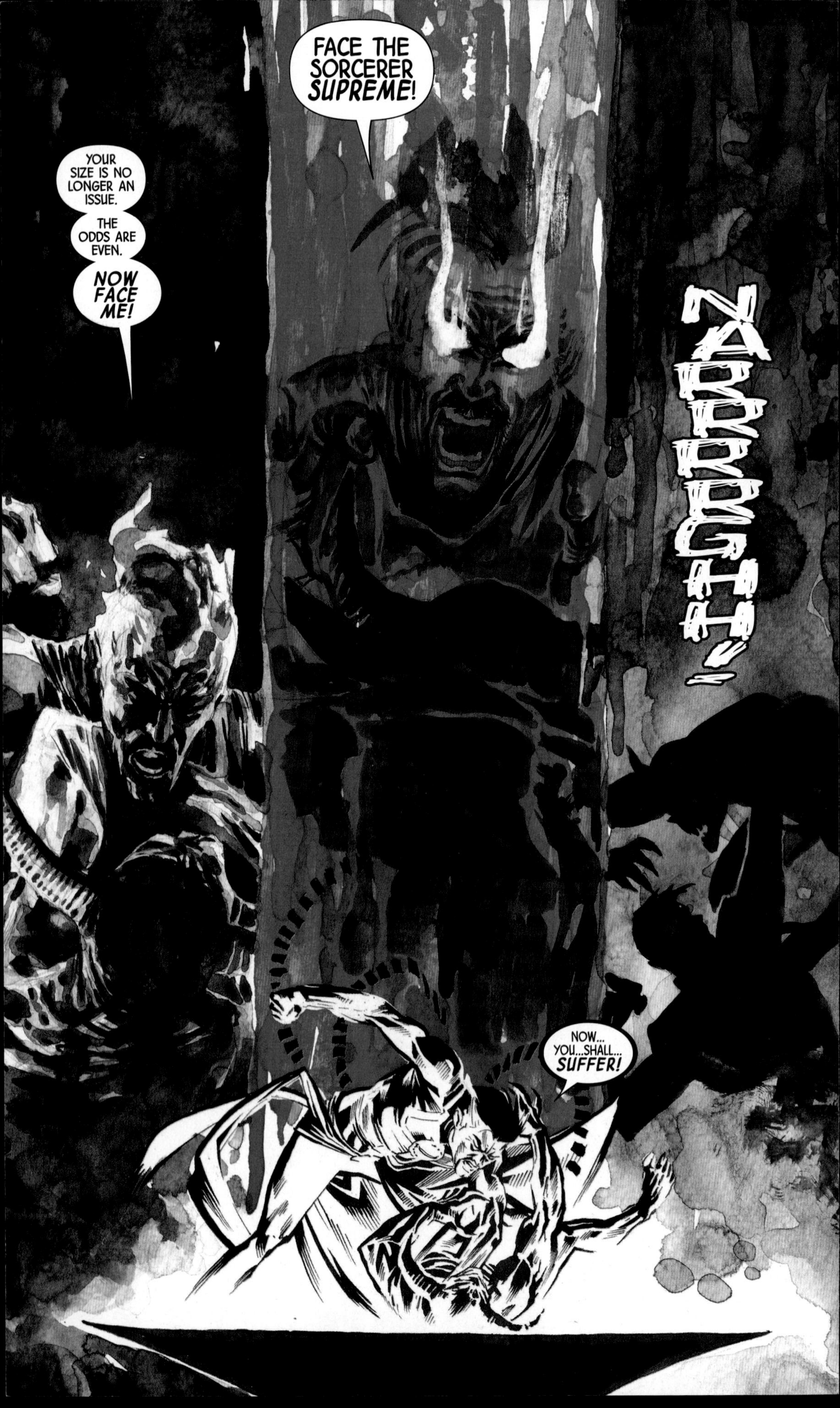
YOUR SIZE IS NO LONGER AN ISSUE.
THE ODDS ARE EVEN.
NOW FACE ME!
FACE THE SORCERER SUPREME!
ZARRRGHH!
NOW... YOU...SHALL... SUFFER!

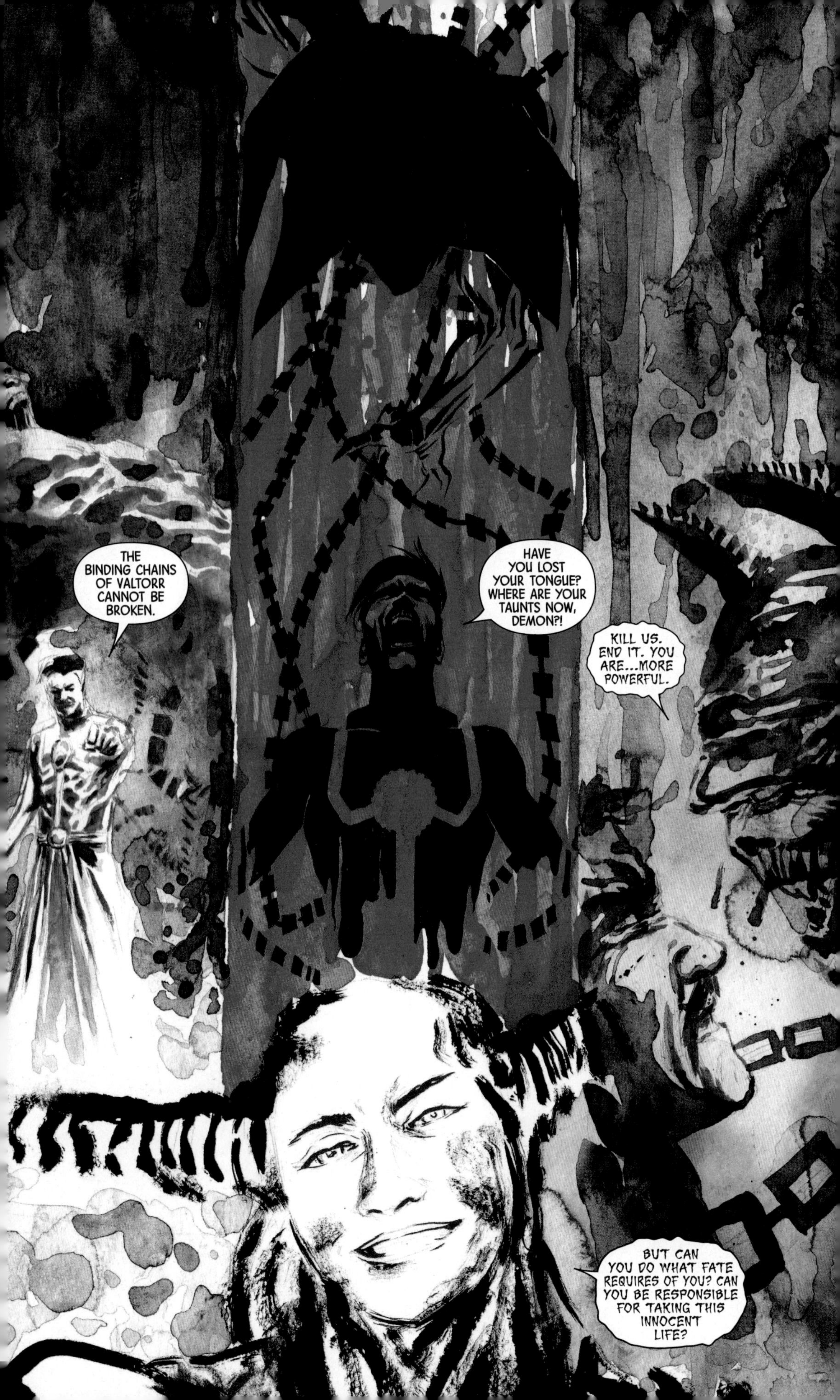
THE BINDING CHAINS OF VALTORR CANNOT BE BROKEN.
HAVE YOU LOST YOUR TONGUE? WHERE ARE YOUR TAUNTS NOW, DEMON?!
KILL US. END IT. YOU ARE...MORE POWERFUL.
BUT CAN YOU DO WHAT FATE REQUIRES OF YOU? CAN YOU BE RESPONSIBLE FOR TAKING THIS INNOCENT LIFE?

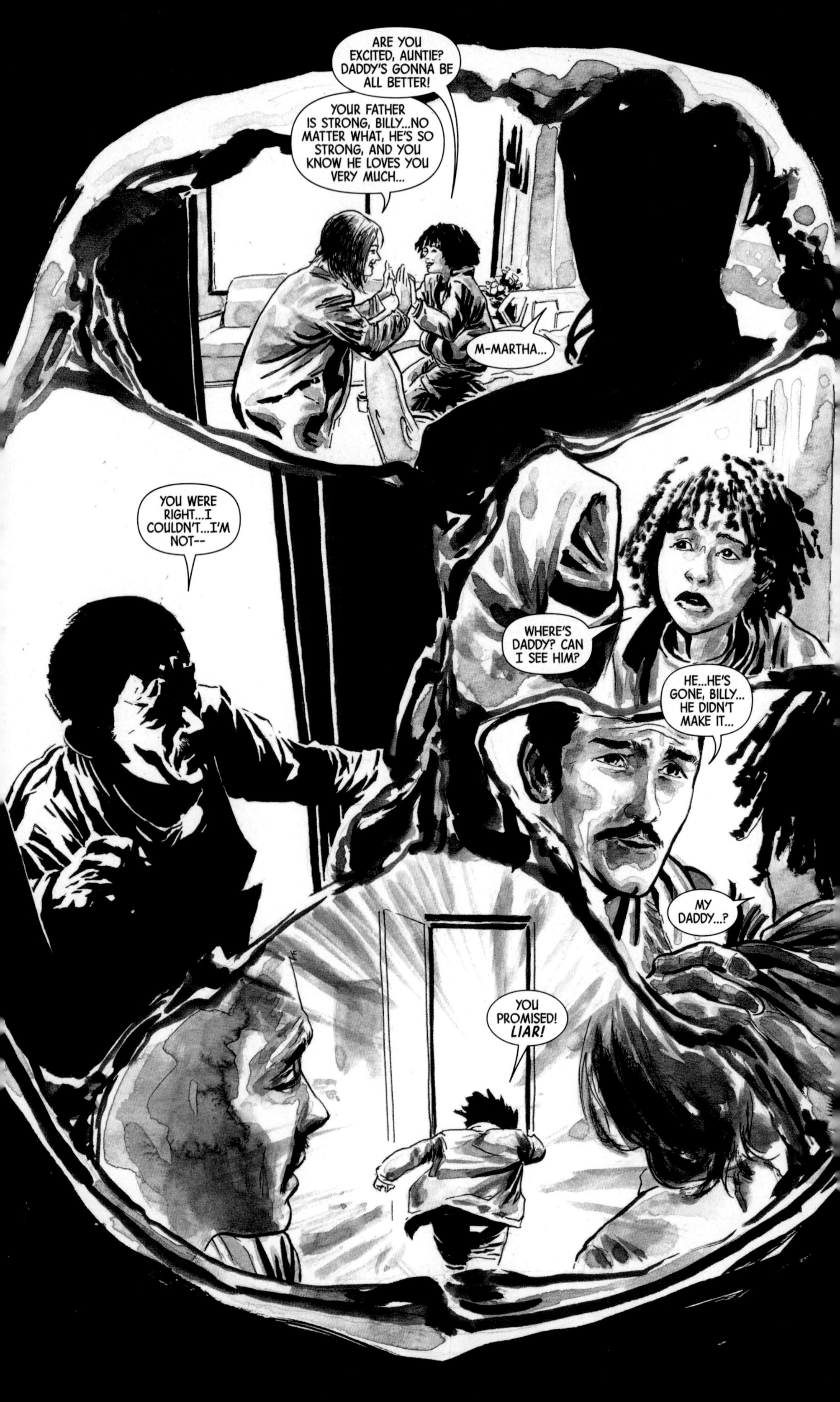
ARE YOU EXCITED, AUNTIE? DADDY'S GONNA BE ALL BETTER!
YOUR FATHER IS STRONG, BILLY...NO MATTER WHAT, HE'S SO STRONG, AND YOU KNOW HE LOVES YOU VERY MUCH...
M-MARTHA...
YOU WERE RIGHT...I COULDN'T...I'M NOT--
WHERE'S DADDY? CAN I SEE HIM?
HE...HE'S GONE, BILLY... HE DIDN'T MAKE IT...
MY DADDY...?
YOU PROMISED! *LIAR!*

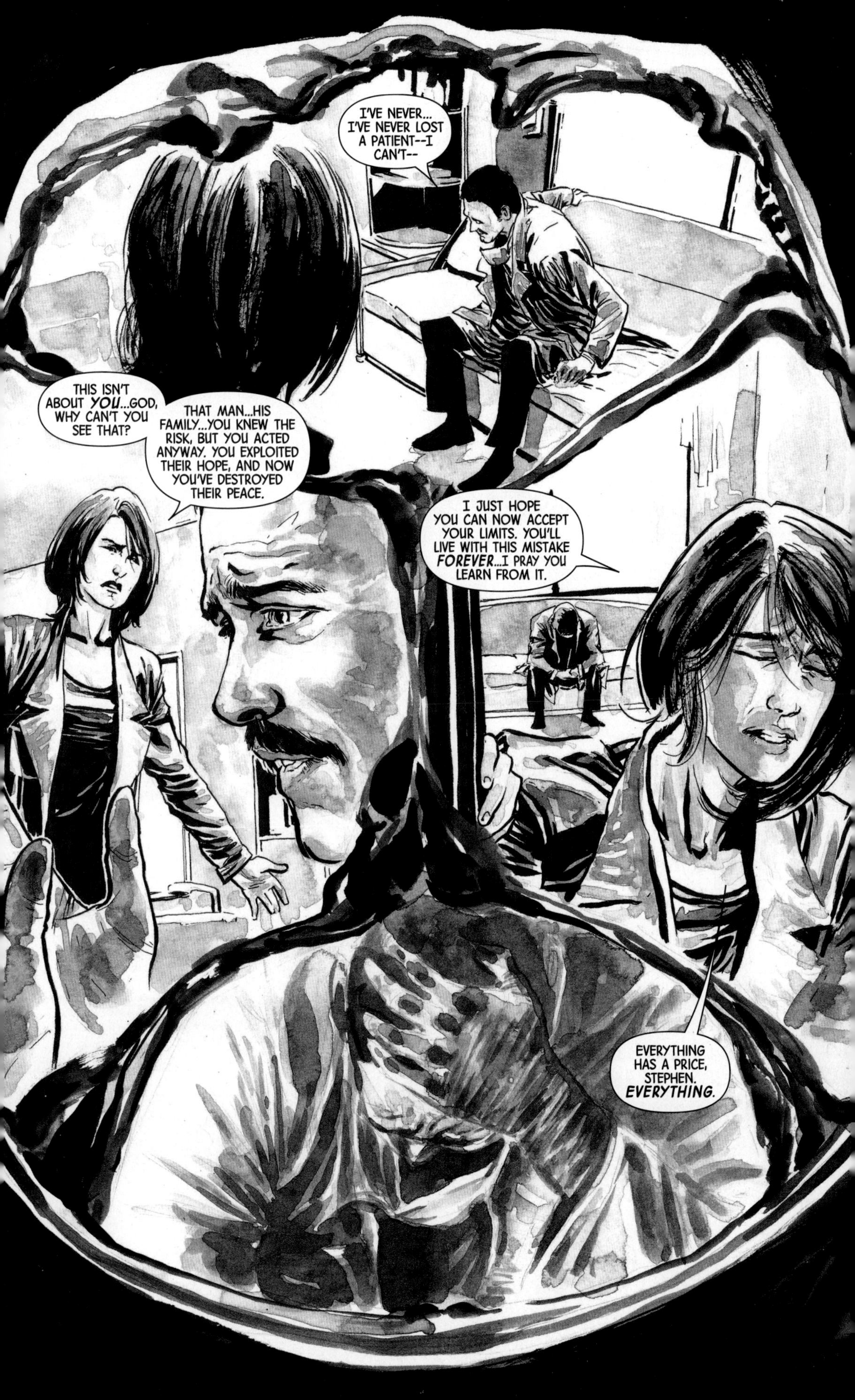
I'VE NEVER... I'VE NEVER LOST A PATIENT--I CAN'T--
THIS ISN'T ABOUT *YOU*...GOD, WHY CAN'T YOU SEE THAT?
THAT MAN...HIS FAMILY...YOU KNEW THE RISK, BUT YOU ACTED ANYWAY. YOU EXPLOITED THEIR HOPE, AND NOW YOU'VE DESTROYED THEIR PEACE.
I JUST HOPE YOU CAN NOW ACCEPT YOUR LIMITS. YOU'LL LIVE WITH THIS MISTAKE *FOREVER*...I PRAY YOU LEARN FROM IT.
EVERYTHING HAS A PRICE, STEPHEN. *EVERYTHING*.

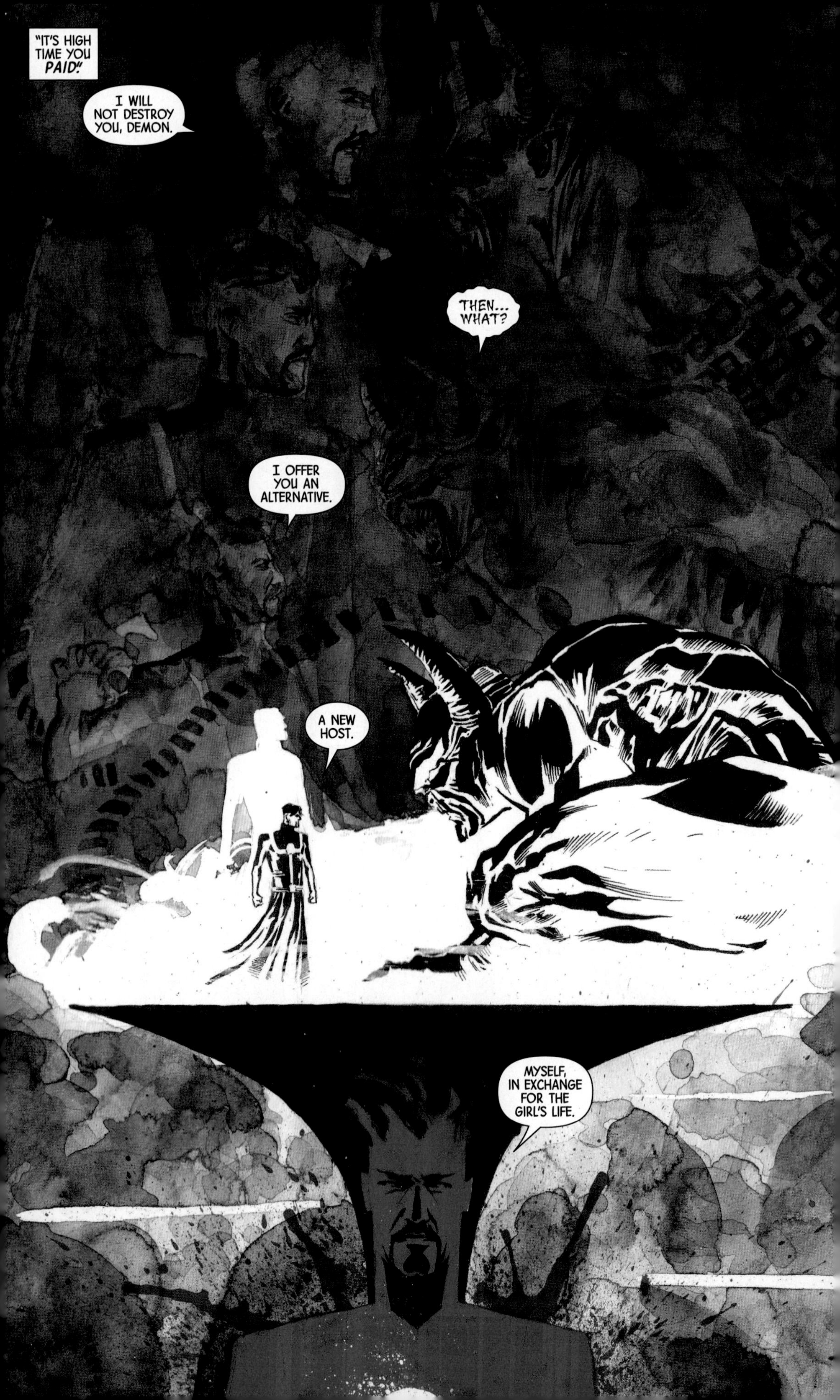
"IT'S HIGH TIME YOU *PAID!*"
I WILL NOT DESTROY YOU, DEMON.
THEN... WHAT?
I OFFER YOU AN ALTERNATIVE.
A NEW HOST.
MYSELF, IN EXCHANGE FOR THE GIRL'S LIFE.

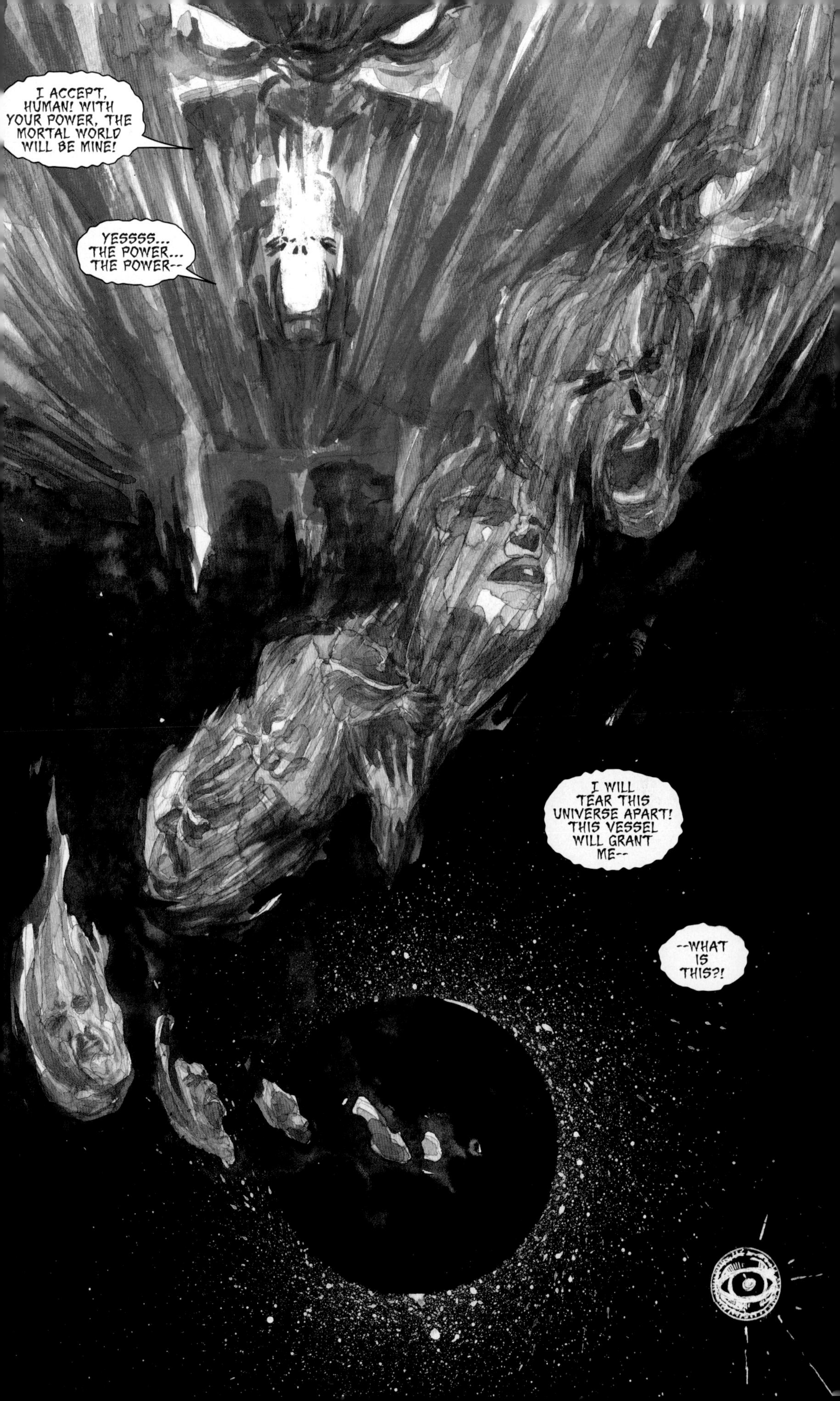
I ACCEPT, HUMAN! WITH YOUR POWER, THE MORTAL WORLD WILL BE MINE!
YESSSS... THE POWER... THE POWER--
I WILL TEAR THIS UNIVERSE APART! THIS VESSEL WILL GRANT ME--
--WHAT IS THIS?!

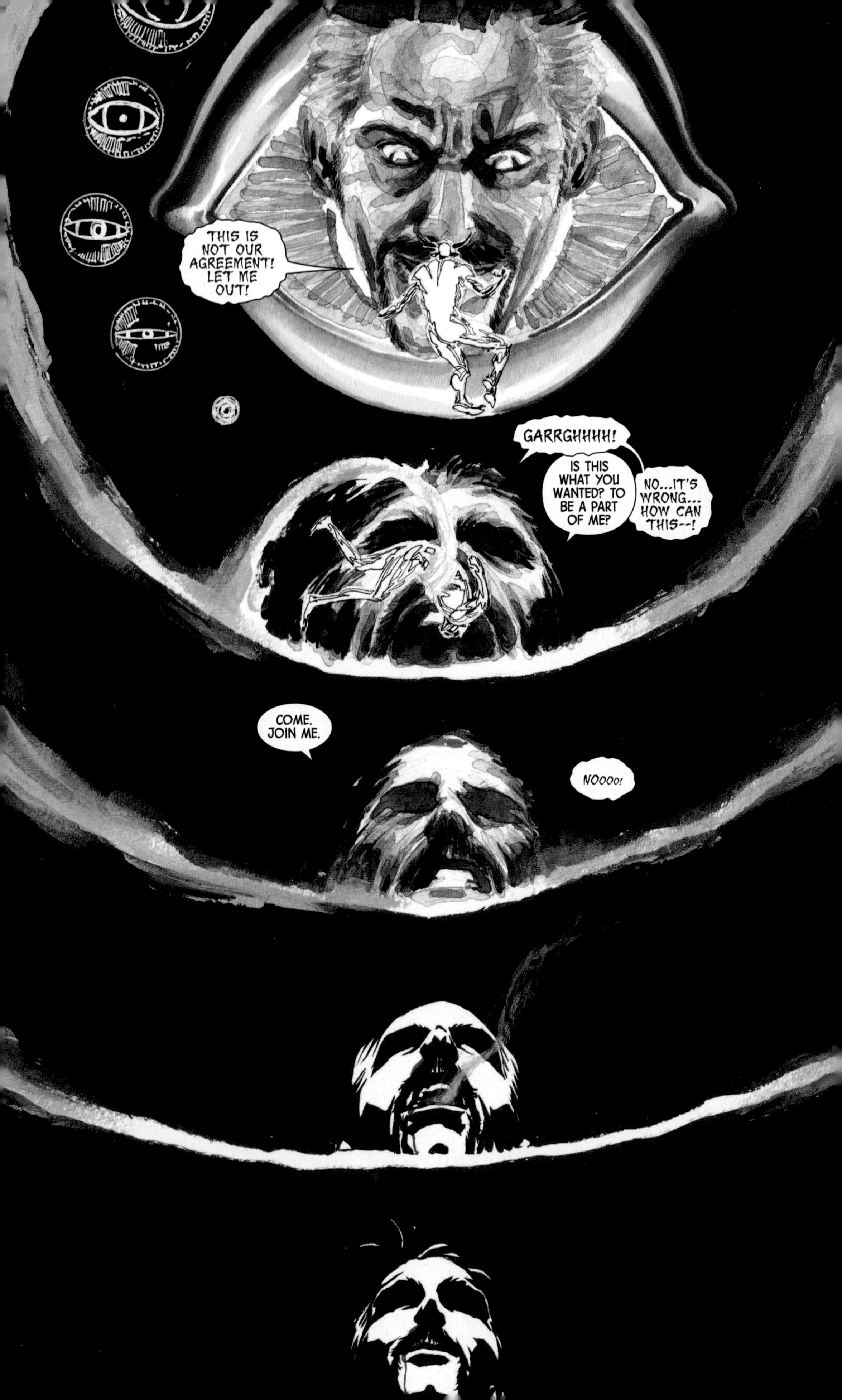
THIS IS NOT OUR AGREEMENT! LET ME OUT!
GARRGHHHH!
IS THIS WHAT YOU WANTED? TO BE A PART OF ME?
NO...IT'S WRONG... HOW CAN THIS--!
COME. JOIN ME.
NOOOO!

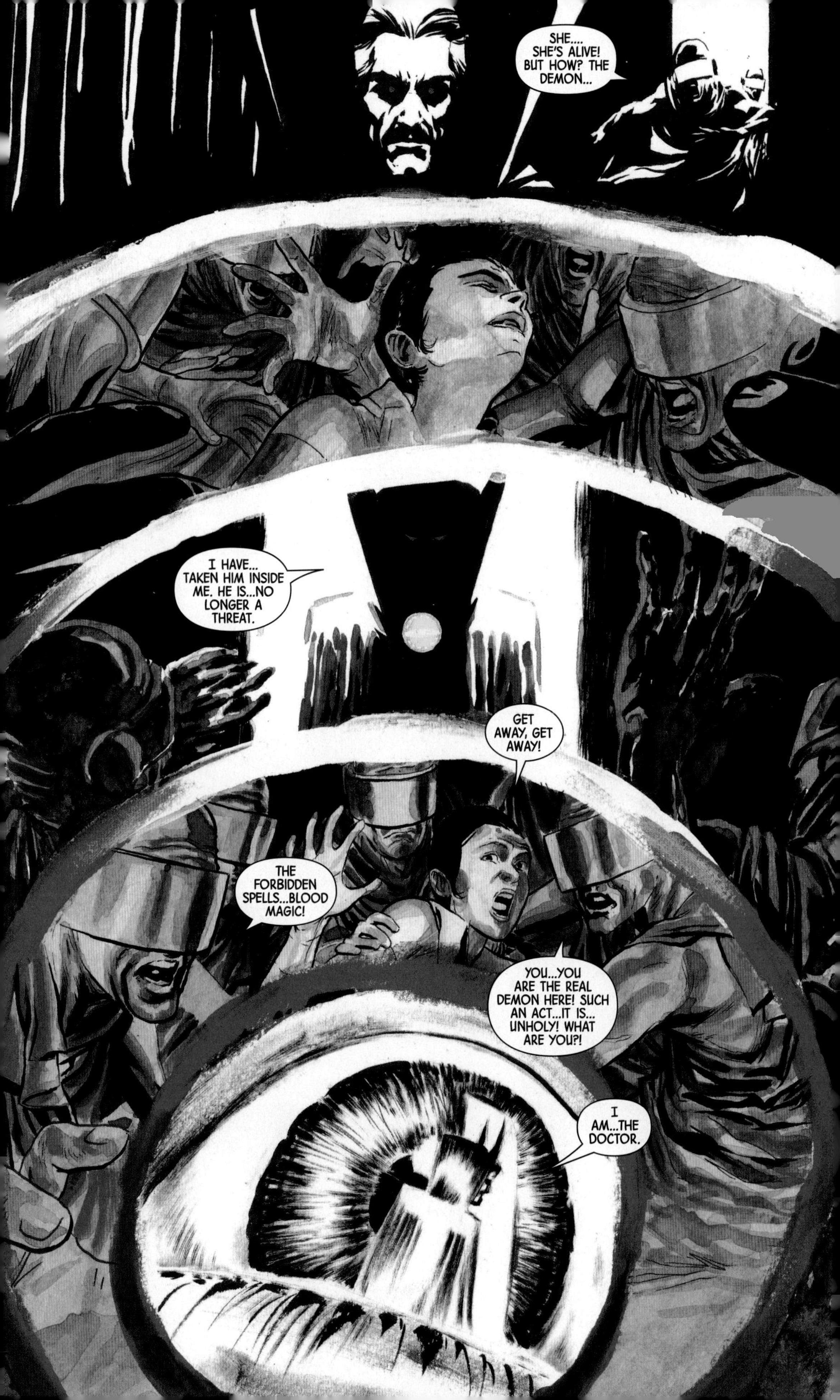

SHE... SHE'S ALIVE! BUT HOW? THE DEMON...
I HAVE... TAKEN HIM INSIDE ME. HE IS...NO LONGER A THREAT.
GET AWAY, GET AWAY!
THE FORBIDDEN SPELLS...BLOOD MAGIC!
YOU...YOU ARE THE REAL DEMON HERE! SUCH AN ACT...IT IS... UNHOLY! WHAT ARE YOU?!
I AM...THE DOCTOR.

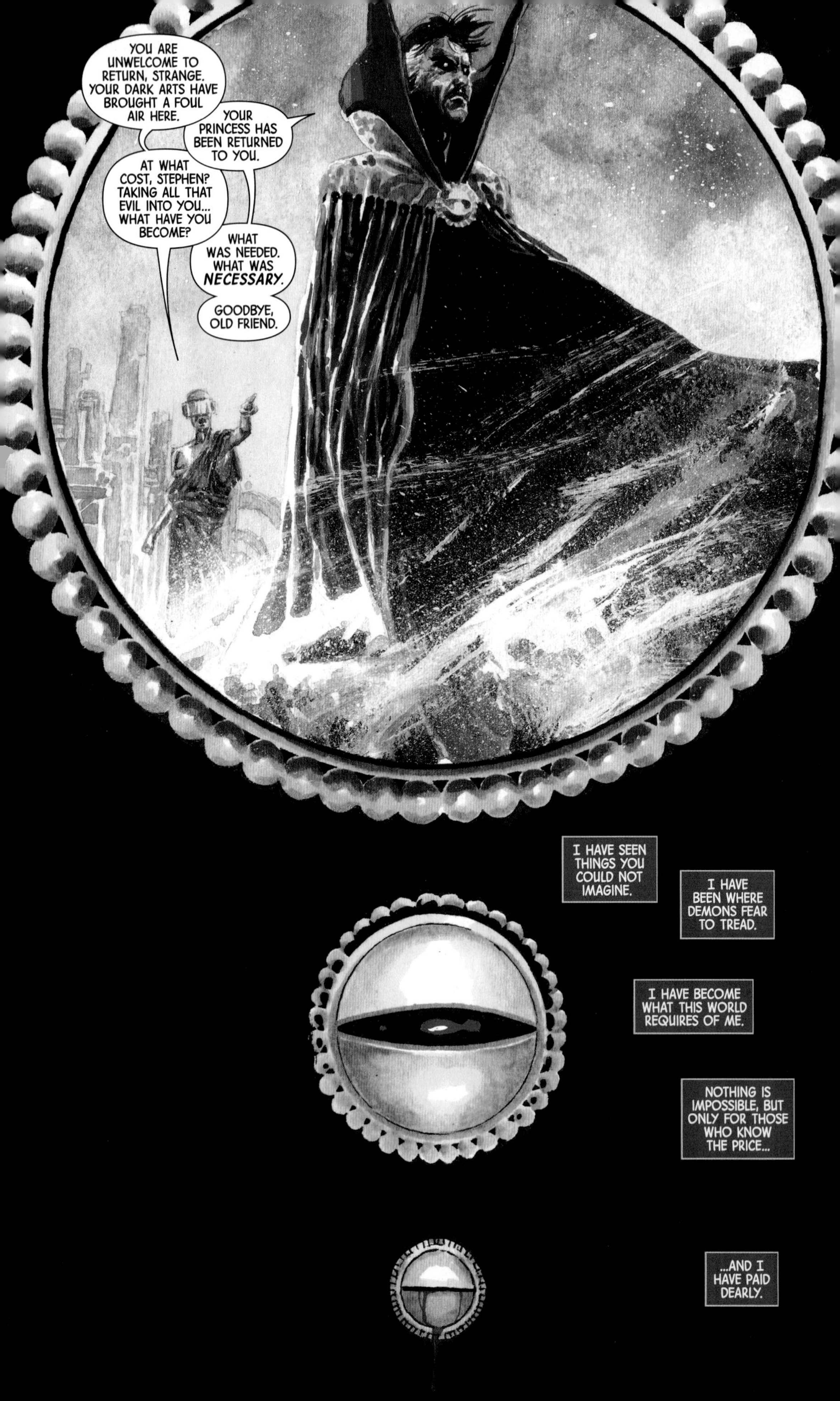

YOU ARE UNWELCOME TO RETURN, STRANGE. YOUR DARK ARTS HAVE BROUGHT A FOUL AIR HERE.
YOUR PRINCESS HAS BEEN RETURNED TO YOU.
AT WHAT COST, STEPHEN? TAKING ALL THAT EVIL INTO YOU... WHAT HAVE YOU BECOME?
WHAT WAS NEEDED. WHAT WAS *NECESSARY*.
GOODBYE, OLD FRIEND.
I HAVE SEEN THINGS YOU COULD NOT IMAGINE.
I HAVE BEEN WHERE DEMONS FEAR TO TREAD.
I HAVE BECOME WHAT THIS WORLD REQUIRES OF ME.
NOTHING IS IMPOSSIBLE, BUT ONLY FOR THOSE WHO KNOW THE PRICE...
...AND I HAVE PAID DEARLY.

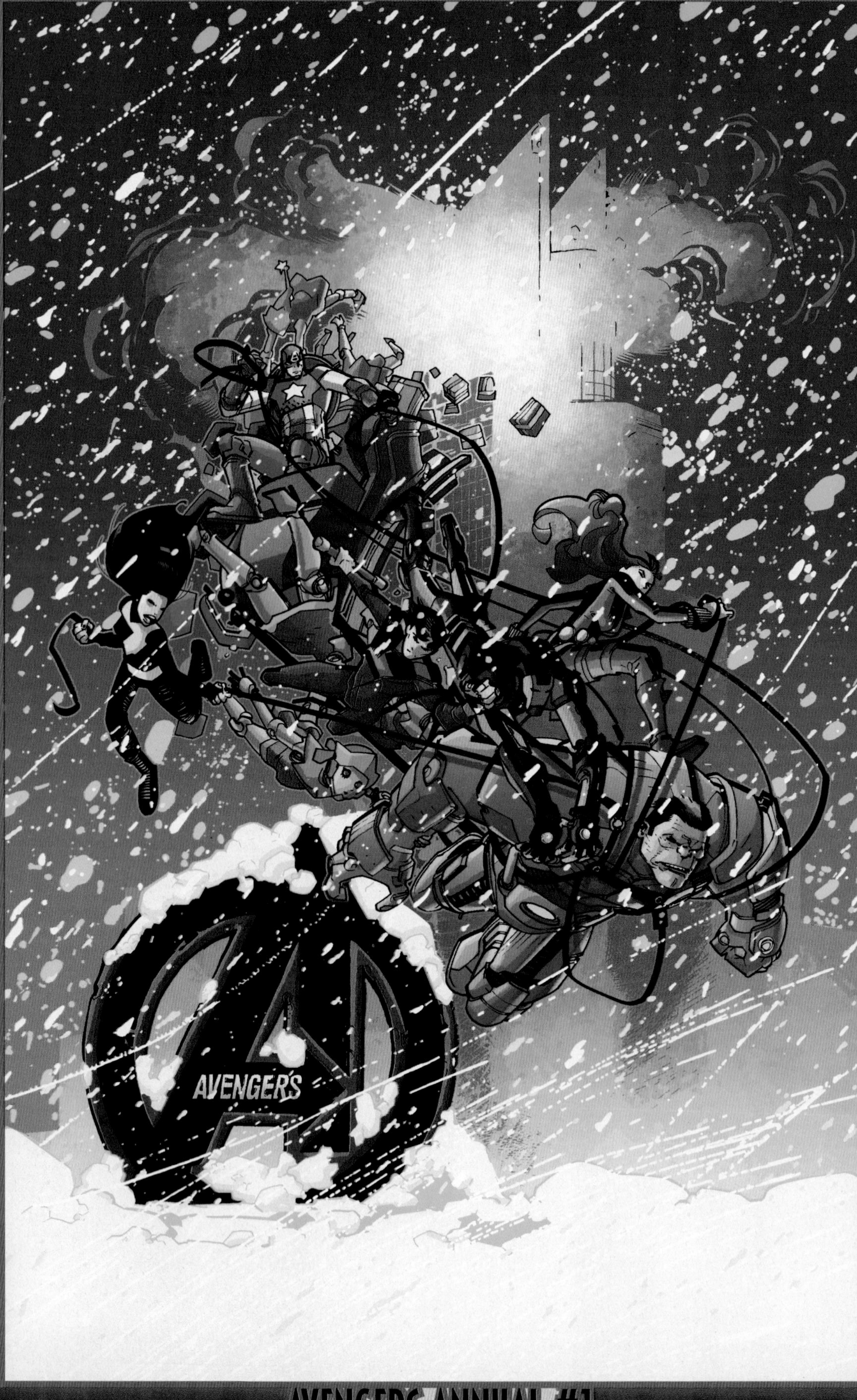
AVENGERS

AVENGERS ANNUAL #1

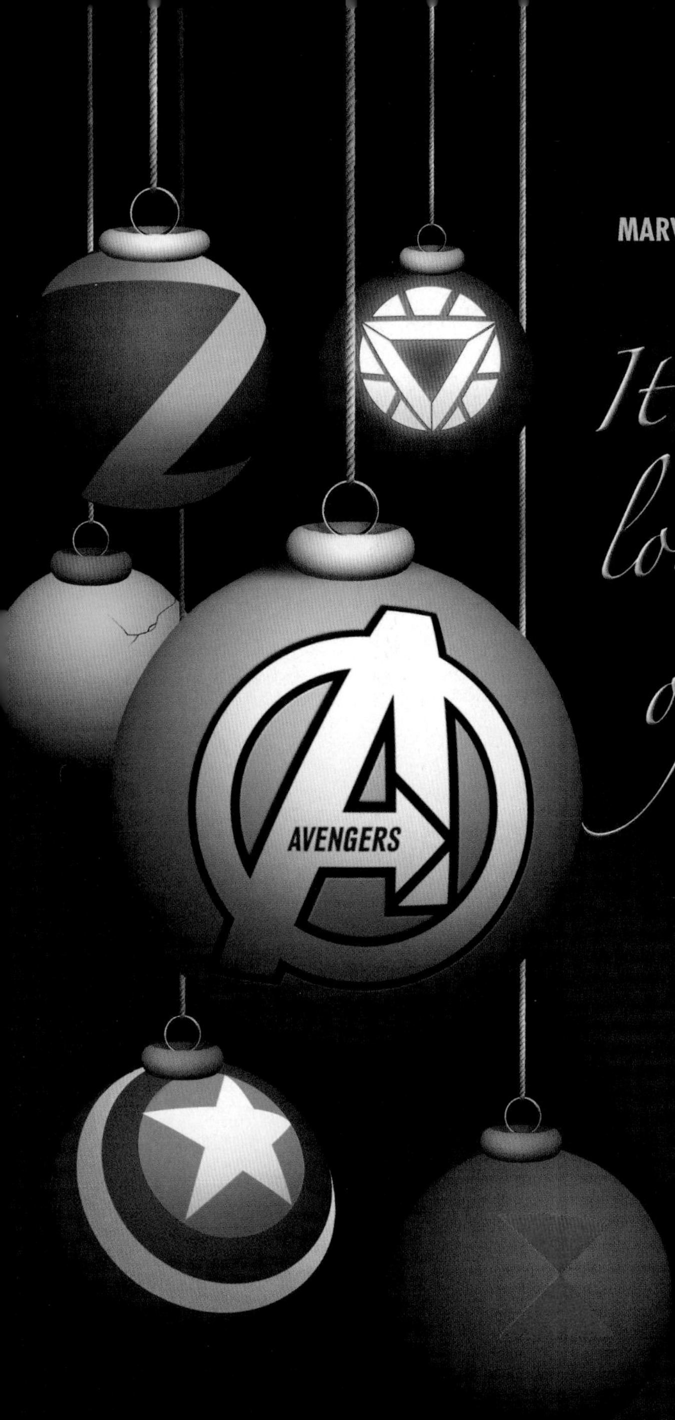
AVENGERS

MARVEL COMICS cordially invites you to…

It's the most loneliest time of the year!

A festive holiday event filled with cheer, joy, balloons, robots, lasers and 'splosions!

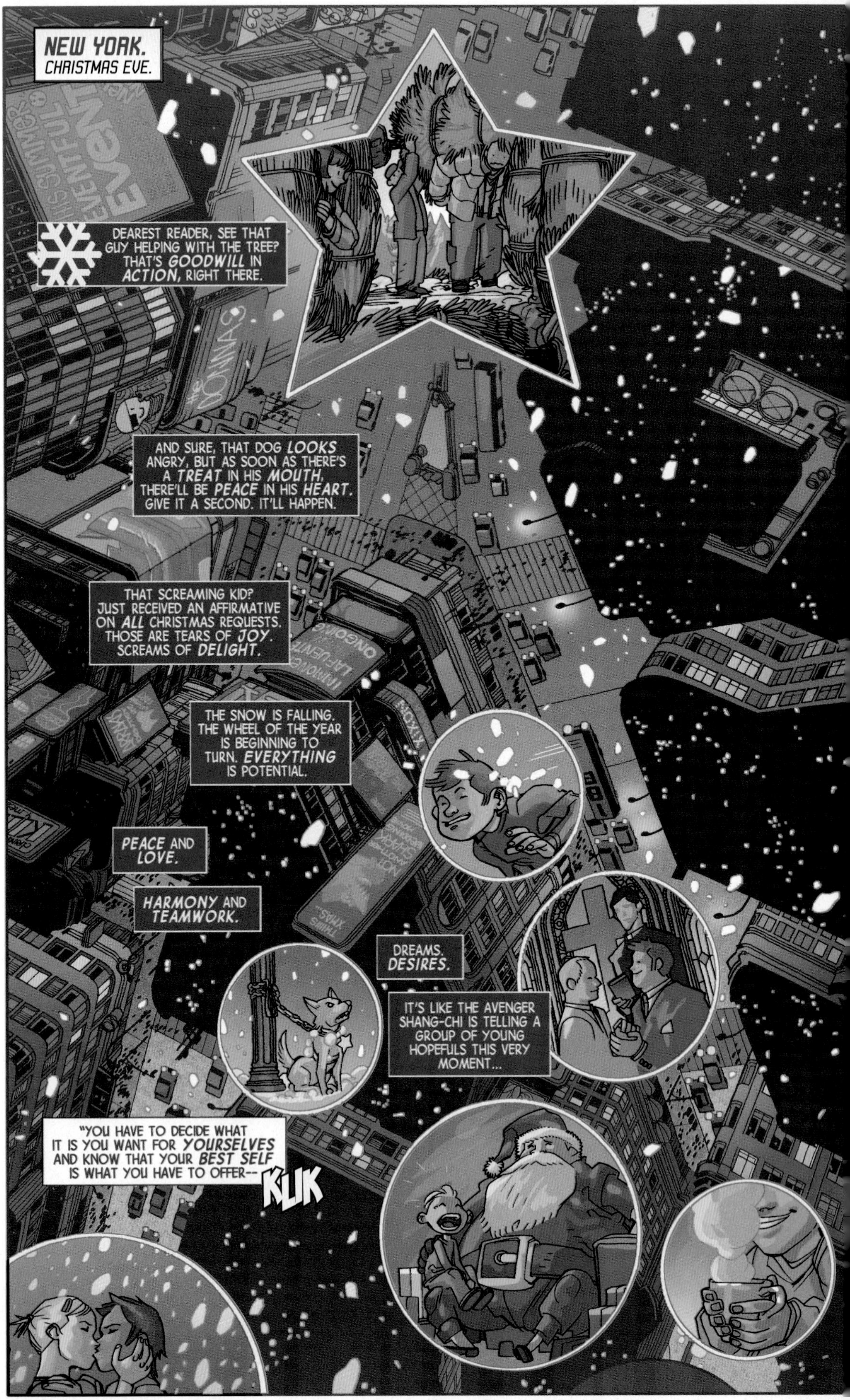

NEW YORK.
CHRISTMAS EVE.
DEAREST READER, SEE THAT GUY HELPING WITH THE TREE? THAT'S GOODWILL IN ACTION, RIGHT THERE.
AND SURE, THAT DOG LOOKS ANGRY, BUT AS SOON AS THERE'S A TREAT IN HIS MOUTH, THERE'LL BE PEACE IN HIS HEART. GIVE IT A SECOND. IT'LL HAPPEN.
THAT SCREAMING KID? JUST RECEIVED AN AFFIRMATIVE ON ALL CHRISTMAS REQUESTS. THOSE ARE TEARS OF JOY. SCREAMS OF DELIGHT.
THE SNOW IS FALLING. THE WHEEL OF THE YEAR IS BEGINNING TO TURN. EVERYTHING IS POTENTIAL.
PEACE AND LOVE.
HARMONY AND TEAMWORK.
DREAMS. DESIRES.
IT'S LIKE THE AVENGER SHANG-CHI IS TELLING A GROUP OF YOUNG HOPEFULS THIS VERY MOMENT...
"YOU HAVE TO DECIDE WHAT IT IS YOU WANT FOR YOURSELVES AND KNOW THAT YOUR BEST SELF IS WHAT YOU HAVE TO OFFER--
KLIK

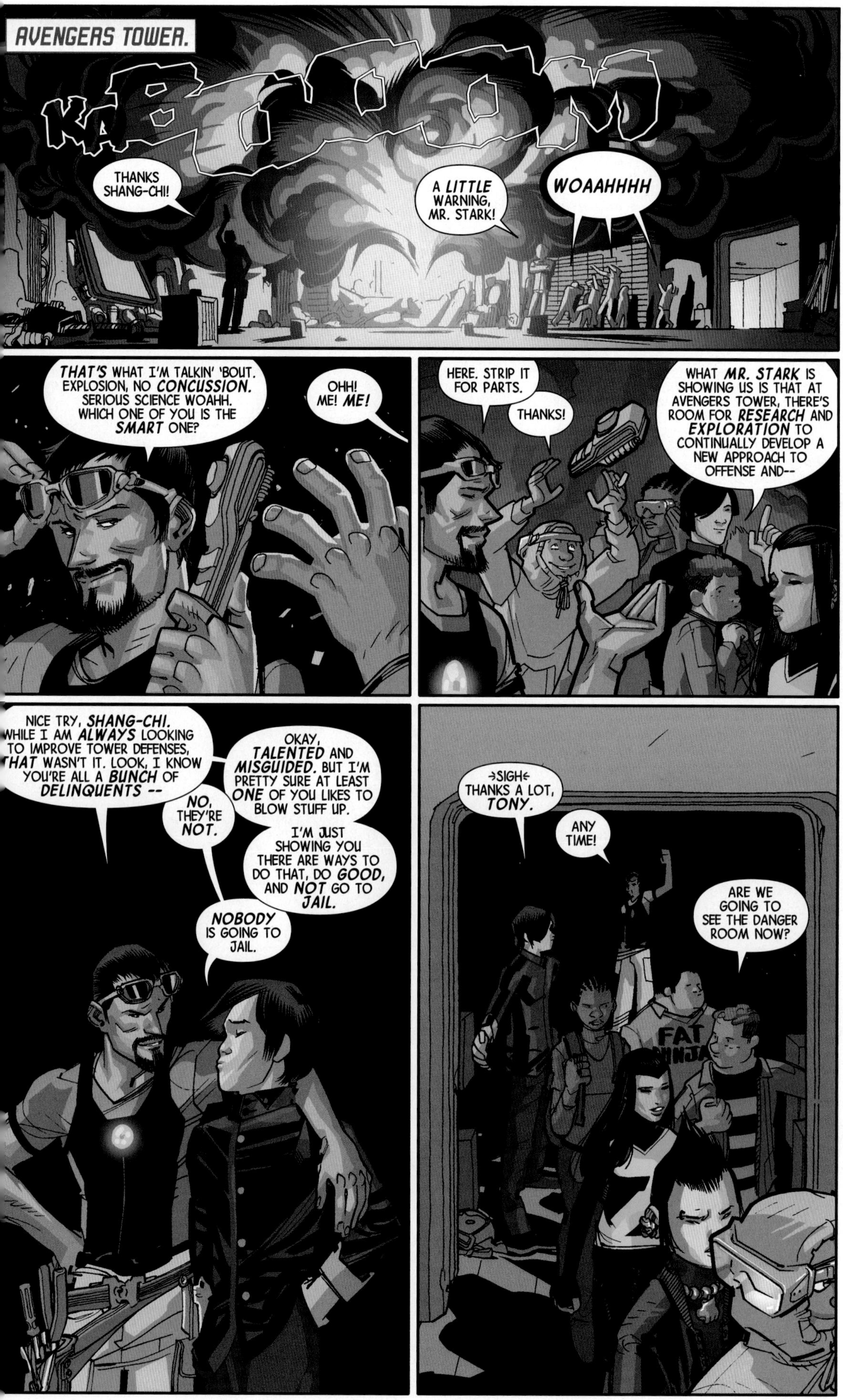

AVENGERS TOWER.
KABOOOOM
THANKS SHANG-CHI!
A LITTLE WARNING, MR. STARK!
WOAAHHHH
THAT'S WHAT I'M TALKIN' 'BOUT. EXPLOSION, NO CONCUSSION. SERIOUS SCIENCE WOAHH. WHICH ONE OF YOU IS THE SMART ONE?
OHH! ME! ME!
HERE. STRIP IT FOR PARTS.
THANKS!
WHAT MR. STARK IS SHOWING US IS THAT AT AVENGERS TOWER, THERE'S ROOM FOR RESEARCH AND EXPLORATION TO CONTINUALLY DEVELOP A NEW APPROACH TO OFFENSE AND--
NICE TRY, SHANG-CHI. WHILE I AM ALWAYS LOOKING TO IMPROVE TOWER DEFENSES, THAT WASN'T IT. LOOK, I KNOW YOU'RE ALL A BUNCH OF DELINQUENTS --
NO, THEY'RE NOT.
OKAY, TALENTED AND MISGUIDED. BUT I'M PRETTY SURE AT LEAST ONE OF YOU LIKES TO BLOW STUFF UP.
I'M JUST SHOWING YOU THERE ARE WAYS TO DO THAT, DO GOOD, AND NOT GO TO JAIL.
NOBODY IS GOING TO JAIL.
→SIGH← THANKS A LOT, TONY.
ANY TIME!
ARE WE GOING TO SEE THE DANGER ROOM NOW?
FAT NINJA

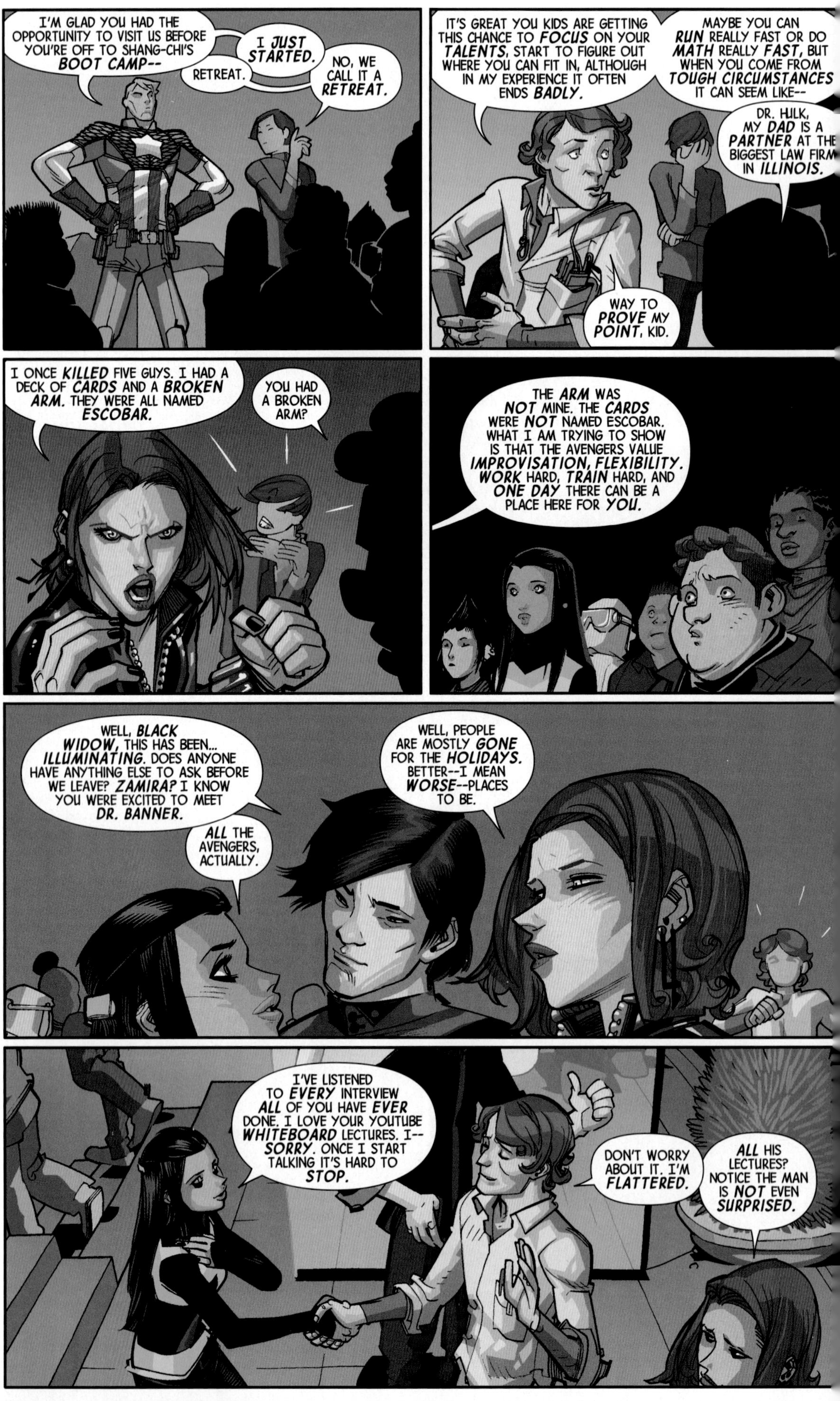

I'M GLAD YOU HAD THE OPPORTUNITY TO VISIT US BEFORE YOU'RE OFF TO SHANG-CHI'S BOOT CAMP--
I JUST STARTED.
RETREAT.
NO, WE CALL IT A RETREAT.
IT'S GREAT YOU KIDS ARE GETTING THIS CHANCE TO FOCUS ON YOUR TALENTS, START TO FIGURE OUT WHERE YOU CAN FIT IN, ALTHOUGH IN MY EXPERIENCE IT OFTEN ENDS BADLY.
MAYBE YOU CAN RUN REALLY FAST OR DO MATH REALLY FAST, BUT WHEN YOU COME FROM TOUGH CIRCUMSTANCES IT CAN SEEM LIKE--
DR. HULK, MY DAD IS A PARTNER AT THE BIGGEST LAW FIRM IN ILLINOIS.
WAY TO PROVE MY POINT, KID.
I ONCE KILLED FIVE GUYS. I HAD A DECK OF CARDS AND A BROKEN ARM. THEY WERE ALL NAMED ESCOBAR.
YOU HAD A BROKEN ARM?
THE ARM WAS NOT MINE. THE CARDS WERE NOT NAMED ESCOBAR. WHAT I AM TRYING TO SHOW IS THAT THE AVENGERS VALUE IMPROVISATION, FLEXIBILITY. WORK HARD, TRAIN HARD, AND ONE DAY THERE CAN BE A PLACE HERE FOR YOU.
WELL, BLACK WIDOW, THIS HAS BEEN... ILLUMINATING. DOES ANYONE HAVE ANYTHING ELSE TO ASK BEFORE WE LEAVE? ZAMIRA? I KNOW YOU WERE EXCITED TO MEET DR. BANNER.
ALL THE AVENGERS, ACTUALLY.
WELL, PEOPLE ARE MOSTLY GONE FOR THE HOLIDAYS. BETTER--I MEAN WORSE--PLACES TO BE.
I'VE LISTENED TO EVERY INTERVIEW ALL OF YOU HAVE EVER DONE. I LOVE YOUR YOUTUBE WHITEBOARD LECTURES. I-- SORRY. ONCE I START TALKING IT'S HARD TO STOP.
DON'T WORRY ABOUT IT. I'M FLATTERED.
ALL HIS LECTURES? NOTICE THE MAN IS NOT EVEN SURPRISED.

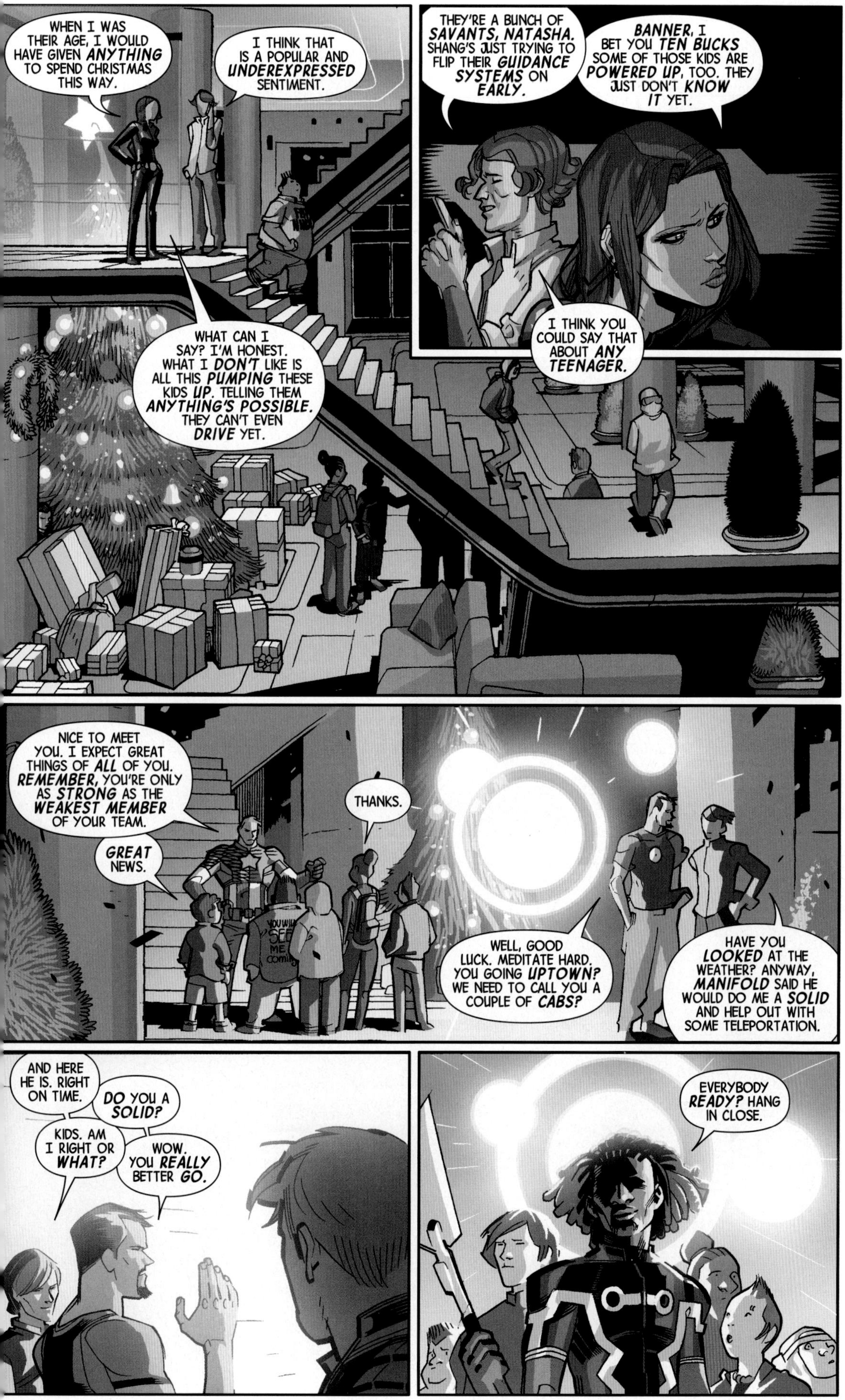
WHEN I WAS THEIR AGE, I WOULD HAVE GIVEN ANYTHING TO SPEND CHRISTMAS THIS WAY.
I THINK THAT IS A POPULAR AND UNDEREXPRESSED SENTIMENT.
WHAT CAN I SAY? I'M HONEST. WHAT I DON'T LIKE IS ALL THIS PUMPING THESE KIDS UP. TELLING THEM ANYTHING'S POSSIBLE. THEY CAN'T EVEN DRIVE YET.
THEY'RE A BUNCH OF SAVANTS, NATASHA. SHANG'S JUST TRYING TO FLIP THEIR GUIDANCE SYSTEMS ON EARLY.
BANNER, I BET YOU TEN BUCKS SOME OF THOSE KIDS ARE POWERED UP, TOO. THEY JUST DON'T KNOW IT YET.
I THINK YOU COULD SAY THAT ABOUT ANY TEENAGER.
NICE TO MEET YOU. I EXPECT GREAT THINGS OF ALL OF YOU. REMEMBER, YOU'RE ONLY AS STRONG AS THE WEAKEST MEMBER OF YOUR TEAM.
GREAT NEWS.
THANKS.
YOU WILL SEE ME coming
WELL, GOOD LUCK. MEDITATE HARD. YOU GOING UPTOWN? WE NEED TO CALL YOU A COUPLE OF CABS?
HAVE YOU LOOKED AT THE WEATHER? ANYWAY, MANIFOLD SAID HE WOULD DO ME A SOLID AND HELP OUT WITH SOME TELEPORTATION.
AND HERE HE IS. RIGHT ON TIME.
DO YOU A SOLID?
KIDS. AM I RIGHT OR WHAT?
WOW. YOU REALLY BETTER GO.
EVERYBODY READY? HANG IN CLOSE.

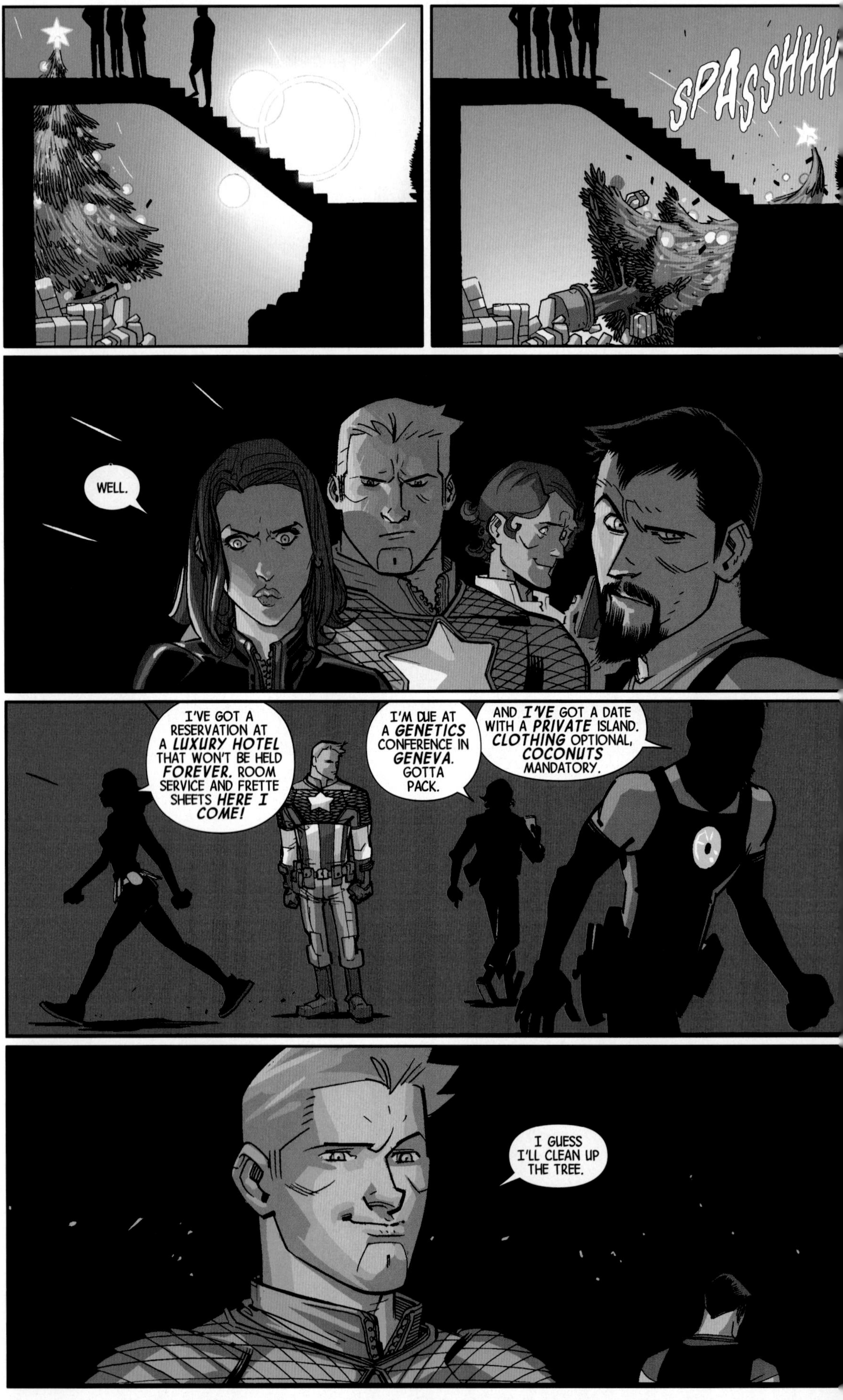

SPASSHHH
WELL.
I'VE GOT A RESERVATION AT A LUXURY HOTEL THAT WON'T BE HELD FOREVER. ROOM SERVICE AND FRETTE SHEETS HERE I COME!
I'M DUE AT A GENETICS CONFERENCE IN GENEVA. GOTTA PACK.
AND I'VE GOT A DATE WITH A PRIVATE ISLAND. CLOTHING OPTIONAL, COCONUTS MANDATORY.
I GUESS I'LL CLEAN UP THE TREE.

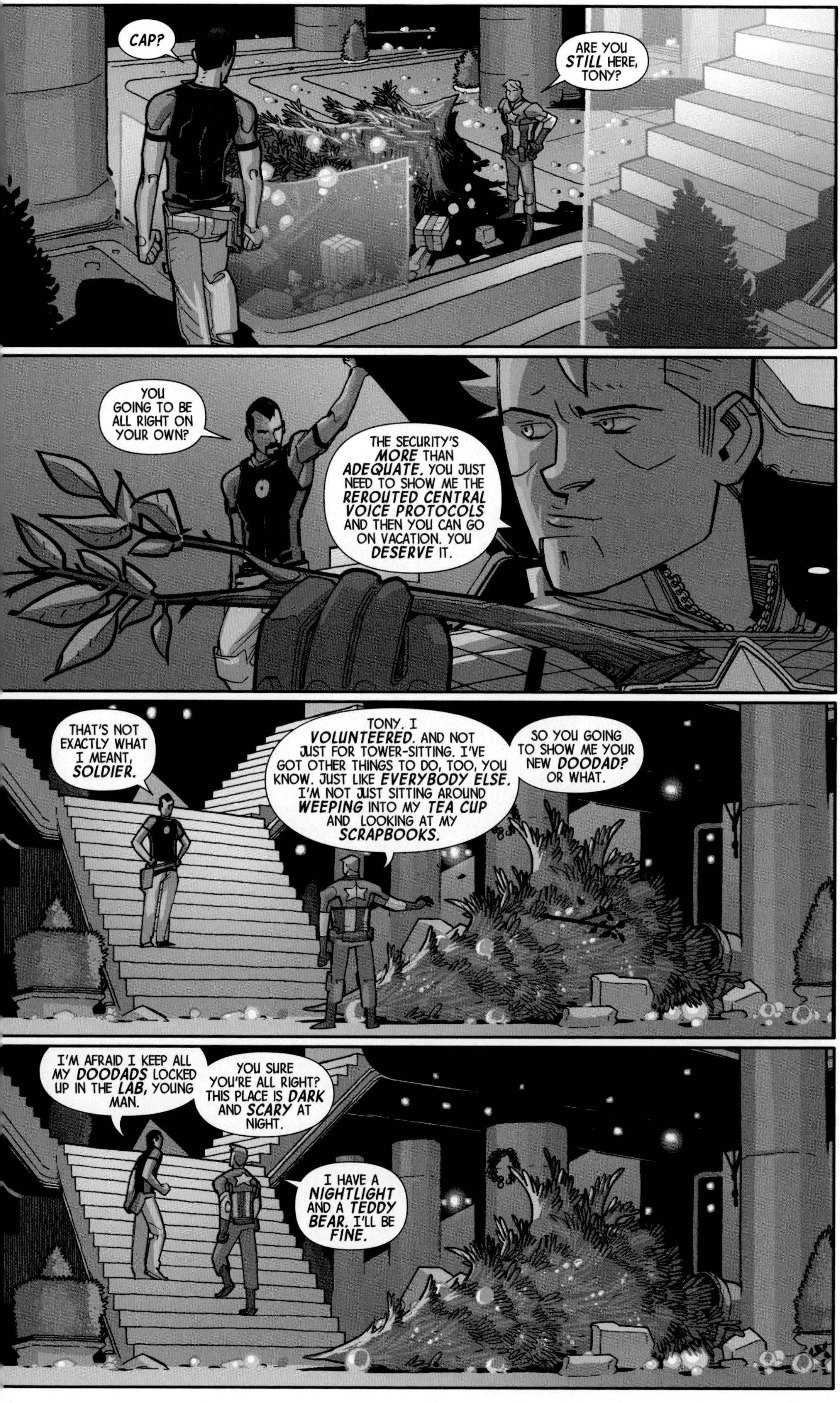
CAP?
ARE YOU STILL HERE, TONY?
YOU GOING TO BE ALL RIGHT ON YOUR OWN?
THE SECURITY'S MORE THAN ADEQUATE. YOU JUST NEED TO SHOW ME THE REROUTED CENTRAL VOICE PROTOCOLS AND THEN YOU CAN GO ON VACATION. YOU DESERVE IT.
THAT'S NOT EXACTLY WHAT I MEANT, SOLDIER.
TONY. I VOLUNTEERED. AND NOT JUST FOR TOWER-SITTING. I'VE GOT OTHER THINGS TO DO, TOO, YOU KNOW. JUST LIKE EVERYBODY ELSE. I'M NOT JUST SITTING AROUND WEEPING INTO MY TEA CUP AND LOOKING AT MY SCRAPBOOKS.
SO YOU GOING TO SHOW ME YOUR NEW DOODAD? OR WHAT.
I'M AFRAID I KEEP ALL MY DOODADS LOCKED UP IN THE LAB, YOUNG MAN.
YOU SURE YOU'RE ALL RIGHT? THIS PLACE IS DARK AND SCARY AT NIGHT.
I HAVE A NIGHTLIGHT AND A TEDDY BEAR. I'LL BE FINE.

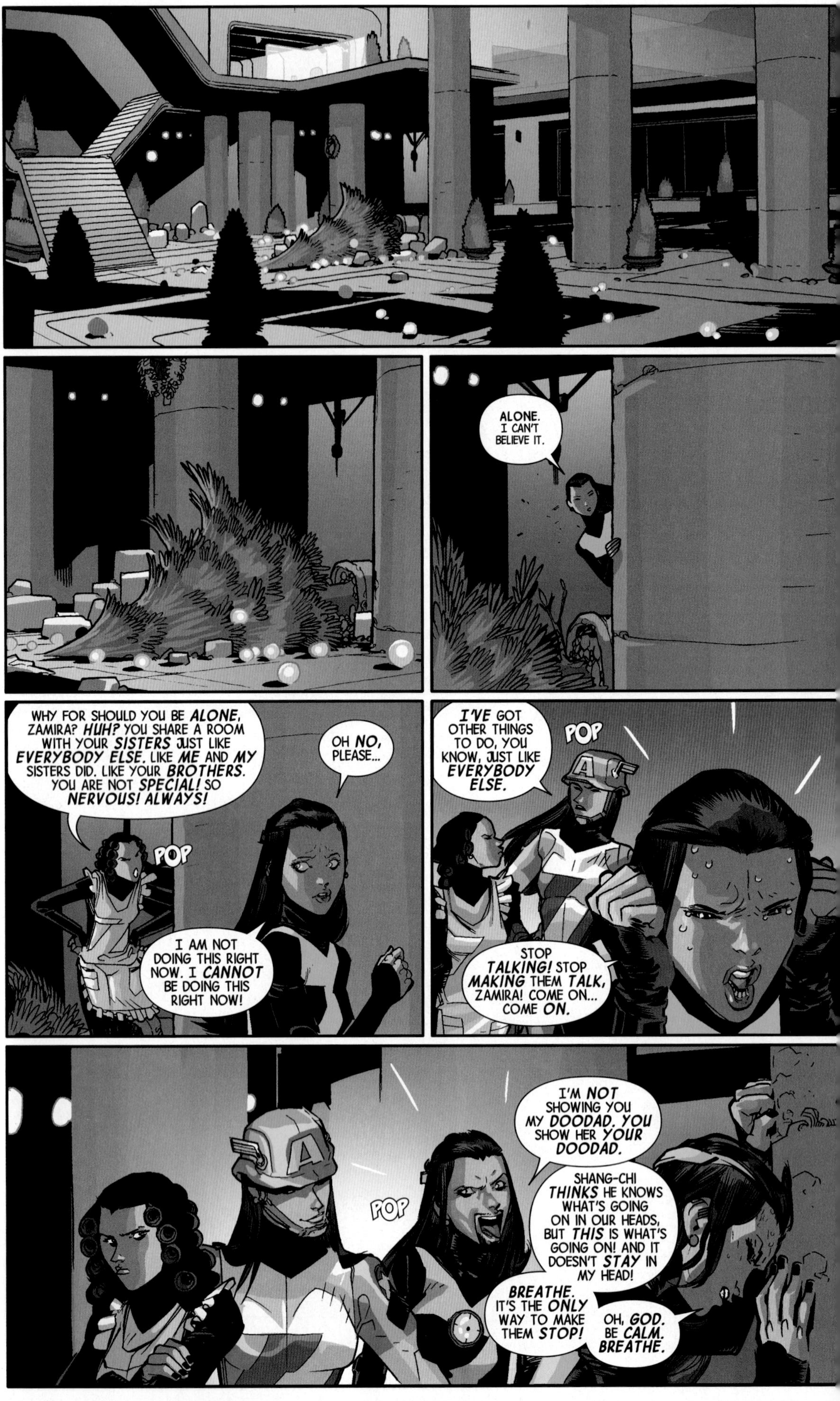

ALONE. I CAN'T BELIEVE IT.
WHY FOR SHOULD YOU BE ALONE, ZAMIRA? HUH? YOU SHARE A ROOM WITH YOUR SISTERS JUST LIKE EVERYBODY ELSE. LIKE ME AND MY SISTERS DID. LIKE YOUR BROTHERS. YOU ARE NOT SPECIAL! SO NERVOUS! ALWAYS!
POP
OH NO, PLEASE...
I AM NOT DOING THIS RIGHT NOW. I CANNOT BE DOING THIS RIGHT NOW!
I'VE GOT OTHER THINGS TO DO, YOU KNOW, JUST LIKE EVERYBODY ELSE.
POP
STOP TALKING! STOP MAKING THEM TALK, ZAMIRA! COME ON... COME ON.
POP
I'M NOT SHOWING YOU MY DOODAD. YOU SHOW HER YOUR DOODAD.
SHANG-CHI THINKS HE KNOWS WHAT'S GOING ON IN OUR HEADS, BUT THIS IS WHAT'S GOING ON! AND IT DOESN'T STAY IN MY HEAD!
BREATHE. IT'S THE ONLY WAY TO MAKE THEM STOP!
OH, GOD. BE CALM. BREATHE.

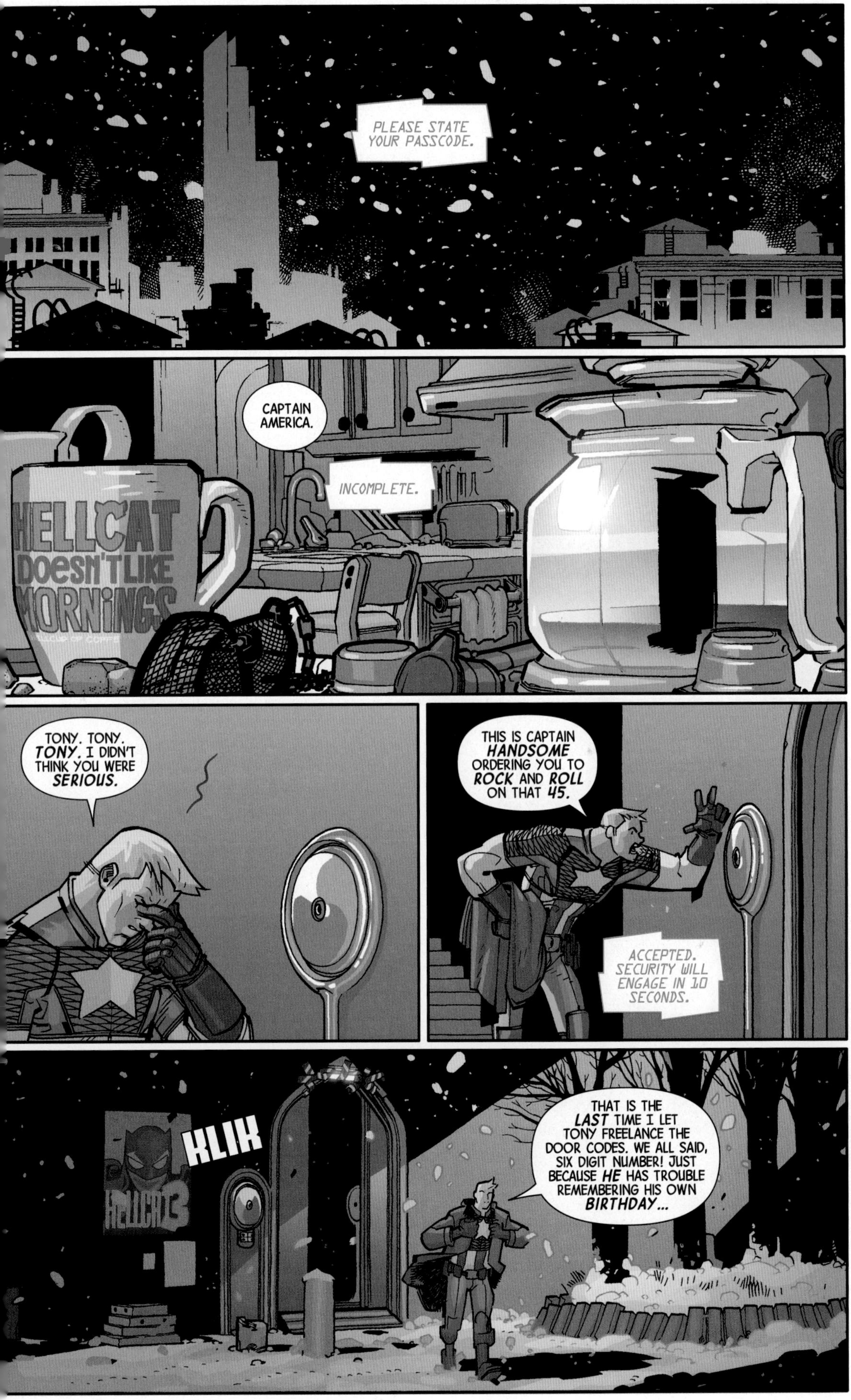
PLEASE STATE YOUR PASSCODE.
CAPTAIN AMERICA.
INCOMPLETE.
HELLCAT DOESN'T LIKE MORNINGS
TONY. TONY. TONY. I DIDN'T THINK YOU WERE SERIOUS.
THIS IS CAPTAIN HANDSOME ORDERING YOU TO ROCK AND ROLL ON THAT 45.
ACCEPTED. SECURITY WILL ENGAGE IN 10 SECONDS.
HELLCAT 3
KLIK
THAT IS THE LAST TIME I LET TONY FREELANCE THE DOOR CODES. WE ALL SAID, SIX DIGIT NUMBER! JUST BECAUSE HE HAS TROUBLE REMEMBERING HIS OWN BIRTHDAY...

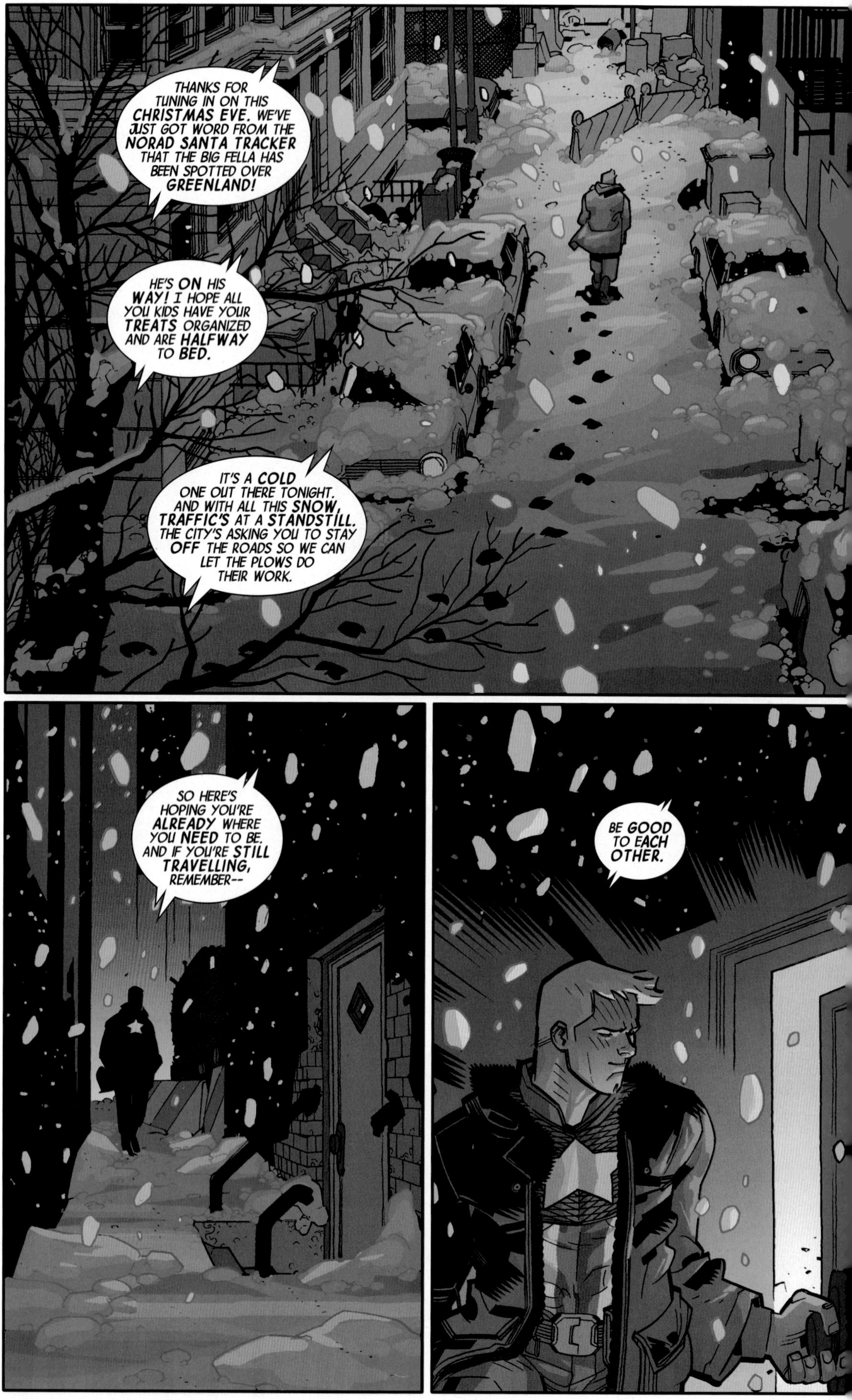
THANKS FOR TUNING IN ON THIS CHRISTMAS EVE. WE'VE JUST GOT WORD FROM THE NORAD SANTA TRACKER THAT THE BIG FELLA HAS BEEN SPOTTED OVER GREENLAND!
HE'S ON HIS WAY! I HOPE ALL YOU KIDS HAVE YOUR TREATS ORGANIZED AND ARE HALFWAY TO BED.
IT'S A COLD ONE OUT THERE TONIGHT. AND WITH ALL THIS SNOW, TRAFFIC'S AT A STANDSTILL. THE CITY'S ASKING YOU TO STAY OFF THE ROADS SO WE CAN LET THE PLOWS DO THEIR WORK.
SO HERE'S HOPING YOU'RE ALREADY WHERE YOU NEED TO BE. AND IF YOU'RE STILL TRAVELLING, REMEMBER--
BE GOOD TO EACH OTHER.

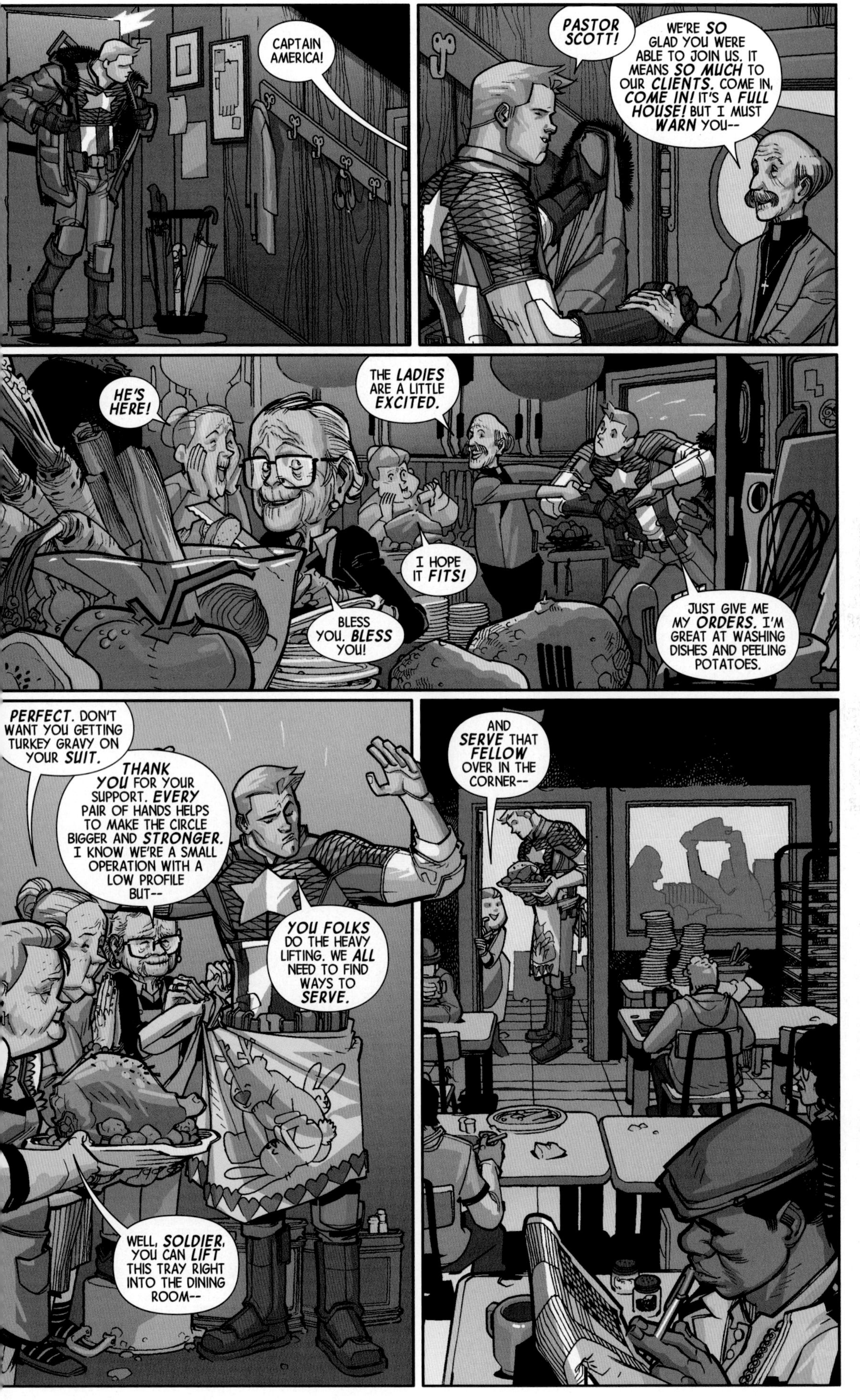
CAPTAIN AMERICA!
PASTOR SCOTT!
WE'RE SO GLAD YOU WERE ABLE TO JOIN US. IT MEANS SO MUCH TO OUR CLIENTS. COME IN, COME IN! IT'S A FULL HOUSE! BUT I MUST WARN YOU--
HE'S HERE!
THE LADIES ARE A LITTLE EXCITED.
I HOPE IT FITS!
BLESS YOU. BLESS YOU!
JUST GIVE ME MY ORDERS. I'M GREAT AT WASHING DISHES AND PEELING POTATOES.
PERFECT. DON'T WANT YOU GETTING TURKEY GRAVY ON YOUR SUIT.
THANK YOU FOR YOUR SUPPORT. EVERY PAIR OF HANDS HELPS TO MAKE THE CIRCLE BIGGER AND STRONGER. I KNOW WE'RE A SMALL OPERATION WITH A LOW PROFILE BUT--
YOU FOLKS DO THE HEAVY LIFTING. WE ALL NEED TO FIND WAYS TO SERVE.
WELL, SOLDIER, YOU CAN LIFT THIS TRAY RIGHT INTO THE DINING ROOM--
AND SERVE THAT FELLOW OVER IN THE CORNER--

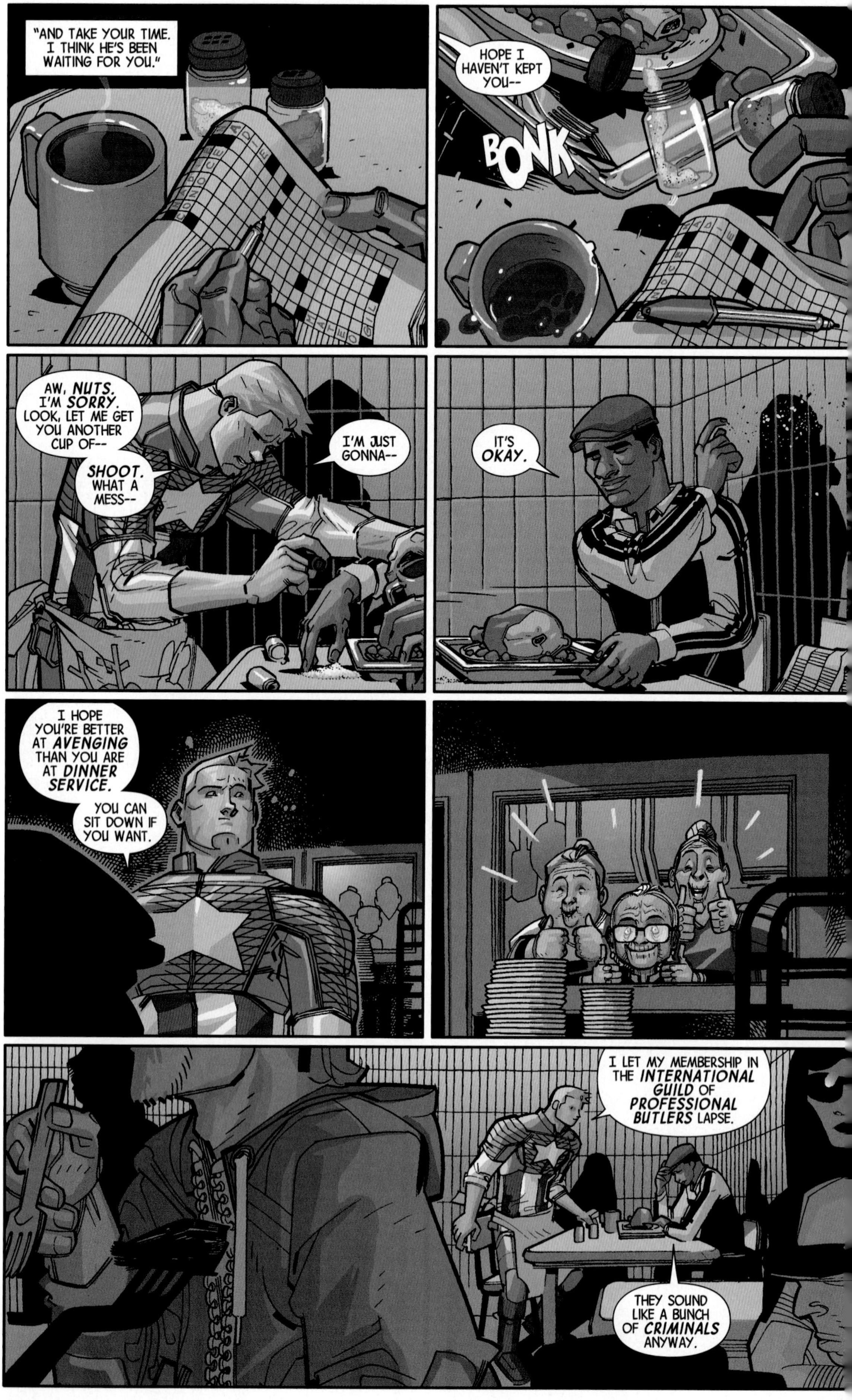

"AND TAKE YOUR TIME. I THINK HE'S BEEN WAITING FOR YOU."
HOPE I HAVEN'T KEPT YOU--
BONK
AW, NUTS. I'M SORRY. LOOK, LET ME GET YOU ANOTHER CUP OF--
SHOOT. WHAT A MESS--
I'M JUST GONNA--
IT'S OKAY.
I HOPE YOU'RE BETTER AT AVENGING THAN YOU ARE AT DINNER SERVICE.
YOU CAN SIT DOWN IF YOU WANT.
I LET MY MEMBERSHIP IN THE INTERNATIONAL GUILD OF PROFESSIONAL BUTLERS LAPSE.
THEY SOUND LIKE A BUNCH OF CRIMINALS ANYWAY.

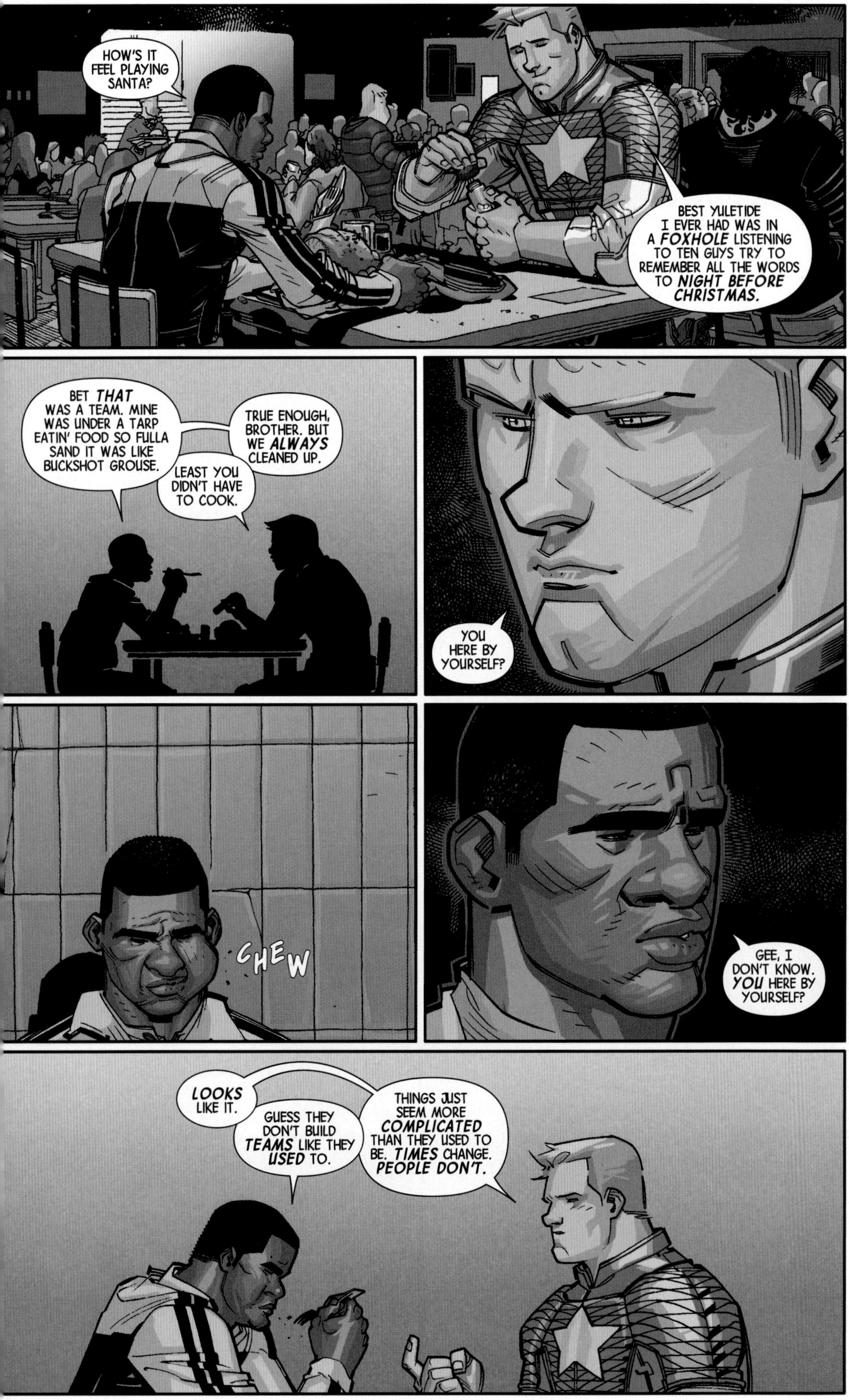
HOW'S IT FEEL PLAYING SANTA?
BEST YULETIDE I EVER HAD WAS IN A FOXHOLE LISTENING TO TEN GUYS TRY TO REMEMBER ALL THE WORDS TO NIGHT BEFORE CHRISTMAS.
BET THAT WAS A TEAM. MINE WAS UNDER A TARP EATIN' FOOD SO FULLA SAND IT WAS LIKE BUCKSHOT GROUSE.
TRUE ENOUGH, BROTHER. BUT WE ALWAYS CLEANED UP.
LEAST YOU DIDN'T HAVE TO COOK.
YOU HERE BY YOURSELF?
CHEW
GEE, I DON'T KNOW. YOU HERE BY YOURSELF?
LOOKS LIKE IT.
GUESS THEY DON'T BUILD TEAMS LIKE THEY USED TO.
THINGS JUST SEEM MORE COMPLICATED THAN THEY USED TO BE. TIMES CHANGE. PEOPLE DON'T.

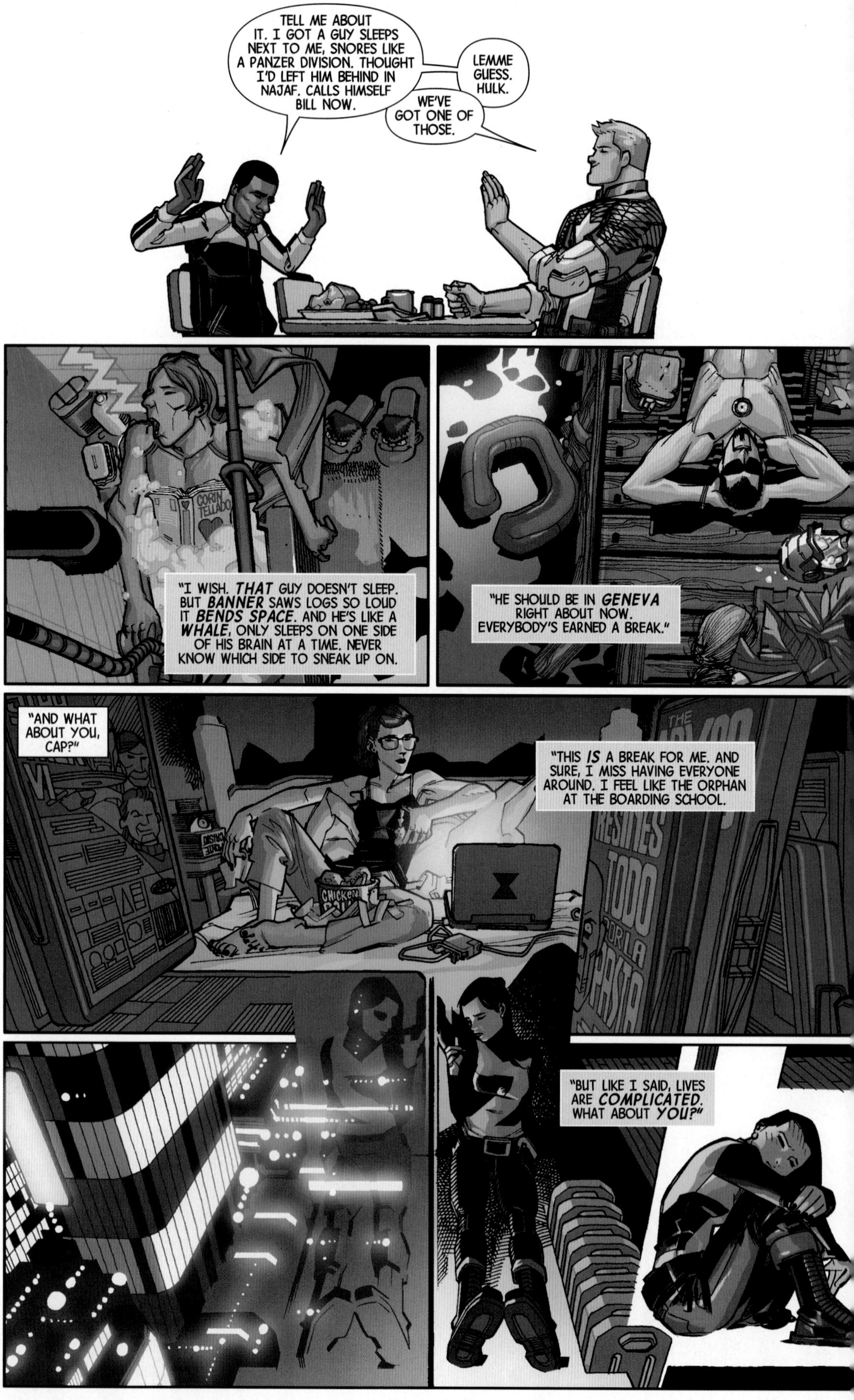
TELL ME ABOUT IT. I GOT A GUY SLEEPS NEXT TO ME, SNORES LIKE A PANZER DIVISION. THOUGHT I'D LEFT HIM BEHIND IN NAJAF. CALLS HIMSELF BILL NOW.
LEMME GUESS. HULK.
WE'VE GOT ONE OF THOSE.
"I WISH. THAT GUY DOESN'T SLEEP. BUT BANNER SAWS LOGS SO LOUD IT BENDS SPACE. AND HE'S LIKE A WHALE, ONLY SLEEPS ON ONE SIDE OF HIS BRAIN AT A TIME. NEVER KNOW WHICH SIDE TO SNEAK UP ON.
"HE SHOULD BE IN GENEVA RIGHT ABOUT NOW. EVERYBODY'S EARNED A BREAK."
"AND WHAT ABOUT YOU, CAP?"
"THIS IS A BREAK FOR ME. AND SURE, I MISS HAVING EVERYONE AROUND. I FEEL LIKE THE ORPHAN AT THE BOARDING SCHOOL.
"BUT LIKE I SAID, LIVES ARE COMPLICATED. WHAT ABOUT YOU?"

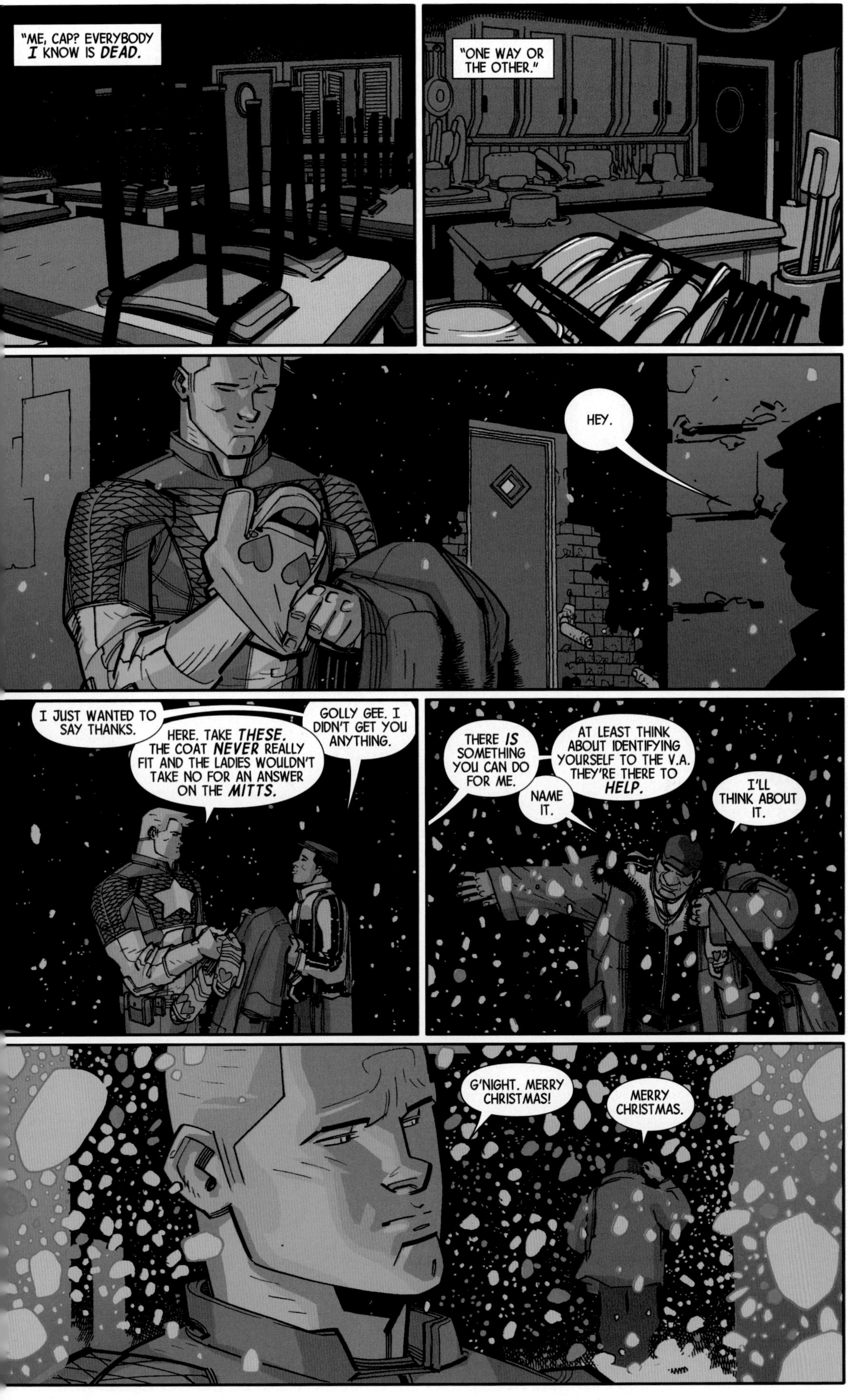
"ME, CAP? EVERYBODY I KNOW IS DEAD.
"ONE WAY OR THE OTHER."
HEY.
I JUST WANTED TO SAY THANKS.
GOLLY GEE. I DIDN'T GET YOU ANYTHING.
HERE. TAKE THESE. THE COAT NEVER REALLY FIT AND THE LADIES WOULDN'T TAKE NO FOR AN ANSWER ON THE MITTS.
THERE IS SOMETHING YOU CAN DO FOR ME.
NAME IT.
AT LEAST THINK ABOUT IDENTIFYING YOURSELF TO THE V.A. THEY'RE THERE TO HELP.
I'LL THINK ABOUT IT.
G'NIGHT. MERRY CHRISTMAS!
MERRY CHRISTMAS.

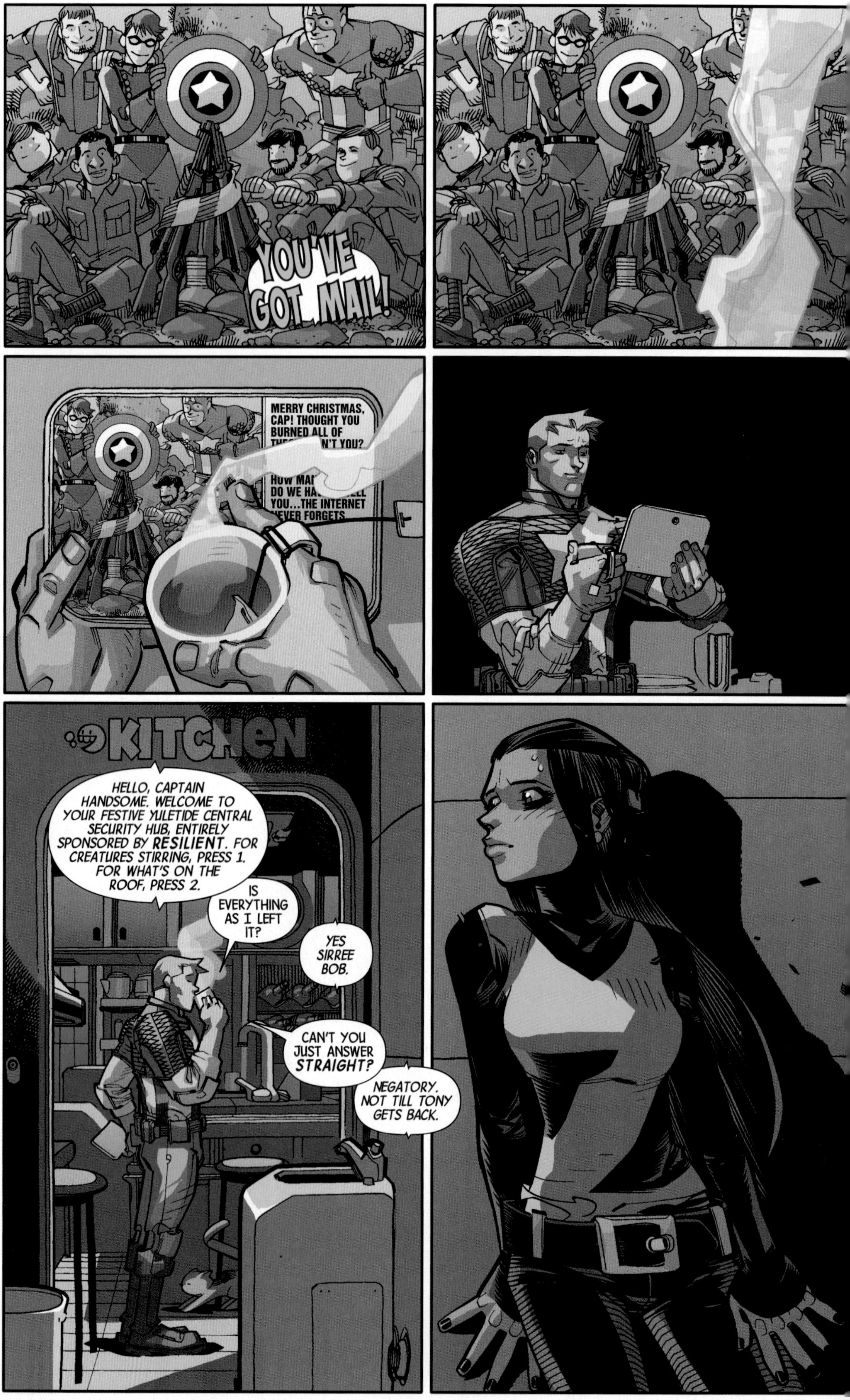

YOU'VE GOT MAIL!
MERRY CHRISTMAS, CAP! THOUGHT YOU BURNED ALL OF
HOW MA
DO WE HA
YOU...THE INTERNET
NEVER FORGETS
KITCHEN
HELLO, CAPTAIN HANDSOME. WELCOME TO YOUR FESTIVE YULETIDE CENTRAL SECURITY HUB, ENTIRELY SPONSORED BY RESILIENT. FOR CREATURES STIRRING, PRESS 1. FOR WHAT'S ON THE ROOF, PRESS 2.
IS EVERYTHING AS I LEFT IT?
YES SIRREE BOB.
CAN'T YOU JUST ANSWER STRAIGHT?
NEGATORY. NOT TILL TONY GETS BACK.

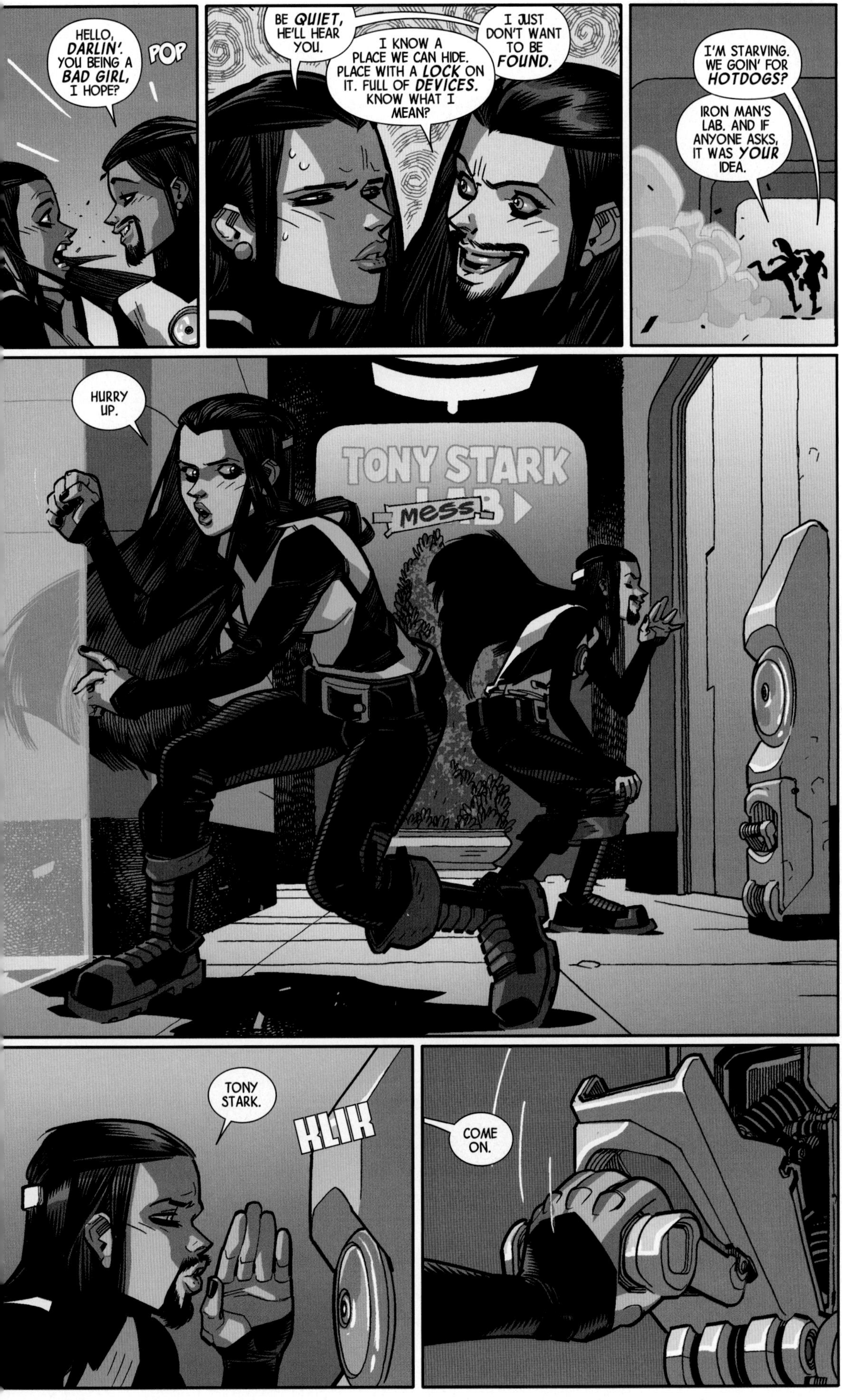

HELLO, DARLIN'. YOU BEING A BAD GIRL, I HOPE?
POP
BE QUIET, HE'LL HEAR YOU.
I JUST DON'T WANT TO BE FOUND.
I KNOW A PLACE WE CAN HIDE. PLACE WITH A LOCK ON IT. FULL OF DEVICES. KNOW WHAT I MEAN?
I'M STARVING. WE GOIN' FOR HOTDOGS?
IRON MAN'S LAB. AND IF ANYONE ASKS, IT WAS YOUR IDEA.
HURRY UP.
TONY STARK
MESS
LAB
TONY STARK.
KLIK
COME ON.

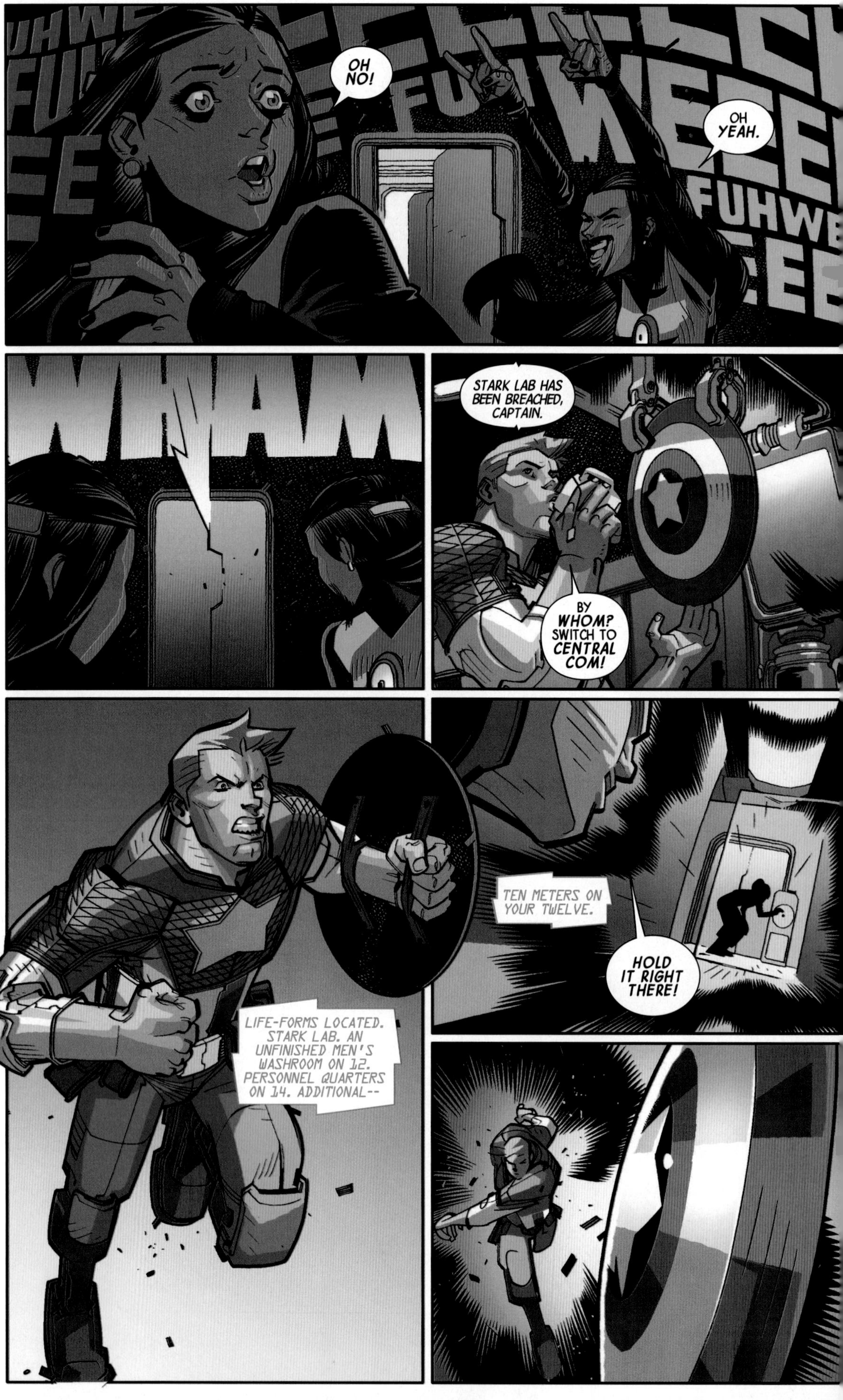
FUHWEEE
OH NO!
OH YEAH.
WHAM
STARK LAB HAS BEEN BREACHED, CAPTAIN.
BY WHOM? SWITCH TO CENTRAL COM!
LIFE-FORMS LOCATED. STARK LAB. AN UNFINISHED MEN'S WASHROOM ON 12. PERSONNEL QUARTERS ON 14. ADDITIONAL--
TEN METERS ON YOUR TWELVE.
HOLD IT RIGHT THERE!

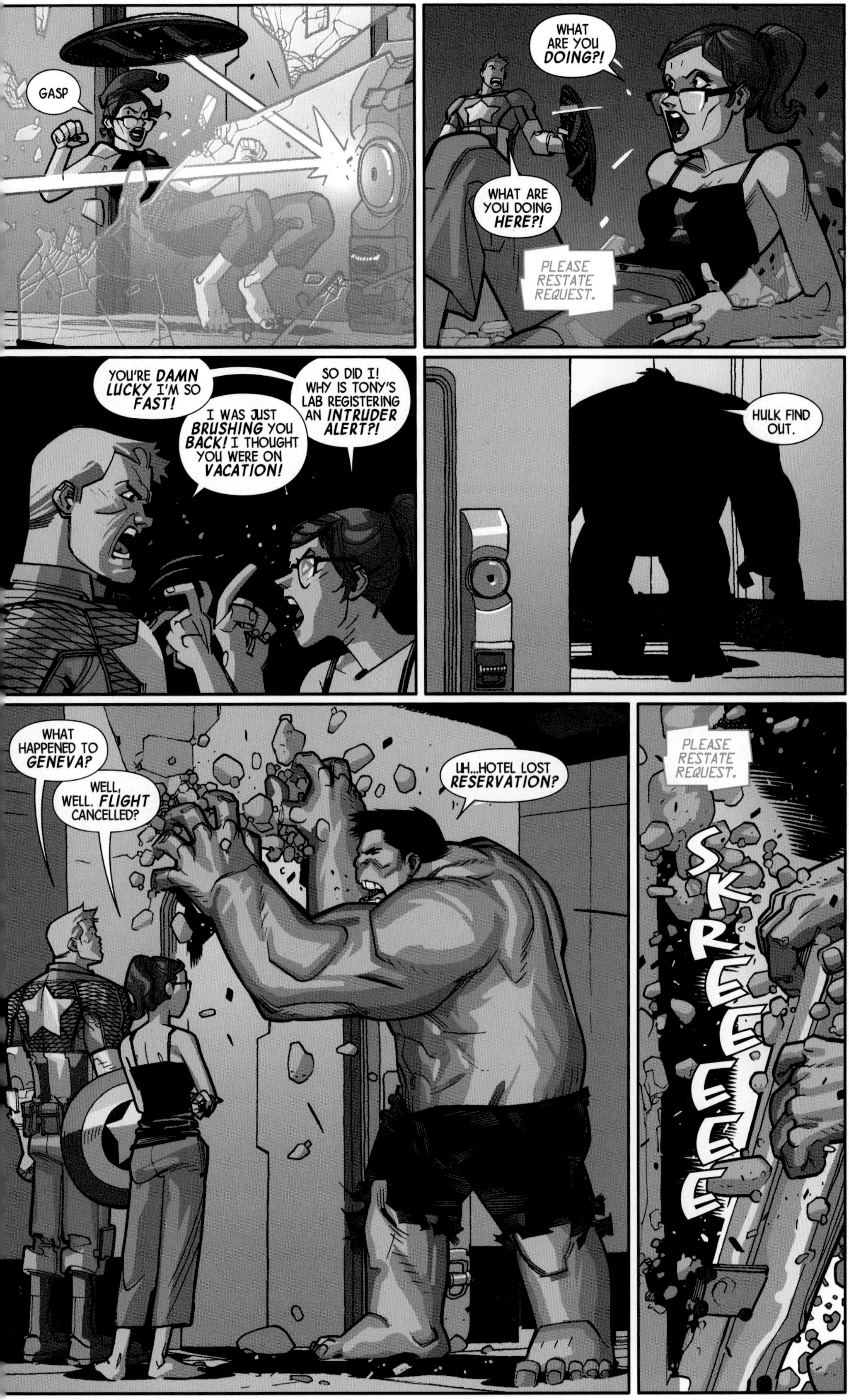
GASP
WHAT ARE YOU DOING?!
WHAT ARE YOU DOING HERE?!
PLEASE RESTATE REQUEST.
YOU'RE DAMN LUCKY I'M SO FAST!
I WAS JUST BRUSHING YOU BACK! I THOUGHT YOU WERE ON VACATION!
SO DID I! WHY IS TONY'S LAB REGISTERING AN INTRUDER ALERT?!
HULK FIND OUT.
WHAT HAPPENED TO GENEVA?
WELL, WELL. FLIGHT CANCELLED?
UH...HOTEL LOST RESERVATION?
PLEASE RESTATE REQUEST.
SKREEEEEE

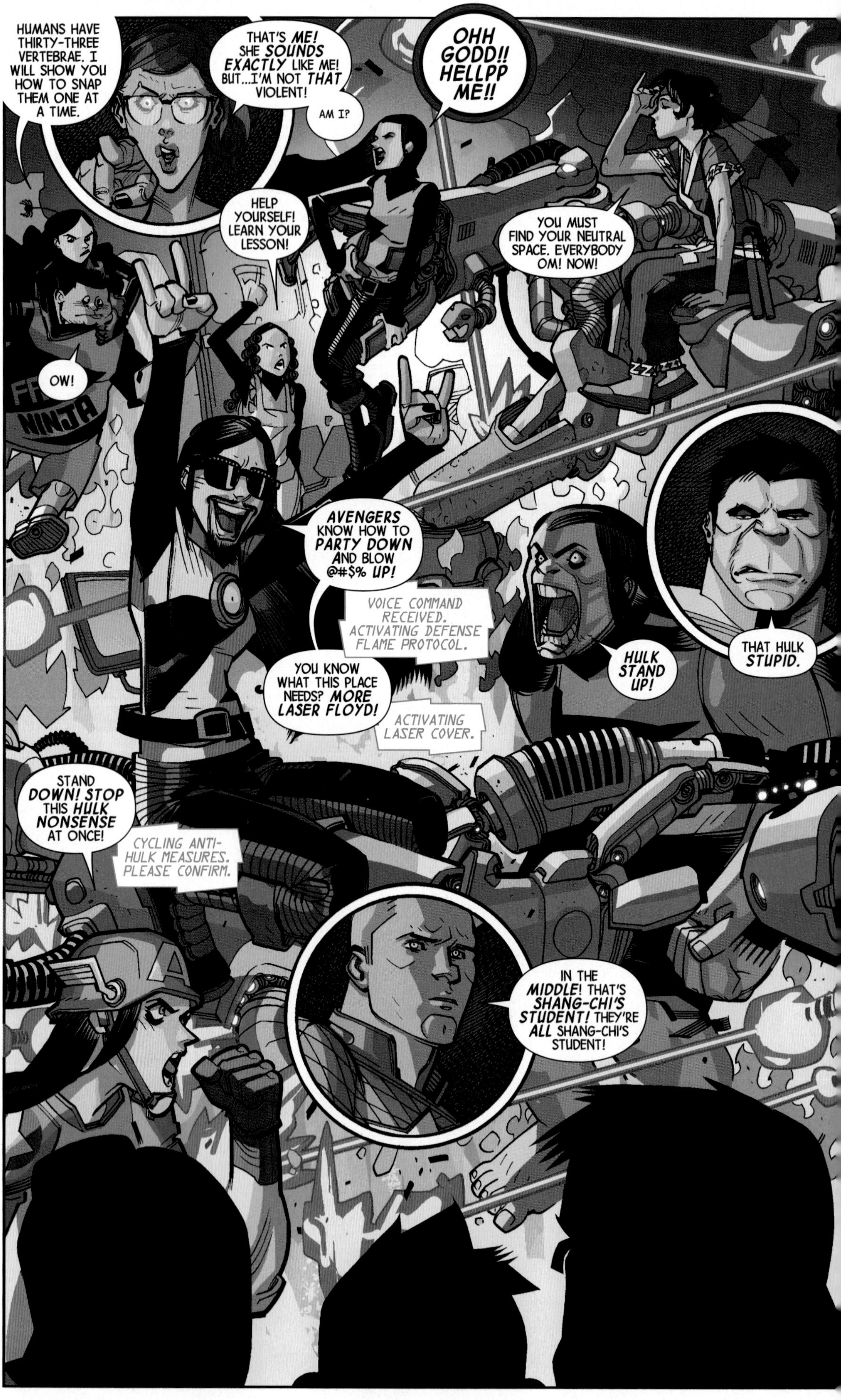
HUMANS HAVE THIRTY-THREE VERTEBRAE. I WILL SHOW YOU HOW TO SNAP THEM ONE AT A TIME.
THAT'S ME! SHE SOUNDS EXACTLY LIKE ME! BUT...I'M NOT THAT VIOLENT!
AM I?
OHH GODD!! HELLPP ME!!
HELP YOURSELF! LEARN YOUR LESSON!
YOU MUST FIND YOUR NEUTRAL SPACE. EVERYBODY OM! NOW!
OW!
FR NINJA
AVENGERS KNOW HOW TO PARTY DOWN AND BLOW @#$% UP!
VOICE COMMAND RECEIVED. ACTIVATING DEFENSE FLAME PROTOCOL.
YOU KNOW WHAT THIS PLACE NEEDS? MORE LASER FLOYD!
ACTIVATING LASER COVER.
HULK STAND UP!
THAT HULK STUPID.
STAND DOWN! STOP THIS HULK NONSENSE AT ONCE!
CYCLING ANTI-HULK MEASURES. PLEASE CONFIRM.
IN THE MIDDLE! THAT'S SHANG-CHI'S STUDENT! THEY'RE ALL SHANG-CHI'S STUDENT!

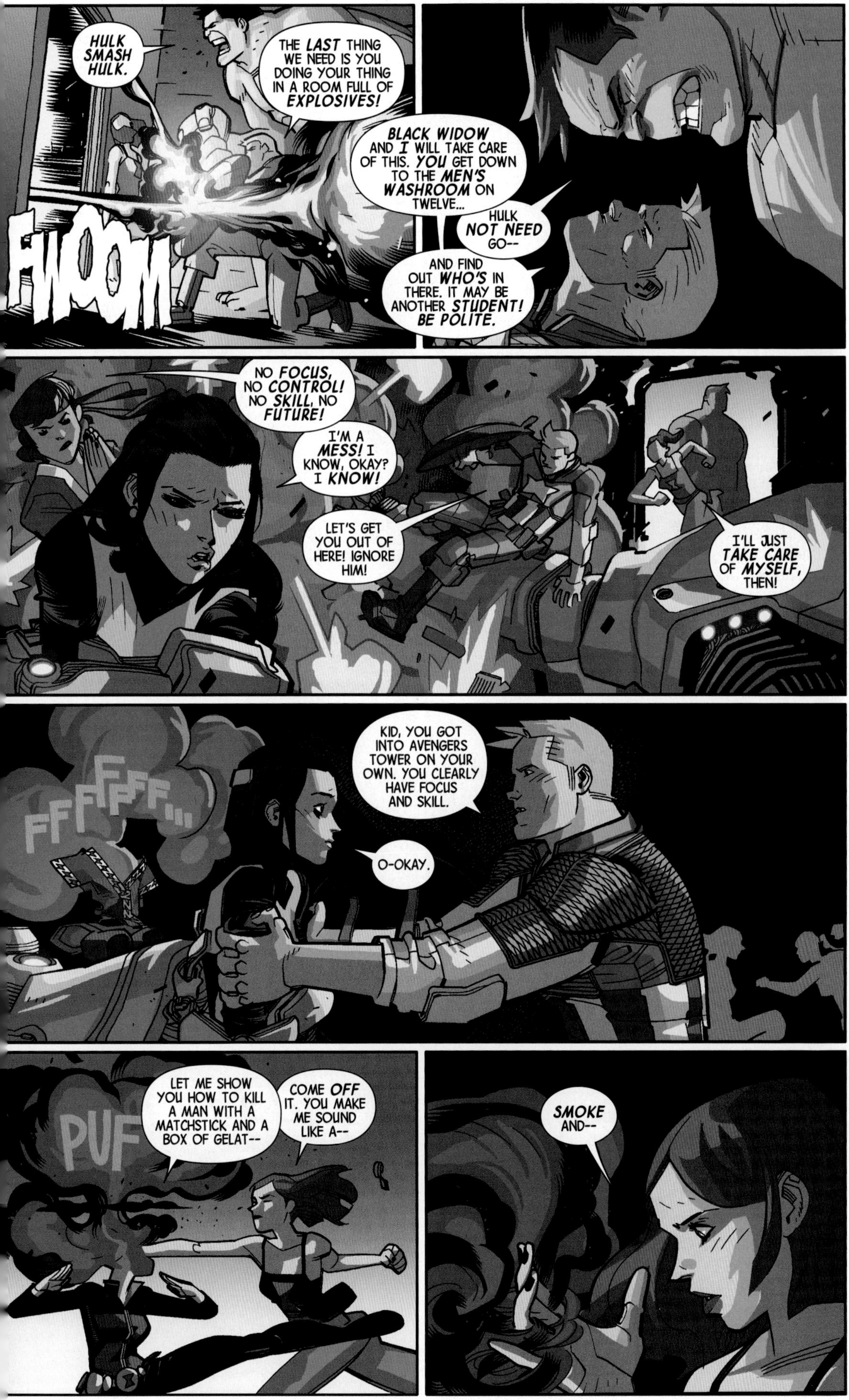
HULK SMASH HULK.
THE LAST THING WE NEED IS YOU DOING YOUR THING IN A ROOM FULL OF EXPLOSIVES!
FWOOM
BLACK WIDOW AND I WILL TAKE CARE OF THIS. YOU GET DOWN TO THE MEN'S WASHROOM ON TWELVE...
HULK NOT NEED GO--
AND FIND OUT WHO'S IN THERE. IT MAY BE ANOTHER STUDENT! BE POLITE.
NO FOCUS, NO CONTROL! NO SKILL, NO FUTURE!
I'M A MESS! I KNOW, OKAY? I KNOW!
LET'S GET YOU OUT OF HERE! IGNORE HIM!
I'LL JUST TAKE CARE OF MYSELF, THEN!
FFFFFFF...
KID, YOU GOT INTO AVENGERS TOWER ON YOUR OWN. YOU CLEARLY HAVE FOCUS AND SKILL.
O-OKAY.
PUF
LET ME SHOW YOU HOW TO KILL A MAN WITH A MATCHSTICK AND A BOX OF GELAT--
COME OFF IT. YOU MAKE ME SOUND LIKE A--
SMOKE AND--

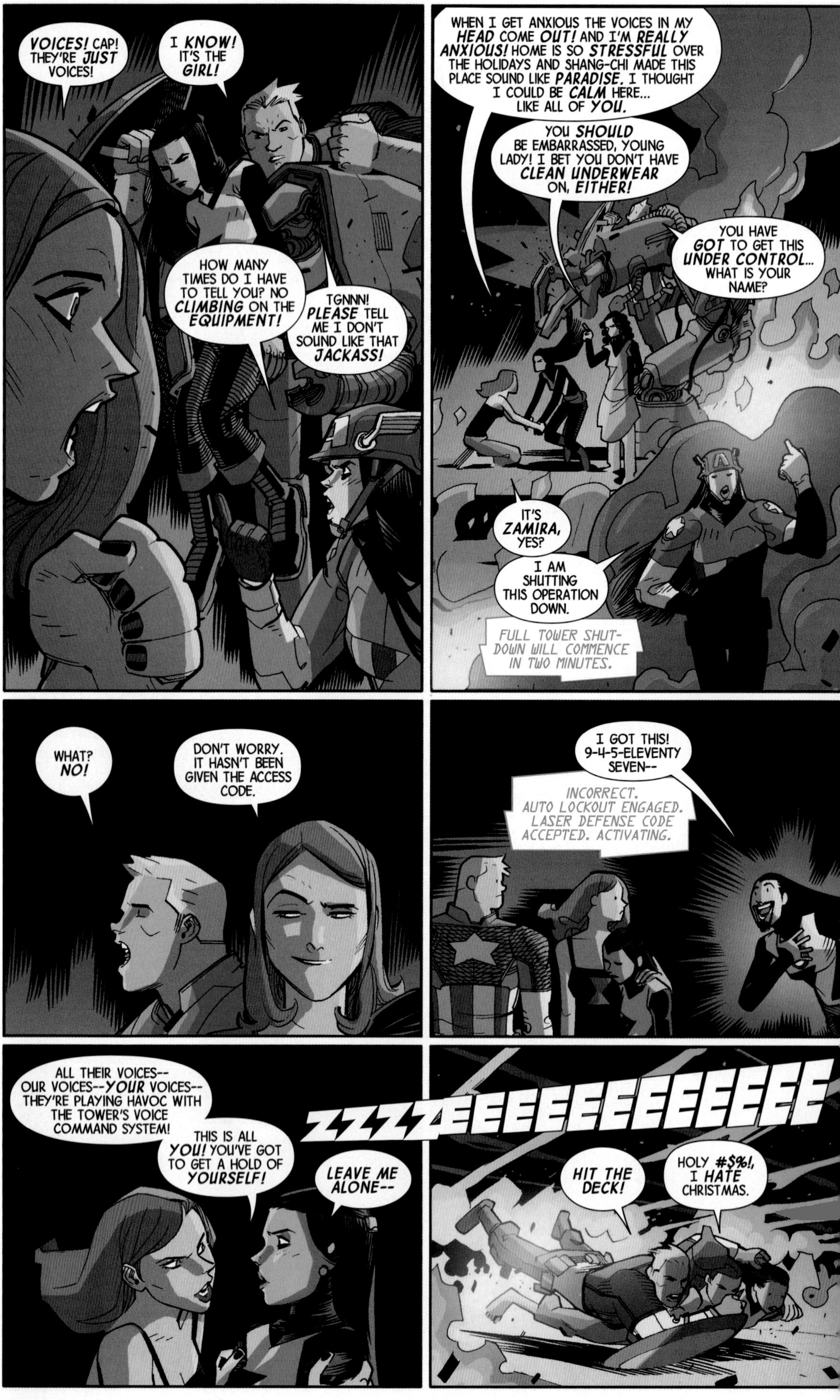

VOICES! CAP! THEY'RE JUST VOICES!
I KNOW! IT'S THE GIRL!
HOW MANY TIMES DO I HAVE TO TELL YOU? NO CLIMBING ON THE EQUIPMENT!
TGNNN! PLEASE TELL ME I DON'T SOUND LIKE THAT JACKASS!
WHEN I GET ANXIOUS THE VOICES IN MY HEAD COME OUT! AND I'M REALLY ANXIOUS! HOME IS SO STRESSFUL OVER THE HOLIDAYS AND SHANG-CHI MADE THIS PLACE SOUND LIKE PARADISE. I THOUGHT I COULD BE CALM HERE... LIKE ALL OF YOU.
YOU SHOULD BE EMBARRASSED, YOUNG LADY! I BET YOU DON'T HAVE CLEAN UNDERWEAR ON, EITHER!
YOU HAVE GOT TO GET THIS UNDER CONTROL... WHAT IS YOUR NAME?
IT'S ZAMIRA, YES?
I AM SHUTTING THIS OPERATION DOWN.
FULL TOWER SHUT-DOWN WILL COMMENCE IN TWO MINUTES.
WHAT? NO!
DON'T WORRY. IT HASN'T BEEN GIVEN THE ACCESS CODE.
I GOT THIS! 9-4-5-ELEVENTY SEVEN--
INCORRECT. AUTO LOCKOUT ENGAGED. LASER DEFENSE CODE ACCEPTED. ACTIVATING.
ALL THEIR VOICES-- OUR VOICES--YOUR VOICES-- THEY'RE PLAYING HAVOC WITH THE TOWER'S VOICE COMMAND SYSTEM!
THIS IS ALL YOU! YOU'VE GOT TO GET A HOLD OF YOURSELF!
LEAVE ME ALONE--
ZZZZEEEEEEEEEEEEEEE
HIT THE DECK!
HOLY #$%!, I HATE CHRISTMAS.

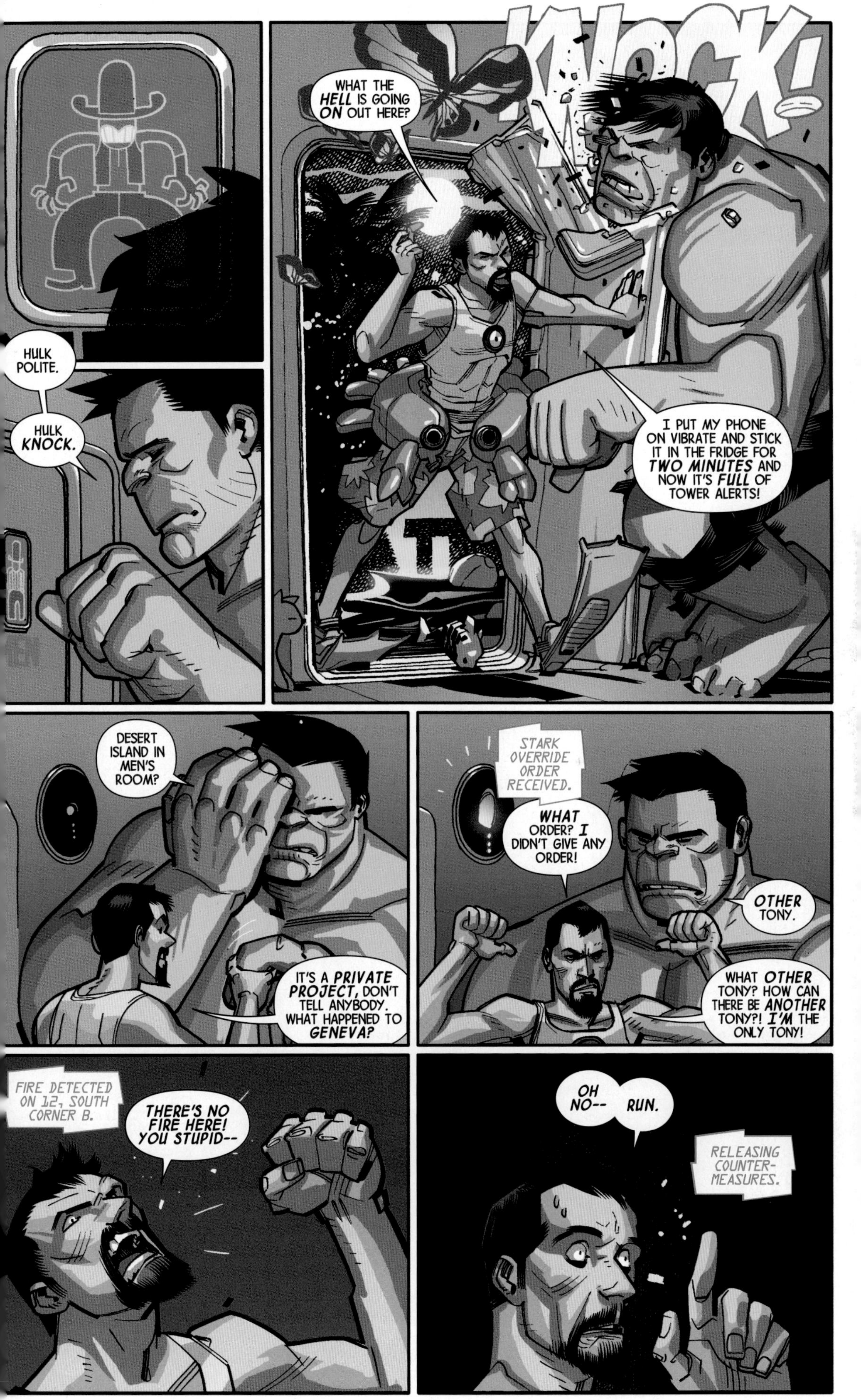
KNOCK!
WHAT THE HELL IS GOING ON OUT HERE?
HULK POLITE.
HULK KNOCK.
I PUT MY PHONE ON VIBRATE AND STICK IT IN THE FRIDGE FOR TWO MINUTES AND NOW IT'S FULL OF TOWER ALERTS!
DESERT ISLAND IN MEN'S ROOM?
IT'S A PRIVATE PROJECT, DON'T TELL ANYBODY. WHAT HAPPENED TO GENEVA?
STARK OVERRIDE ORDER RECEIVED.
WHAT ORDER? I DIDN'T GIVE ANY ORDER!
OTHER TONY.
WHAT OTHER TONY? HOW CAN THERE BE ANOTHER TONY?! I'M THE ONLY TONY!
FIRE DETECTED ON 12, SOUTH CORNER B.
THERE'S NO FIRE HERE! YOU STUPID--
OH NO--
RUN.
RELEASING COUNTER-MEASURES.

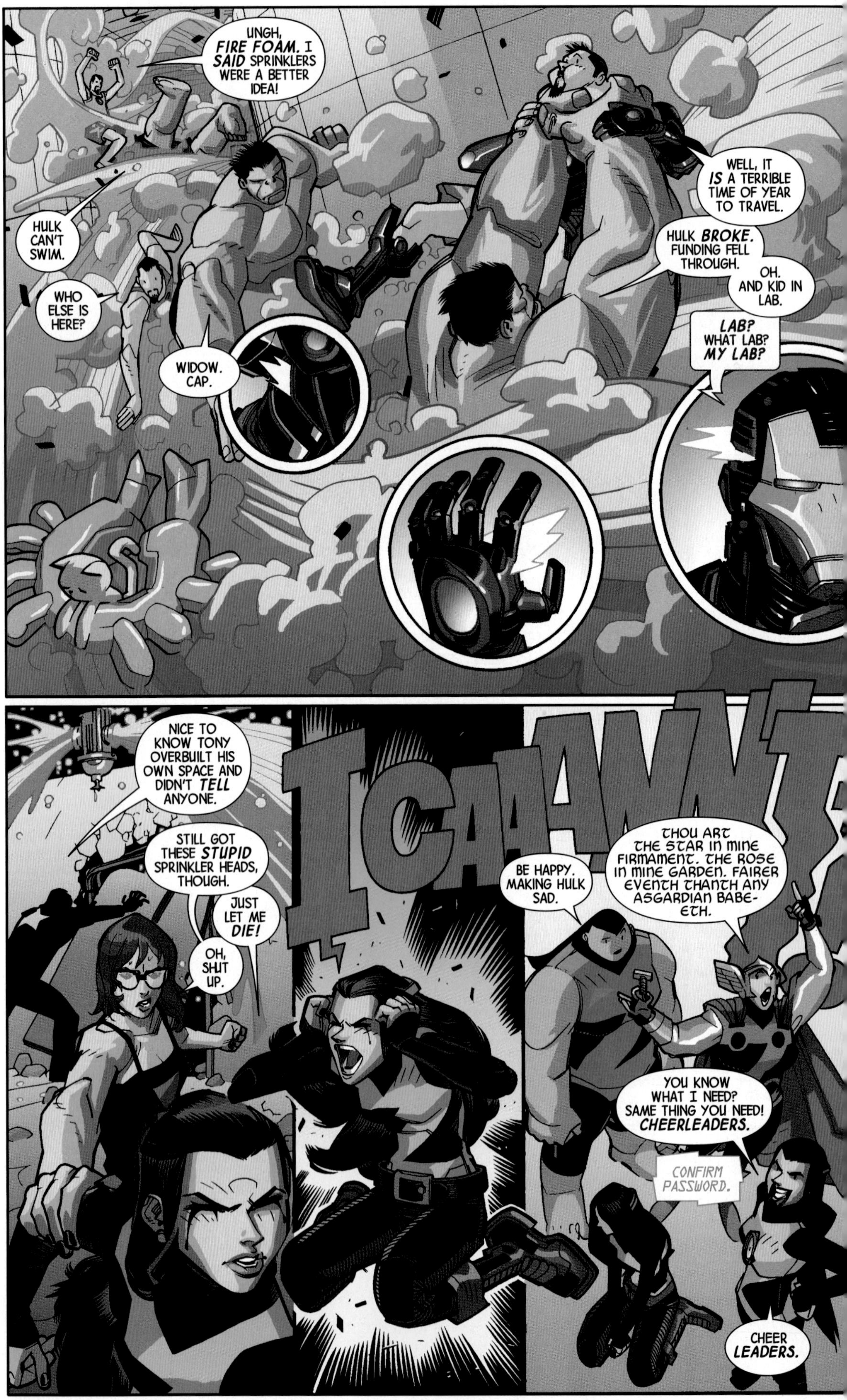
UNGH, FIRE FOAM. I SAID SPRINKLERS WERE A BETTER IDEA!
WELL, IT IS A TERRIBLE TIME OF YEAR TO TRAVEL.
HULK CAN'T SWIM.
HULK BROKE. FUNDING FELL THROUGH.
OH. AND KID IN LAB.
WHO ELSE IS HERE?
WIDOW. CAP.
LAB? WHAT LAB? MY LAB?
NICE TO KNOW TONY OVERBUILT HIS OWN SPACE AND DIDN'T TELL ANYONE.
STILL GOT THESE STUPID SPRINKLER HEADS, THOUGH.
JUST LET ME DIE!
OH, SHUT UP.
I CAAAN'T
BE HAPPY. MAKING HULK SAD.
THOU ART THE STAR IN MINE FIRMAMENT. THE ROSE IN MINE GARDEN. FAIRER EVENTH THANTH ANY ASGARDIAN BABE-ETH.
YOU KNOW WHAT I NEED? SAME THING YOU NEED! CHEERLEADERS.
CONFIRM PASSWORD.
CHEER LEADERS.

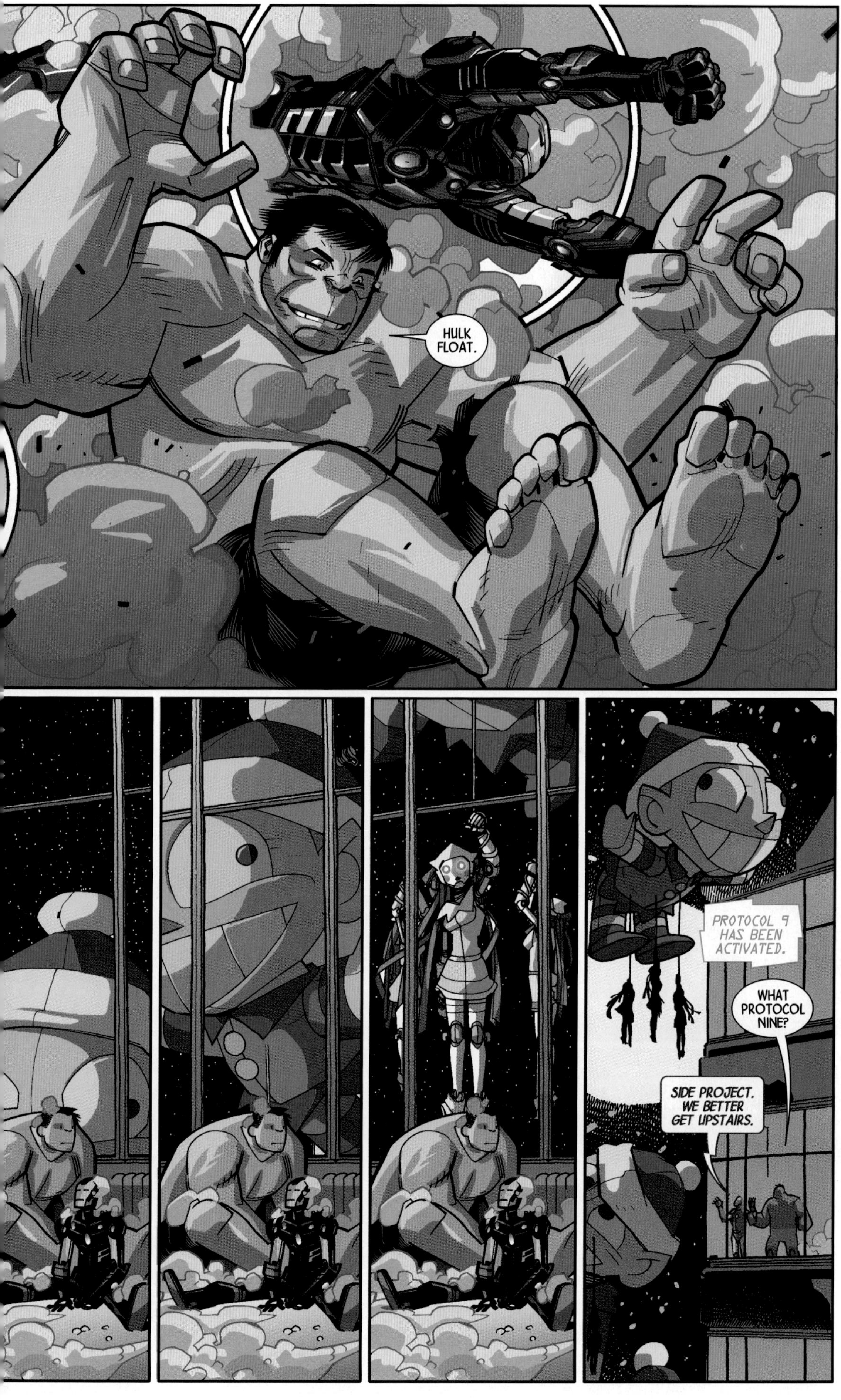
HULK FLOAT.
PROTOCOL 9 HAS BEEN ACTIVATED.
WHAT PROTOCOL NINE?
SIDE PROJECT. WE BETTER GET UPSTAIRS.

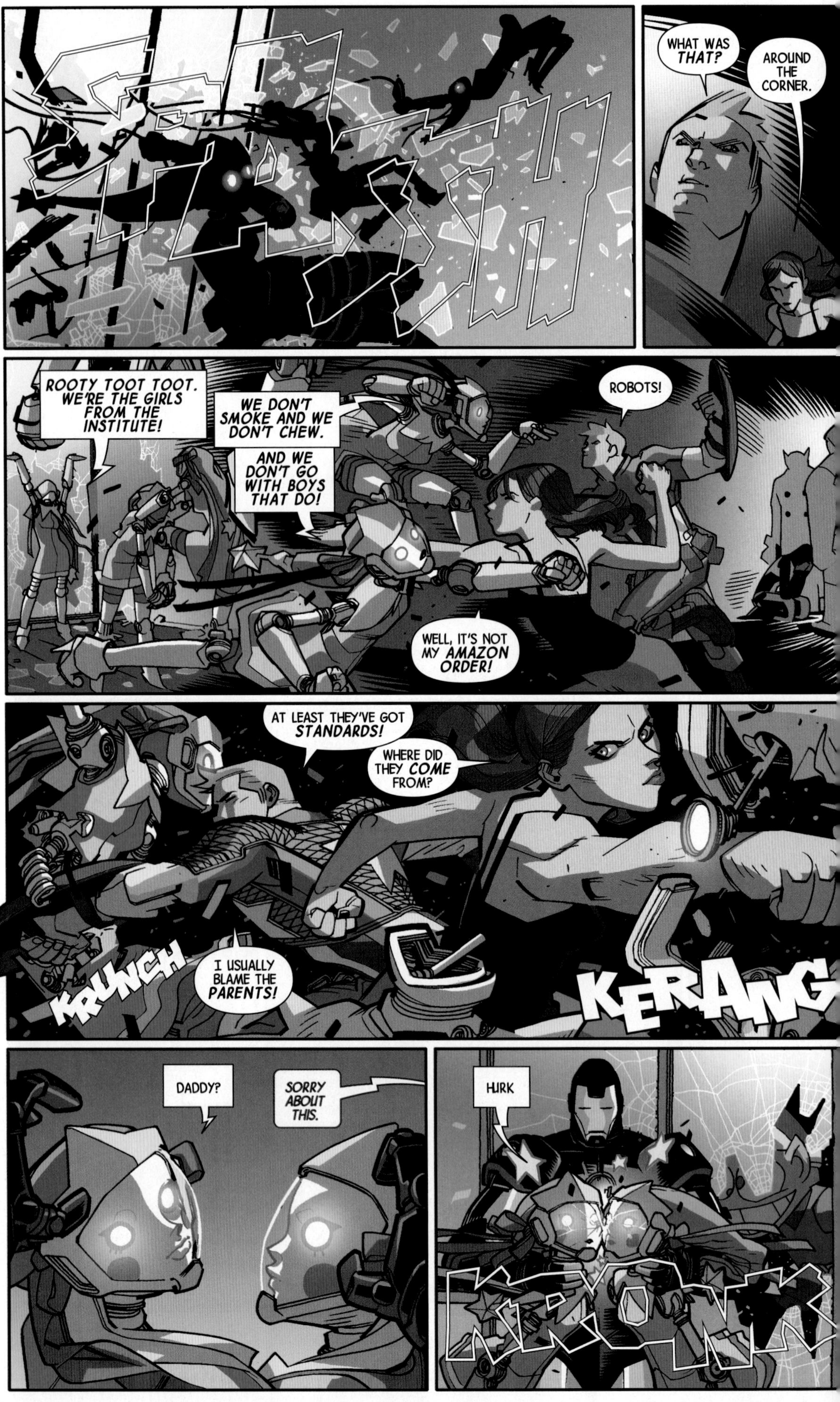
WHAT WAS THAT?
AROUND THE CORNER.
ROOTY TOOT TOOT. WE'RE THE GIRLS FROM THE INSTITUTE!
WE DON'T SMOKE AND WE DON'T CHEW.
AND WE DON'T GO WITH BOYS THAT DO!
ROBOTS!
WELL, IT'S NOT MY AMAZON ORDER!
AT LEAST THEY'VE GOT STANDARDS!
WHERE DID THEY COME FROM?
I USUALLY BLAME THE PARENTS!
KRUNCH
KERANG
DADDY?
SORRY ABOUT THIS.
HURK

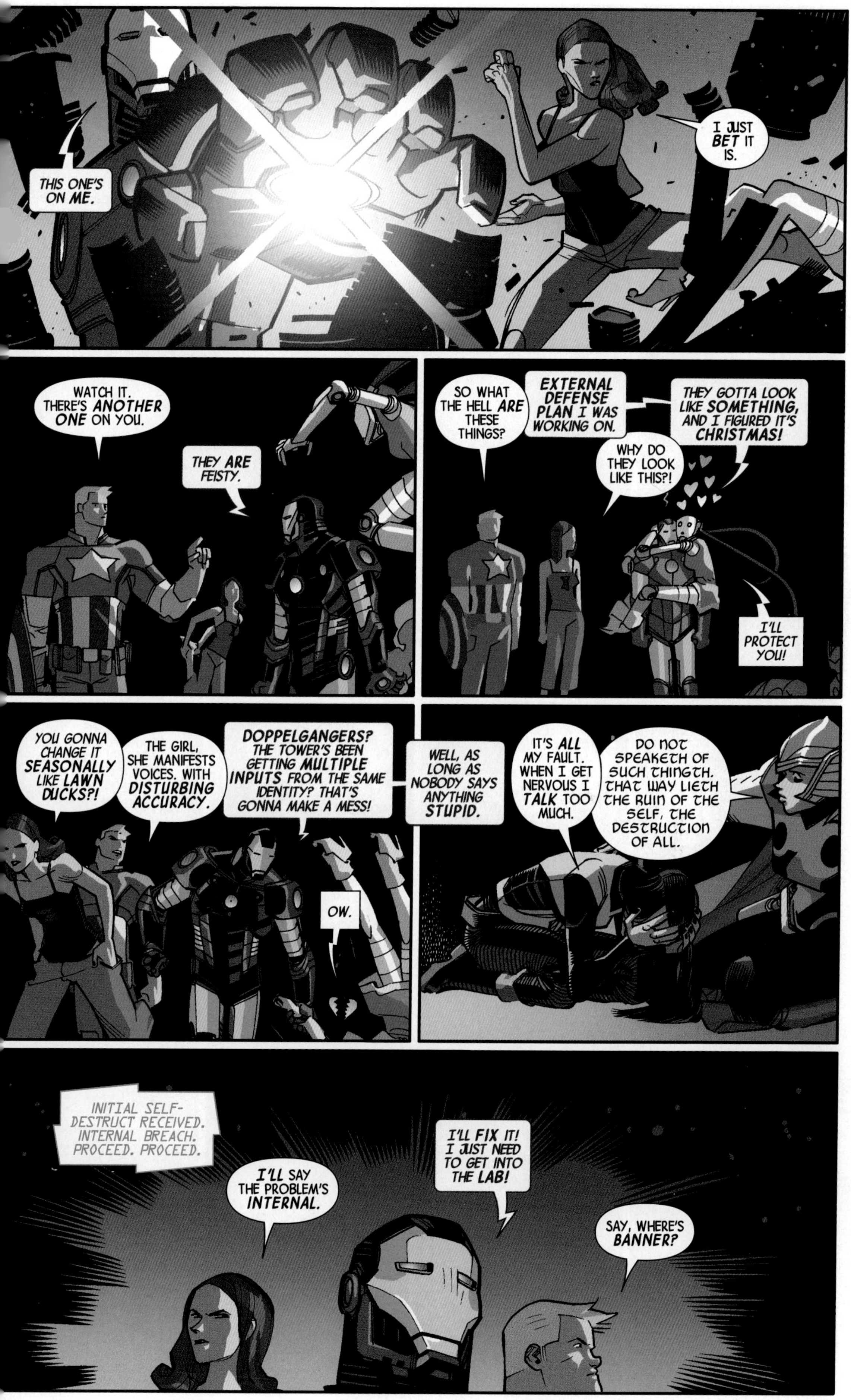
THIS ONE'S ON ME.
I JUST BET IT IS.
WATCH IT. THERE'S ANOTHER ONE ON YOU.
THEY ARE FEISTY.
SO WHAT THE HELL ARE THESE THINGS?
EXTERNAL DEFENSE PLAN I WAS WORKING ON.
THEY GOTTA LOOK LIKE SOMETHING, AND I FIGURED IT'S CHRISTMAS!
WHY DO THEY LOOK LIKE THIS?!
I'LL PROTECT YOU!
YOU GONNA CHANGE IT SEASONALLY LIKE LAWN DUCKS?!
THE GIRL, SHE MANIFESTS VOICES. WITH DISTURBING ACCURACY.
DOPPELGANGERS? THE TOWER'S BEEN GETTING MULTIPLE INPUTS FROM THE SAME IDENTITY? THAT'S GONNA MAKE A MESS!
OW.
WELL, AS LONG AS NOBODY SAYS ANYTHING STUPID.
IT'S ALL MY FAULT. WHEN I GET NERVOUS I TALK TOO MUCH.
DO NOT SPEAKETH OF SUCH THINGTH. THAT WAY LIETH THE RUIN OF THE SELF, THE DESTRUCTION OF ALL.
INITIAL SELF-DESTRUCT RECEIVED. INTERNAL BREACH. PROCEED. PROCEED.
I'LL SAY THE PROBLEM'S INTERNAL.
I'LL FIX IT! I JUST NEED TO GET INTO THE LAB!
SAY, WHERE'S BANNER?

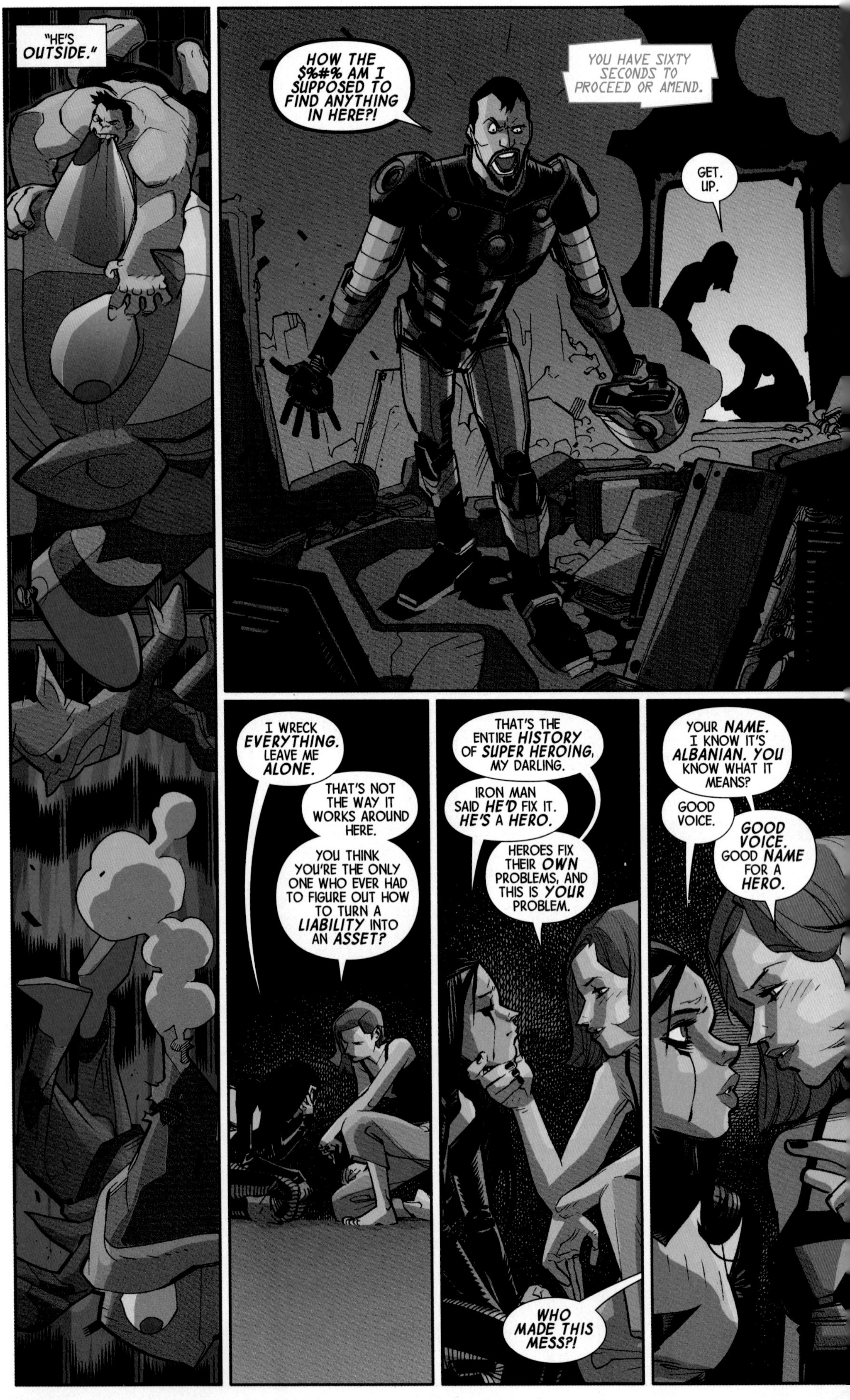
"HE'S OUTSIDE."
HOW THE $%#% AM I SUPPOSED TO FIND ANYTHING IN HERE?!
YOU HAVE SIXTY SECONDS TO PROCEED OR AMEND.
GET. UP.
I WRECK EVERYTHING. LEAVE ME ALONE.
THAT'S NOT THE WAY IT WORKS AROUND HERE.
YOU THINK YOU'RE THE ONLY ONE WHO EVER HAD TO FIGURE OUT HOW TO TURN A LIABILITY INTO AN ASSET?
THAT'S THE ENTIRE HISTORY OF SUPER HEROING, MY DARLING.
IRON MAN SAID HE'D FIX IT. HE'S A HERO.
HEROES FIX THEIR OWN PROBLEMS, AND THIS IS YOUR PROBLEM.
WHO MADE THIS MESS?!
YOUR NAME. I KNOW IT'S ALBANIAN. YOU KNOW WHAT IT MEANS?
GOOD VOICE.
GOOD VOICE. GOOD NAME FOR A HERO.

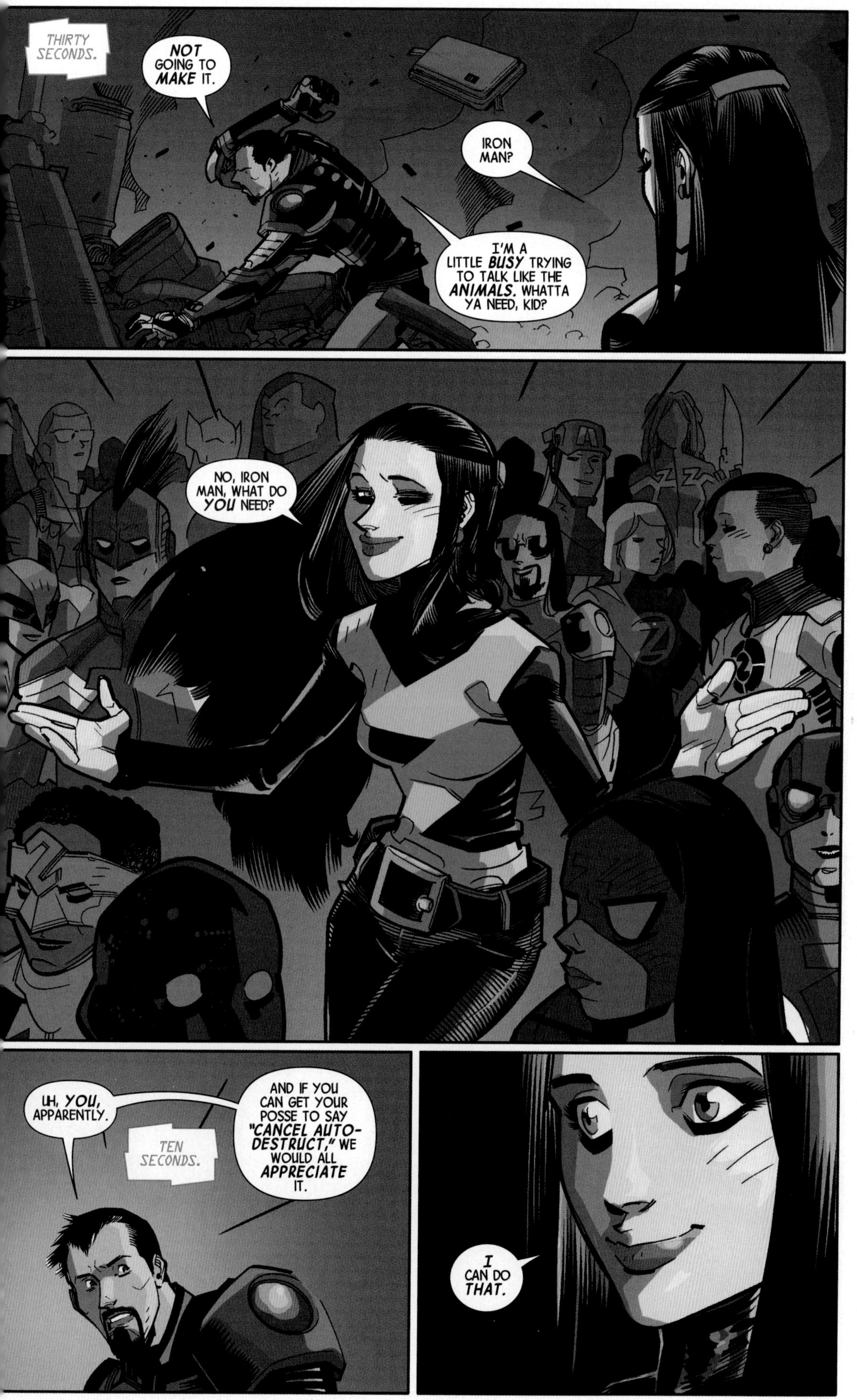
THIRTY SECONDS.
NOT GOING TO MAKE IT.
IRON MAN?
I'M A LITTLE BUSY TRYING TO TALK LIKE THE ANIMALS. WHATTA YA NEED, KID?
NO, IRON MAN, WHAT DO YOU NEED?
UH, YOU, APPARENTLY.
AND IF YOU CAN GET YOUR POSSE TO SAY "CANCEL AUTO-DESTRUCT," WE WOULD ALL APPRECIATE IT.
TEN SECONDS.
I CAN DO THAT.

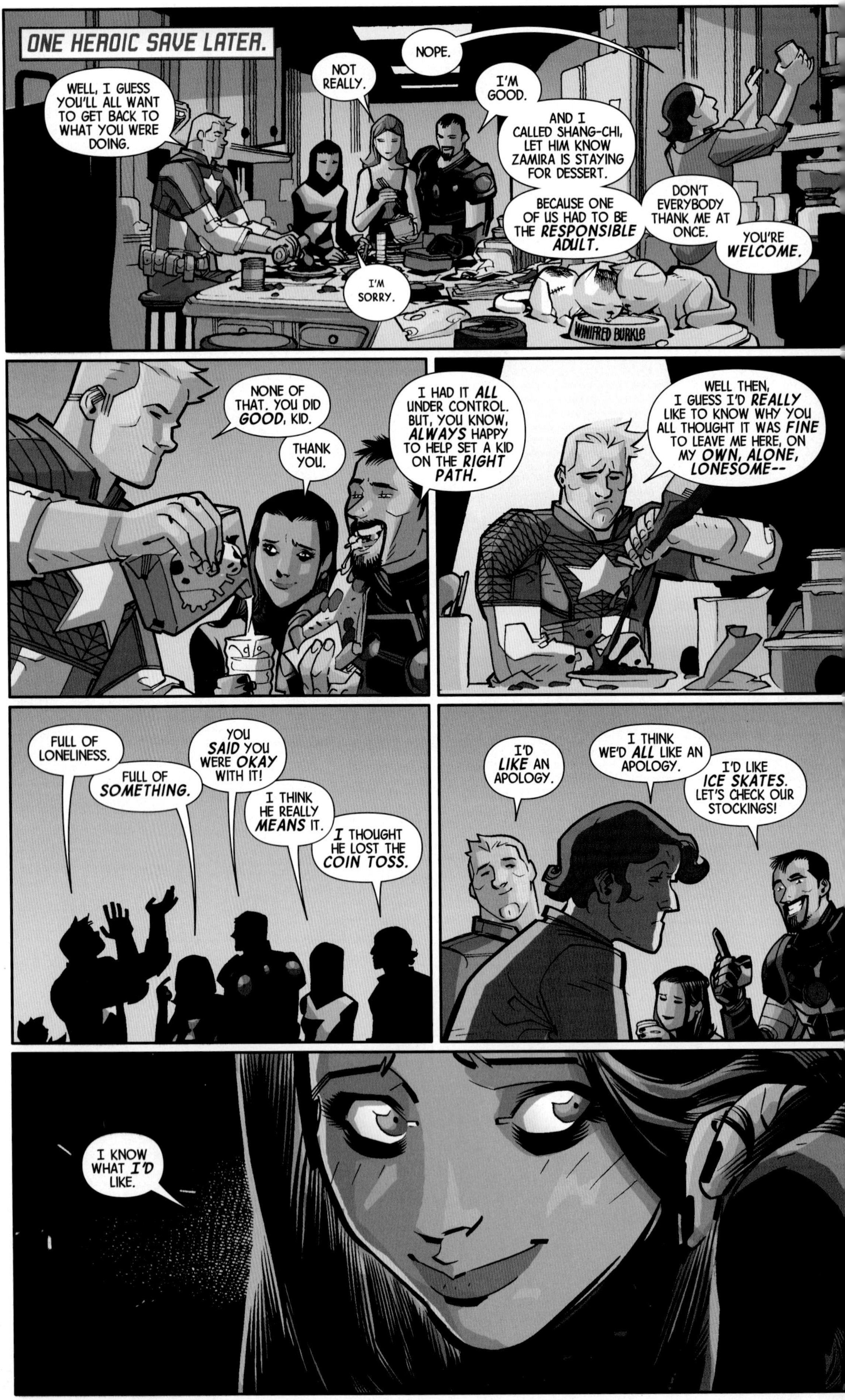
ONE HEROIC SAVE LATER.
WELL, I GUESS YOU'LL ALL WANT TO GET BACK TO WHAT YOU WERE DOING.
NOT REALLY.
NOPE.
I'M GOOD.
AND I CALLED SHANG-CHI, LET HIM KNOW ZAMIRA IS STAYING FOR DESSERT.
BECAUSE ONE OF US HAD TO BE THE RESPONSIBLE ADULT.
DON'T EVERYBODY THANK ME AT ONCE.
YOU'RE WELCOME.
I'M SORRY.
WINIFRED BURKLE
NONE OF THAT. YOU DID GOOD, KID.
THANK YOU.
I HAD IT ALL UNDER CONTROL. BUT, YOU KNOW, ALWAYS HAPPY TO HELP SET A KID ON THE RIGHT PATH.
WELL THEN, I GUESS I'D REALLY LIKE TO KNOW WHY YOU ALL THOUGHT IT WAS FINE TO LEAVE ME HERE, ON MY OWN, ALONE, LONESOME--
FULL OF LONELINESS.
FULL OF SOMETHING.
YOU SAID YOU WERE OKAY WITH IT!
I THINK HE REALLY MEANS IT.
I THOUGHT HE LOST THE COIN TOSS.
I'D LIKE AN APOLOGY.
I THINK WE'D ALL LIKE AN APOLOGY.
I'D LIKE ICE SKATES. LET'S CHECK OUR STOCKINGS!
I KNOW WHAT I'D LIKE.

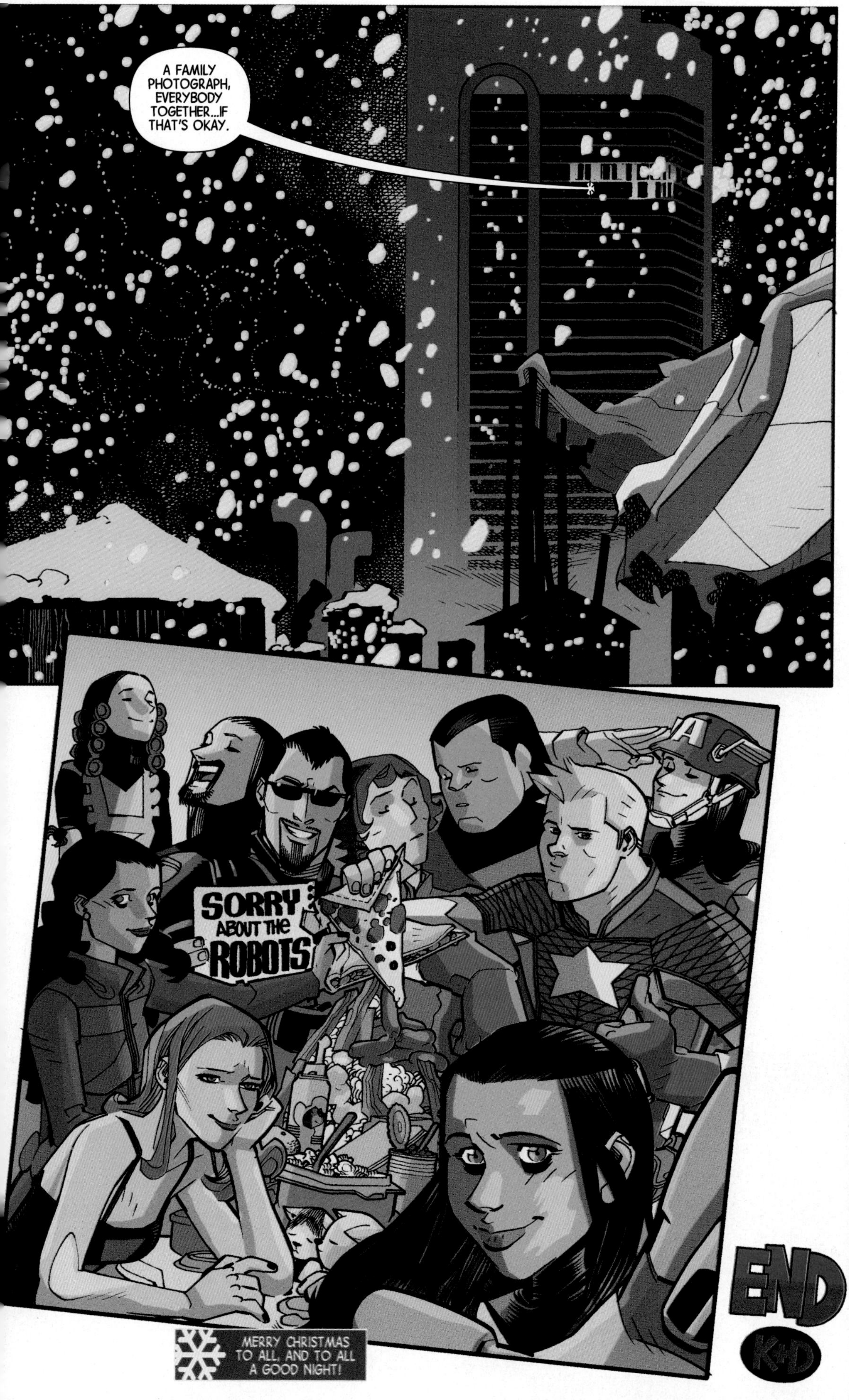
A FAMILY PHOTOGRAPH, EVERYBODY TOGETHER...IF THAT'S OKAY.
SORRY ABOUT THE ROBOTS
END
K+D
MERRY CHRISTMAS TO ALL, AND TO ALL A GOOD NIGHT!

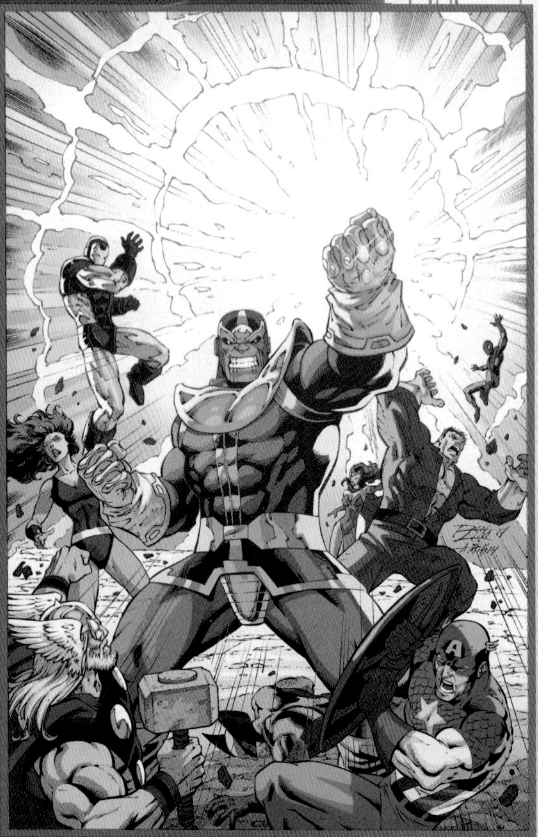

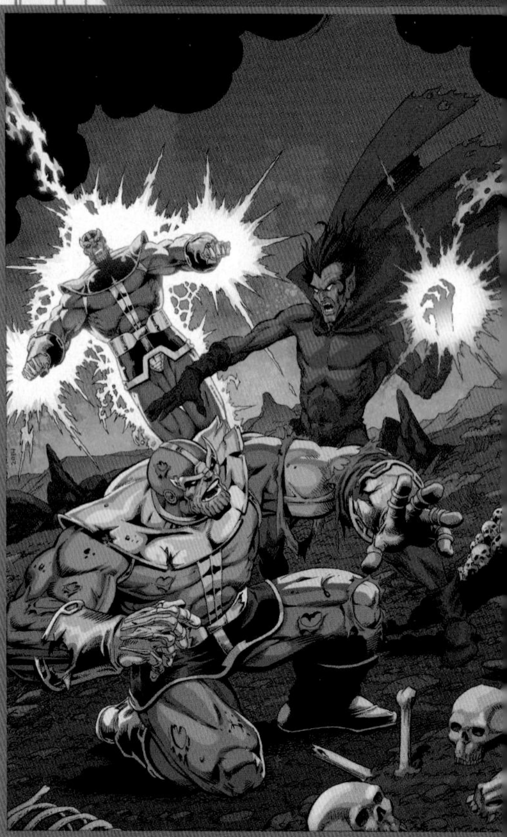

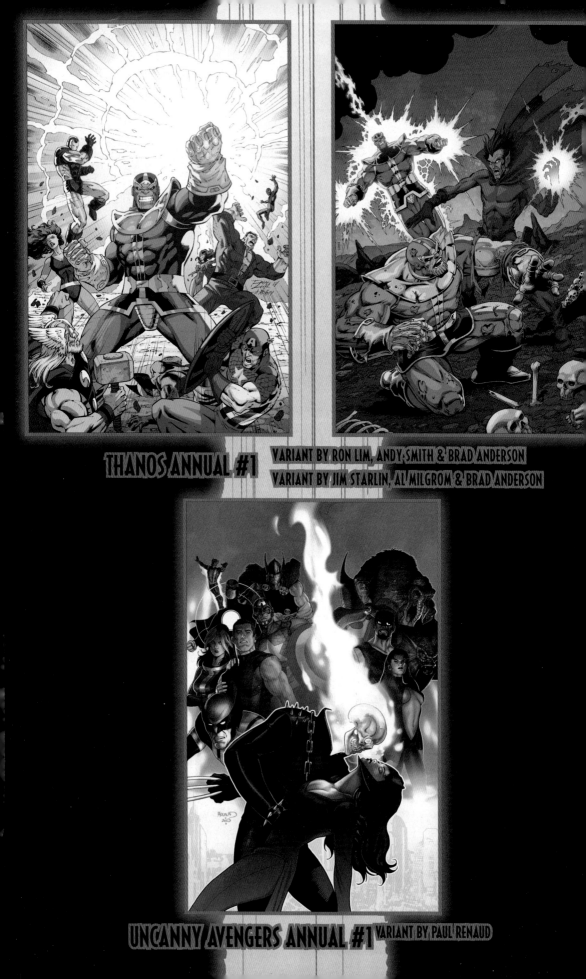

THANOS ANNUAL #1 VARIANT BY RON LIM, ANDY SMITH & BRAD ANDERSON
VARIANT BY JIM STARLIN, AL MILGROM & BRAD ANDERSON

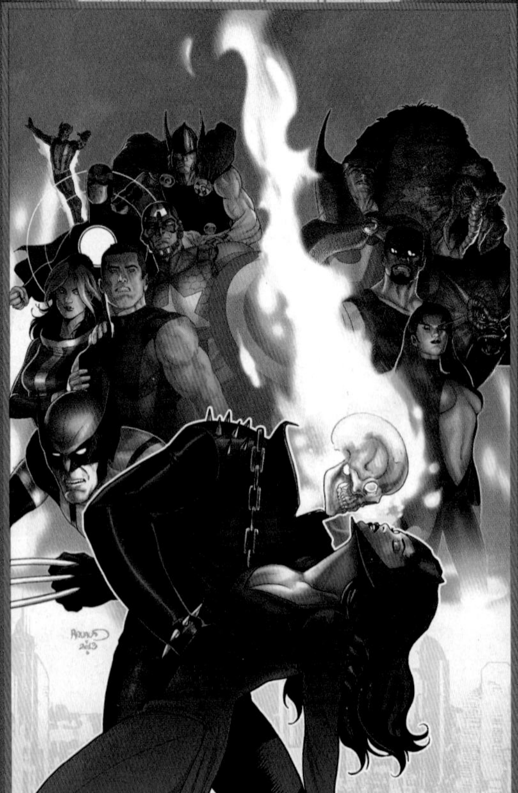

UNCANNY AVENGERS ANNUAL #1 VARIANT BY PAUL RENAUD